DISCARDED

THE GARDEN AND THE MAP

The Garden and the Map

Schizophrenia in Twentieth-Century Literature and Culture

JOHN VERNON

University of Illinois Press
Urbana Chicago London

COLLEGE OF THE SEQUOIAS
LIBRARY

© 1973 by the Board of Trustees of the University of Illinois
Manufactured in the United States of America
Library of Congress Catalog Card No. 72–85612
ISBN 0–252–00256–3

To my father and mother, Elijah and Ruth Vernon

Contents

Preface

This book was originally intended to be an examination of the preoccupation with fantasy in twentieth-century literature. It still is that, but the examination of fantasy has led to an examination of "reality" as well, and both have led to an examination of that culture which opposes fantasy and reality, which defines each by the exclusion of the other. The question of how fantasy differs from reality already contains the brand of that culture—of Western civilization—since it assumes that the two modes of being, fantasy and reality, occupy two mutually exclusive spaces. Since the boundary line between these spaces is absolute, it is apparent that "reality" in this culture is an exclusive term, reserved for certain modes of being—that is, it is a term of approbation. Of course in order to function effectively as a term of approbation, the illusion must be created that "reality" is not merely that. A significant shift in consciousness in the twentieth century has been occurring with the loss of this illusion and the consequent realization that "reality" is simply one structure, one mode of experiencing the world, among many. The literature of fantasy in this century, from Franz Kafka and the surrealists at the beginning, to Alain Robbe-Grillet, John Barth, William S. Burroughs, Theodore Roethke, and others in the second half, can be fully understood only in terms of this shift.

My examination of this literature, then, is not a history, but an interpretative analysis in terms of the cultural shift from which it is inseparable. For this reason I discuss only certain representative authors, and devote a great deal of space to cultural as well as literary analysis, particularly in Chapter One. By "cultural analysis" I mean the analysis of those underlying structures that fill out a culture and make it what it is. Such structures are present not only in the artifacts or literature of a culture, but also in the fundamental relationships between all beings in that culture, between people and people, between people and things, between things and things. When I perform even the simplest acts of orientation, walking across the room or turning around, for example, the culture I exist in interprets everything I see. Actually "interpret" is a misleading word, since it implies a translation of what I see into the terms of that culture. There is no translation; rather, the very manifestation of the things I see accomplishes that interpretation. Perception creates and organizes as well as records, and it does so with structures that are inseparable from the structures of a culture. Our perception of space, for example, is inseparable from the philosophy of Democritus or the science of Newton—or if it is separable from them, it is because of the cultural shift at the beginning of this century represented by Einstein and relativity physics. A culture is the most pervading organization of experience for each of us; it is what, after childhood, makes the perceptions of a few accessible to the many, and also what enslaves us to those perceptions.

This enslavement is so strongly rooted in our culture that those who escape it are usually called "insane," a term that is therefore more a political or social label (as R. D. Laing asserts) than a medical one. The examination of fantasy has led me also to an examination of madness, for the same culture that creates the absolute reality-fantasy division also creates an absolute sanity-madness division. And as in the case of "reality," "sanity" is thus a term of approbation, reserved for culturally approved modes of being. This is one of Michel Foucault's major points in *Madness and Civilization,* and as he hints throughout that work, a culture that makes such an absolute dichotomy in its experience of the world—approving a major chunk of it, dis-

approving and consequently repressing another chunk of it—
is itself mad. This is the defining characteristic of Western culture: it is schizophrenic, in that it chooses to fragment its
experience and seal certain areas off from each other. It drains
the fantastic, the mad, and the subjective out of their unity with
the self and the world, out of the condition by which they are
not even differentiated yet, and locks them in a common inaccessible space.

The advantage of this is obvious: the chunk of reality left behind, which is then the only reality, is more manageable, cleaner,
safer, more "objective," since it has been cleansed of the emotional, the qualitative, the unpredictable. But the disadvantage
should be obvious also: a whole area of experience, an area that
should not be self-enclosed but should drench and fill out objective reality, has been made inaccessible. This area of experience, the fantastic and the mad, does fill out all aspects of
being-in-the-world for cultures other than our own, to the extent
that it cannot be termed an "area." But in the West it is a pure
separate space, and one can connect with it only by withdraw-
ing from reality, by becoming insane. Of course the reality one
withdraws from is equally insane, equally unreal, since it is an
incomplete chunk of the real feigning completeness. This is the
"double bind" that Bateson, Laing, and others see as a major
manifestation of schizophrenia: each mode of being, the real
and the fantastic, the sane and the insane, excludes the other,
and each is intolerable because of that exclusion.

The truth is that the culture that has invented such classes of
being as fantasy and madness is mad. Madness in this sense is
not simply an aberration of motor phenomena (as Erwin Straus
points out), but a basic alteration of one's being-in-the-world.
It is that alteration which tears one's being out of the world,
which alienates the self by fragmenting it. Heidegger's term
"being-in-the-world" presumes that there is a unity of oneself
and the world, but the structures of Western culture repress
that unity by separating reality and fantasy, object and subject,
world and self. The first three chapters of this study are devoted
to an examination of this repression as it is manifest in literature,

particularly in realism. The "map" of the title *The Garden and the Map* refers to that schizophrenic structure whereby areas of experience are extricated from each other and arranged in discrete spaces beside each other, often as opposites. As we shall see, the appropriateness of the metaphor of the map becomes apparent when the structure of space in the realistic and naturalistic novel is analyzed.

The term "garden" in the title refers to a structure the opposite of the map, one that unites opposites and enables all areas of experience to be accessible to each other. A major discovery of my analysis of the preoccupation with fantasy in twentieth-century literature is that this preoccupation deals with the reality of fantasy, hence with the unity of fantasy and reality. The cultural shift that twentieth-century consciousness is undergoing is thus a shift from the map to the garden, from the separation of opposites and the fragmentation of experience to the unity of opposites and the wholeness of experience. This shift is a kind of progression, but it is also, in a sense, a regression, since as we shall see in Chapter One, the garden is the structure of primitive cultures as well. The garden is also the structure of primary experience, of the world of the child; it is the structure of our perceptions when those perceptions are freed from cultural repression. I should emphasize that this shift from the map to the garden has only begun; in some respects it exists merely as a hope, an ideal. Map structures of fragmentation have today as strong a grip on consciousness as ever (in bureaucracies, land subdivision, racism, in the scientific passion for administration, control, and accumulating facts). But the very fact that this ideal has risen in the imagination of some indicates there is a new world possibly being born out of the old. This world is the subject of the final two chapters.

This world, the world of the garden, is also, like the world of the map, schizophrenic—but in a very different sense. Part of the problem of writing about a cultural shift is finding a point of view to anchor one's concepts in. From the point of view of the garden, the structure of the map—of reality—is insane, or schizophrenic, since it separates opposites that should be united—fantasy and reality, inner and outer, etc.—and consequently disposes of a whole sphere of human experience. But from the point of view of the map, the structure of the garden is insane, since it is inconceivable to map consciousness that such opposites could be united, as they are in the garden. Hence some of the sanest members of Western society have been called insane—William Blake and Christopher Smart, for example. In particular, Blake's insanity has been called schizophrenia. Yet Blake's world is not one in which aspects of experience are polarized, as the world of the map is. In Blake, sanity and madness, reality and fantasy, inner and outer, are all united. This "schizophrenia" belongs to the world of the garden, and it corresponds to the new view of schizophrenia recently taken by some psychologists, a view which asserts that schizophrenia can be a liberated and healthy state of consciousness rather than an alienated and pathological one.

The shift from the map to the garden, then, is a shift from one kind of schizophrenia to another, from an insane sanity to a sane insanity, from the polarization of aspects of experience to their unity. Since we are, in a sense, midstream in that shift, it is only natural that both of these meanings of the term "schizophrenia" are reflected in contemporary usage. "Schizophrenia" is used both as a term of condemnation—by Eldridge Cleaver and Norman Mailer, for example, in reference to a fragmented, polarized American society—and as a term of approbation—by R. D. Laing and Norman O. Brown, for example, in reference to a liberated state of consciousness. The two writers examined in detail in Chapters Three and Five respectively, William S. Burroughs and Theodore Roethke, have both been diagnosed as schizophrenic, but as we shall see, their worlds are the opposite of each other—one fragmented, violent, and nightmarish, the other whole and free.

The reversal of meaning that the term "schizophrenia" undergoes from the map to the garden is reflected in all the major concepts used in this study. My purpose is to analyze those perceptual structures in literature that reveal the structures of a culture, and there are five major modes of being that I use as touchstones to uncover those structures: the world, the body, objects, space, and time. In moving from the map to the garden, each one of these modes undergoes a reversal of meaning similar to that undergone by the term "schizophrenia." In the map, the world is sealed off from the body, taking the form of a total Other, an absolute, blocklike not-me; but in the garden, the world and the body are united, and more important, united precisely where they are, in the world and in the body. Similarly, in the map, the body is sealed off from the self, whereas in the garden they are united; in the map, objects are inert and one-dimensional, whereas in the garden they are sacred and magical; in the map, time is spatialized and quantified, whereas in the garden it is qualitative and dynamic; and in the map, space is a thing-in-itself, a medium in which objects exist, a container, whereas in the garden it is a qualitative relationship between things, dynamized by time and by the temporal nature of the body. The shift from the map to the garden is a shift in the structure of these fundamental modes—the world, the body, objects, space, and time—a shift taking place in literature from the forms of realism and naturalism to those of symbolism and the fantastic.

A final note on method. Phenomenology is beginning to make inroads in American thought; in criticism, J. Hillis Miller and Susan Sontag are somewhat phenomenological in approach. But their debt is almost entirely to Frenchmen. Georges Poulet, Gaston Bachelard, Roland Barthes, and Jean-Paul Sartre have employed the phenomenological method to its best advantage in the study of literature. However, my own immediate debt is more to the philosophers and psychologists—Husserl, Heidegger, Merleau-Ponty, again Sartre, and Eugene Minkowski, Erwin Straus, and Ludwig Binswanger. It seems to me that the kind of analysis Binswanger performs in "The Case of Ellen West" is perfectly suited to literary criticism—in fact it is a kind of literary criticism, since the bulk of the material upon which he bases his study consists of diary entries and poems.

My analysis of temporality in the novels of William S. Burroughs owes a great deal to Binswanger's analysis of Ellen West's temporality. Binswanger's greatest debt is to Heidegger, and through him to Husserl, the founder of the phenomenological method. This method ideally consists of an unbiased contemplation of phenomena, putting aside any a priori methodological presuppositions or intellectual considerations. In theory, it is a method which is not a method, which has no plan. In this respect it is related to poetry as a way of knowledge, a relationship that becomes explicit in some of the truly poetic passages in Heidegger and Merleau-Ponty. But in practice, most phenomenological thought does fasten upon certain modes in the analysis of phenomena, the most important ones being spatiality and temporality. The aim is always to reconstruct the inner world of an experience, and for this reason phenomenology has been particularly suited to the study of mental disorders.

This method can and should be applied to the study of literature also. Too often we overlay the world of a novel or poem with our own perceptual presuppositions, an error that has contributed to monumental misunderstandings of primitive literature and the literature of other cultures. Given the radical shifts our own culture is undergoing, it is easy to repeat this kind of error in the study of Western literature. My purpose in this work is to avoid that error, to uncover the world of a work of literature, or—in the case of realism or symbolism—of a school of literature, according to its own inner structural coordinates. Only in this manner can we apprehend the underlying structures of the culture from which that literature is inseparable.

I gratefully acknowledge permission from the following publishers to quote from works that are under copyright: Atheneum Publishers, for *The Lice* by W. S. Merwin; Doubleday & Company, Inc., for *The Collected Poems of Theodore Roethke*; Grove Press, for William Burroughs' *Naked Lunch*, *The Soft Machine*, *The Ticket That Exploded*, and *Nova Express*; Alfred A. Knopf, Inc., for lines from the poetry of Wallace Stevens; and Wesleyan University Press, for lines from "Falling" by James Dickey. Thanks also to the *Iowa Review*, which originally published Chapters Three and Five of this book in slightly altered form, and to *Poetry Northwest,* in which my "We Are All One" originally appeared.

I would like to thank Michael Harper of Brown University and Michael Hoffman of the University of California at Davis, both of whom read the manuscript and encouraged me greatly, Karl Shapiro of Davis and Henry Taylor of American University, who offered helpful suggestions, and Joseph Lyons of Davis, who guided me through the maze of research on schizophrenia. Above all, I thank Thomas Hanzo of Davis, whose inspiration as a teacher helped make this book possible, and my wife, Ann, whose love helped make it actual.

. . . soon we saw seven houses of brick, one we
enterd; in it were a number of monkeys, baboons,
and all of that species chaind by the middle, grinning and snatching at one another, but withheld
by the shortness of their chains: however I saw
that they sometimes grew numerous, and then the
weak were caught by the strong and with a grinning aspect, first coupled with and then devourd,
by plucking off first one limb and then another
till the body was left a helpless trunk. This after
grinning and kissing it with seeming fondness they
devourd too; and here and there I saw one savour-
ily picking the flesh off of his own tail; as the
stench terribly annoyd us both we went into the
mill, and I in my hand brought the skeleton of a
body, which in the mill was Aristotles Analytics.

BLAKE, *The Marriage of Heaven and Hell*

1 / The Garden and the Map

God was the first schizophrenic. In India every god has a "terrible form" as well as a benevolent one. The Bulgarians say that Satan arose from God's shadow and convinced God to divide the world between the two of them. The Finns say that God asked his reflection in the water how to make the world.[1] Reflections and shadows are schizophrenic images; when they step out of their relation of dependence and seize their own autonomy, a split occurs (in Greek, *schizein* means "to split").

If the action of "splitting" or the state of "being split" isn't explicitly present in the concepts of God of most primitive peoples, it is virtually present in all of their creation myths. Creation is always a "fall" from wholeness, a separation, a dividing. When divinity is pictured as an indivisible totality, a whole, the creation of the world becomes a breaking down of this totality. Thus the world often stems from a cosmogonic egg or sphere that cracks open, enabling the sky to separate from the earth.[2] Or the primeval state of the world is represented by an Androgyne, or an anthropocosmic giant, and the act of creation is a splitting of the Androgyne, or a dismemberment of the body of the giant.[3]

1. Mircea Eliade, *Mephistopheles and the Androgyne*, trans. J. M. Cohen (New York, 1965), pp. 91, 86.

2. Mircea Eliade, *Patterns in Comparative Religion*, trans. Rosemary Sheed (Cleveland, 1963), p. 413.

3. Eliade, *Mephistopheles*, p. 115.

This kind of process, the movement from wholeness to splitting, is a universal one in the act of being human. Erich Neumann sees in it the birth of the ego and the origin of human consciousness.[4] Teilhard de Chardin sees in it the pattern of the evolution of the universe.[5] The purpose of this chapter is to examine some of the ways in which humanity anchors itself in structures of separation, and how those structures become institutionalized in the forms of thought of Western man. I use the terms "anchors" and "institutionalized" purposely. All cultures exhibit organizations of wholeness and splitting, but these organizations are usually fluid; the whole participates in its parts, and vice versa. Where the structure of splitting in such cultures is specifically a splitting in two (as in the Chinese Yin and Yang), the opposites that result are dynamically opposed, in the sense that each participates in the tension of the other, each sustains the other.

In contrast, the unique property of Western thought, of what Husserl calls philosophy-science,[6] is that it anchors the very forms of its thought, that it detemporalizes them and seals them off from each other. In the West, parts become discrete, atomized, and the whole becomes a sum, not a unity, of its parts. Opposites are static in their opposition; they are mutually exclusive. Examples of such dualisms in Western thought are endless: subject and object, fantasy and reality, spirit and matter, sacred and profane, soul and body, knower and known, self and world, etc. There is no *coincidentia oppositorum*, no unity of opposites, in classical Western thought, as there is in almost all primitive cultures. The function of static exclusiveness and separation is established at the very heart of Western civilization, and in this sense that civilization can be called schizophrenic.

The most powerful expression of the fall from wholeness for the Western tradition occurs in Genesis. The fall of Adam and

4. *The Origins and History of Consciousness*, trans. R. F. C. Hull (New York, 1962), I, 102ff.

5. *The Phenomenon of Man*, trans. Bernard Wall (London, 1959), p. 222.

6. *Phenomenology and the Crisis of Philosophy*, trans. Quentin Lauer (New York, 1965), p. 159.

Eve stems from and confirms itself in knowledge, and thus provides a dramatic miniature of the evolution from primitive (mythical-religious) to modern (philosophical-scientific) man —from the condition of the garden to the condition of the map. The garden and the map are the structures that illustrate most clearly the difference between the two modes of the wholeness-splitting process, the dynamic mode of Eastern and primitive cultures and the static one of Western culture.

I want to emphasize that they are structures in order to make it clear that my method in the following discussion, particularly the discussion of Genesis, is not historical criticism or scriptural exegesis but structural analysis. I include variants of the Genesis story, commentaries upon it, and comments by anthropologists on primitive thought, not for the purpose of establishing an ur-myth or an ideal source of religious beliefs, or anything of the type, but simply in order to uncover the structure that means "garden." Similarly, the analysis of early Greek thought in the second section constitutes an attempt to reveal the structure that means "map," and to justify the application of the term "schizophrenic" to that structure. Finally, in the third section, I will analyze some aspects of modern Western culture by examining these metaphors, garden and map, in a seminal work of modern literature, Conrad's *Heart of Darkness*.

1

In the Garden of Eden, Adam and Eve live in a proximate and fluid environment. There is an aspect of wholeness to this life, a naive direct participation of all forms of life in each other, a synthetic function to all of experience. Actually the term "synthetic" is misleading. What is synthetic from our point of view, i.e., a unity of previously differentiated opposites, is the natural and real condition of the Garden before the schizophrenic opposites of subject and object, inner and outer, left and right, etc., are born. Anthropologists such as Levi-Bruhl and Durkheim, and thinkers such as Cassirer, Neumann, or Eliade, who have analyzed myth and the rudimentary forms of consciousness, have all emphasized this synthetic aspect of consciousness previous to formal knowledge.

The world after the Fall, outside of the Garden, is essentially colorless, neutral, impersonal. It has been separated from the person; there is no longer a synthesis. Objects confine themselves in their locations in a kind of homogeneous map space rather than a magic, expressive space. In the Garden, objects are sacred, invested with human and divine significance. "Things are taken for the incarnation of what they express, because their human significance is compressed into them and presents itself literally as what they mean."[7] The world of sacred objects manifests everywhere the mystery of incarnation, the "coexistence of contradictory essences."[8] The sacred *means*, it *manifests* itself. It is not inert, "there"; it lives and speaks. Everything has a significance; there is, in Jacob Boehme's phrase, a "signature of all things."[9] Outside of the Garden, significance is always referential; it stands behind or beside an object, externally attached to it. Significance and meaning assume a map function; they are assigned in one-to-one correspondences, just as a map creates a one-to-one correspondence between visual symbols and an actual landscape.

In the Garden, significance exists in a constant state of being unlocked by the proliferation of forms. In particular, Eliade asserts, plants represent the appearance of forms, the act of manifestation (as opposed to water, which represents the potential, the undifferentiated).[10] The Tree of Life is the best symbol of this act of manifestation. The Tree reenacts the whole cosmos; it "*is* the universe, and it *is* so because it reproduces it."[11] The Tree has no "location"; its organization is growth itself, the fluid unity of part and whole, by which every part manifests the whole. The Tree represents the very rhythm of life, the act of expanding and contracting, of breathing and exhaling, of

7. Maurice Merleau-Ponty, *The Phenomenology of Perception*, trans. Colin Smith (London, 1962), p. 290.

8. Eliade, *Patterns*, p. 29.

9. This is the English title of one of Boehme's works.

10. Eliade, *Patterns*, p. 281.

11. Ibid., p. 269.

being drawn up into itself and freely producing itself, at one and the same time. The limbs of the Tree are its visible lines of growth, and their relationship to the trunk is that of a gradation of actions to an actor, a gradation of dynamic forms from the very small to the very large.

The kind of organization represented by the Tree cannot be emphasized too much. Cassirer, and Neumann after him, sees the basic model of human thought in the opposition of night and day.[12] But this kind of bipolar model is a condition attained outside the Garden, after the Fall, when distance has inserted itself into consciousness and enabled man to neutralize time and apprehend night and day simultaneously in a kind of map space. Before the Fall, the models for thought are proximate rather than distant ones: the root, the flower, the Tree, the body. And all these models represent integrative rather than segregative structures: they are all fluid organizations of part and whole, by which the whole centers itself in each part, just as the world centers itself in every finite grain of sand for Blake. The Tree carries the imprint of itself in all its parts, in the root, the leaf, the stem, the branch, the limb. The body too reproduces its organization in all its limbs. Both represent, or are, structures that unify the whole and its parts, unity and multiplicity, rather than separate them.

The experience of this unity is carried by the body. The "resurrection of the body" in contemporary thought (Norman O. Brown, Maurice Merleau-Ponty) represents specifically a reaction against bipolar, schizophrenic structures that occur with the fall into Western civilization. Merleau-Ponty's analysis of the body could be called an analysis of the way in which we carry within us the virtual unity of the Garden, even if that unity has been repressed by the schizophrenic forms of classical psychology and physics. "I do not bring together one by one the parts of my body; this translation and this unification are performed once and for all within me: they are my body itself."[13]

---

12. Ernst Cassirer, *The Philosophy of Symbolic Forms*, trans. Ralph Manheim (New Haven, 1955), III, 96. See also Neumann, *Origins*, I, 107.

13. Merleau-Ponty, *Phenomenology*, p. 150.

The parts of Adam's world dovetail against the ground of the body's unity. They are not localized according to a system of coordinates but arrange themselves in a dynamic synthesis around the body, as potential expressions of the body, as elements of the body's space.

This sense of the unity of the body in the Garden has found expression in the assertion that Adam was androgynous. One rabbinical commentary asserts that Adam "was a man on his right side, a woman on his left; but God split him into two halves."[14] Thus some traditions have seen a "First Fall" in the creation of Eve out of Adam. The apocryphal Gospel of Philip asserts this, as does Jacob Boehme, the seventeenth-century German mystic. According to Boehme, "when Eve was made out of Adam during his sleep, this was done in the fiat, in the *spiritus mundi.* There they were made into creatures of the outer world, that is, fashioned into the external natural life, into mortality, with bestial members, and also a carcass or worm-bag to hold earthly food."[15] The separation of Adam and Eve is a fall into the objective body, the body deprived of its unity. Before the Fall, eating is a magic act that doesn't require a digestive cycle.[16] But with the Fall, objects outside the body become objects of desire and consumption; and the body too becomes an object.

In fact, as Boehme asserts, it was the carrying of eating into the body that constitutes what we normally consider the Fall.[17] The Fall consists not in what was eaten but in the act of eating. The apple was the first commodity, in the sense that it embodied the pure act of being a commodity, of existing to be wanted; and Satan was the first salesman. The apple was the first object divested of human significance, the first object pushed into the furthest extreme of its definition, as something separate, objective. It could thus be approached only by the furthest extreme of human gestures toward the world: ownership and consumption. This kind of schizophrenia constitutes the Fall, for in the

14. Cited in Eliade, *Patterns*, p. 423.
15. Jacob Boehme, *On the Election of Grace*, trans. John Rolleston Earle (London, 1930), p. 92.
16. Ibid., p. 77.
17. Ibid., p. 96.

schizophrenic world everything flies into the outcome of its meaning: to acquire, William Burroughs shows, is to devour; to give of oneself is to be devoured.

In this sense, the apple devours Adam and Eve as well as vice versa, for desire is a radical surrender of one's self as well as a radical act of acquisition. The Fall consists in the person's making himself a commodity, because, as Burroughs points out, the salesman sells the customer to the product.[18] Adam and Eve become the first consumers, and their bodies become objects. This is true in a sexual sense too, as Augustine and Milton make explicit in their accounts of the Fall. The close association between eating and sexual intercourse that Claude Lévi-Strauss notes in primitive thought[19] is part of the dynamic of the Fall. Both eating and copulating externalize themselves in the objective body; both cease to be magic acts.

Outside of the Garden all of man's relationships to his needs and his world externalize themselves and become processes with separate structures. Man becomes the object of law, the object of the social contract, the object of knowledge, the object of the circulation of goods. The Fall in particular is a fall into economic relationships, since the body has first and foremost become an object of need and desire. God curses the ground, and Adam has to extract out of it through toil what was naturally present to him before the Fall. This process itself has separate structures: there is one before produce reaches the body, one for the body itself, and one after it leaves.

In the Garden there is an immediate satisfaction of needs, to such an extent that to speak of needs is misleading. But outside the Garden, a radical distance has been inserted between man and his environment; objects sacred to him become mere "objects of consumption" and have to be separated into the open, captured, plucked, shelled, packaged, transported, and received. In the Garden, man literally feels himself "born from" the earth; as Eliade points out, primitive peoples usually believe the fetus or seed enters a woman's womb from wells, trees, crocodiles,

18. *Naked Lunch* (New York, 1966), p. xxix.
19. *The Savage Mind*, trans. George Weidenfeld (Chicago, 1966), p. 105.

swans, caves, etc.[20] There are sacred spaces in the Garden, areas that are qualitatively related to the body.[21] But outside the Garden, space arranges itself economically; there is an area for work, an area for play, an area to live in, etc., and these occur beside each other, in a homogeneous map arrangement, into which the body enters.

An economy that is redistributive rather than reciprocal[22] requires various centers, stores, into which goods flow and out of which they spread. And these require transportation routes and roads, a map arrangement of one's environment. A map represents the mechanization of the Tree organization: it relates the whole to its parts as an addition of discrete entities rather than as a fluid unity of transformations. The image of the map and of its counterpart, the labyrinth, becomes a common one in the modern novel. It is an image, John Barth points out, of exhaustion,[23] of Western thought structures that have lost their cohesive force. This lack of cohesive force is implicit in the Fall itself, in structures that find their expression in the discreteness represented by property relationships. In the Garden, every location is a potential center.[24] Outside the Garden, locations become "property," discrete entities connected to people externally in a map space by relationships of containment and ownership, relationships of having.

Of course the circulation of goods and the demarcation of property are not the only functions of a map. But the most essential quality of a map—discreteness—is one that it shares with the structure of objects when those objects exist solely for the sake of being owned or consumed. The definition of a map would obviously be destroyed if its parts could penetrate each other. Each area of a map is confined in its location, to the degree that

20. Eliade, *Patterns*, pp. 243–44.

21. See Mircea Eliade, *The Sacred and the Profane*, trans. Willard R. Trask (New York, 1961), pp. 20ff.

22. The distinction is Karl Polanyi's, in "Anthropology and Economic Theory," *Readings in Anthropology* (New York, 1959), II, 169.

23. Barth specifically sees the image of the labyrinth as a dynamic of behavior, a continual production of mutually exclusive choices, in "The Literature of Exhaustion," *Atlantic Monthly*, CXX (August 1967), 34.

24. Eliade, *Patterns*, pp. 373ff.

this assertion constitutes a tautology. Areas on a map are related only at their respective borders, so that no location can exist in itself and in any other location simultaneously. The last statement is simply the Aristotelian Principle of Contradiction in slightly different terms than it was put by Aristotle: "the same attribute cannot at the same time belong and not belong to the same subject and in the same respect."[25] In this regard, the structure of a map is essentially bipolar; it depends upon the separation of Being and Nonbeing.[26] This is what "discreteness" means and why it underlies the relationship of property as well as the structure of a map.

Perhaps the best way to look at it would be through mathematics. Aristotle defines number as "discrete quantity,"[27] and the reason is obvious: when two numbers are added together, they do not merge; rather, it is sufficient to stack them together externally. This is why only two numbers are necessary to generate a mathematics, as in the binary system. The deciding factor is that the distinction between those two numbers is absolute; thus they are totally sealed off from each other, as Being and Nonbeing are. It is this absolute "sealing off" which enables objects as property to be owned, which draws the line between properties themselves and between objects-as-property and *myself* ("having," Marx says, alienates the body[28]). One historian of mathematics claims that mathematics originated with the rise of personal property. "Property had to be taxed; therefore, the chief or leader or king had to know how much property each of his subjects had in order to levy taxes. A picture of each and every object being counted was too cumbersome, and systems of number notation developed—notches on a stick, lines and dots pressed into a clay tablet."[29] Once mathematics is created, property can be manipulated and controlled symbolically, that

25. *Metaphysics* 1005b 19–21.
26. In the language of traditional logic, the absolute separation of Being and Nonbeing occurs when the Law of Contradiction is separated from the Law of Identity.
27. *Categories* 4b 31.
28. "Economic and Philosophical Manuscripts," trans. T. B. Bottomore, in Erich Fromm, *Marx's Concept of Man* (New York, 1961), p. 132.
29. Jane Muir, *Of Men and Numbers* (New York, 1961), p. 8.

is, with map structures, and still retain its discreteness. Mathematics confirms the discreteness of property by reducing it to its own nature: quantity.

Underlying the structure called "map," and underlying mathematics, is the relationship of discreteness; and underlying discreteness is the Principle of Contradiction, the dual mode, the separation of Being and Nonbeing. This is why the wholeness-splitting process in the civilization of the West is not a process but a static state, a map. And this is why the fall from the condition of the Garden is established in knowledge. Formal knowledge bases itself in formal logic, and the Principle of Contradiction is the foundation of formal logic. Its dual system is the antithesis of the integrative organizations of part and whole that existed in the Garden. The Tree of the Knowledge of Good and Evil, which propels Adam and Eve out of the Garden, is the mechanical tree of discreteness and separation, of schizophrenia, the opposite of the Tree of Life. Knowledge is not simply of Good and Evil, but of their separation, their polarity. The radical separation of Being and Nonbeing neutralizes the dialect of experience[30] and arranges the world into mutually exclusive coordinates of zero and one, left and right, good and evil, work and play, self and body, etc.

All of this will be clarified in the following section. Most of Greek philosophy springs from the Principle of Contradiction, either implicitly or explicitly[31] (the notable exception is Heraclitus). And in Greek philosophy the assumptions of the modern "realistic" world are born.

2

When Thales, in what is considered the first act of philosophy, said that everything was water, he was creating a world of mutually exclusive coordinates, a world based on discreteness,

---

30. See Herbert Marcuse, *One-Dimensional Man* (Boston, 1964), p. 137.
31. Aristotle called it the basic principle of philosophy, in *Metaphysics* 1005b 22.

in a naive but prophetic way. To assert that everything is made out of water implies that everything is not made out of itself. The underlying integrity of objects that I take for granted is an illusion; there is something beside or behind things that accounts for them; there is a distinction between what I see and what things are, between appearances and reality, the many and the one. Most of the major themes of Greek philosophy (and perhaps of Greek drama) are implied by Thales' act. And all of the referential epistemologies of the West find their beginnings in Thales. There is a distinction between image and object, sign and significance, and these are connected by a kind of one-to-one mapping function.

There is a gap between the knower and the known; man has to dissolve a veil in order to arrive at substantial reality. Objects no longer manifest themselves; nor are they invested with human expression and significance. Distance intervenes between man and his world, between subject and object. Space becomes uniform, and the subject relinquishes his own point of view in it. To know, the subject places himself outside the world, at a distance. Only then does the veil dissolve; the world falls into order, its clutter collapsing into one homogeneous principle. Thus space no longer has an "accent."[32] It assumes a map aspect and flattens out, as when, from a great distance, the earth itself looks like a map.

The distance inserted between man and his environment by the fall into knowledge is not depth as experienced by the body, but is, in Merleau-Ponty's phrase, "breadth in profile," a geometrized distance that dissolves the fusion of distance and time, and thus neutralizes the potential and actual experience of the body. True depth, says Merleau-Ponty, "announces a certain indissoluble link between things and myself by which I am placed in front of them, whereas breadth can, at first sight, be taken as a relationship between things themselves, in which the perceiving subject is not implied."[33] The world opens up to Thales,

32. The term is Cassirer's, in *Symbolic Forms*, II, 85.
33. Merleau-Ponty, *Phenomenology*, p. 256.

unfolds and releases its secrets; but it unfolds like a map, is independent and indifferent, inert and static. The structure of Adam's fall into the map of the world becomes more clear in Thales' act. The world does not move when he moves; it does not arrange itself around him. It does not change, since, as in a map, the temporal dimension has been eliminated. Erwin Straus, in a study of aphasic patients who are unable to draw a floor plan of the room or house they are in, makes some pertinent remarks about maps and floor plans: "On a floor plan, we transcend without effort the natural barriers of sight, location and distance. . . . Whoever draws a floor plan must be able to emancipate himself from the impact of reality. A change in his I-world relation is required. . . . The direction backward is eliminated and replaced by the dimension side by side. A plan does not represent an abstraction from concrete sight; it translates visible space into the abstract, homogeneous, isometric, impersonal order of geometry."[34]

The plan, the map implied by Thales' act, was the first consistent and rigorous transformation of the world into object in the West, the transformation that enabled concepts such as "nature" and "identity" to arise. It was the first verification of the subject-object dichotomy that occurred with the Fall, for with space completely mapped, the person is either a disembodied subject, observing the world from a distance, or, as Straus remarks, an object with a position on the map, inserted into "the detached order of things."[35] I no longer fill my body; nor does my body fill space, so that "the small can be copied in the large, the distant in the near, and the two are essentially the same."[36] Rather, the near and the distant drain out of each other and solidify their positions, and the ego "begins simultaneously to constellate its independence of nature as independence of the body."[37] "Locality" freezes into a series of Chinese boxes: the

34. Erwin Straus, *Phenomenological Psychology* (New York, 1966), pp. 262–63.

35. Ibid., p. 262.

36. Cassirer, *Symbolic Forms*, II, 92.

37. Neumann, *Origins*, I, 109.

subject contained in the body contained in space. Holes open up in space, as if the structure of our sight, by which we perceive our body from a hole on top of it, were literally true.

And space itself becomes a hole; as Milic Capek shows, classical space is a container, logically prior to the things it contains.[38] Zero enters the world of knowledge, nothing, Nonbeing. Previous to zero there is plenitude, but with it gaps open up between things, and the world congeals into matter and space, density and vacuum, Being and Nonbeing. Zero is what gives mathematics the potential for infinity and carries the Void into the universe. The opposition of Being and Nonbeing becomes with the atomists the opposition of the Plenum and the Void. "By convention there is bitter, by convention hot and cold, by convention color; but in reality there are only atoms and the void."[39] The quality of discreteness injected into objects by the fall out of the Garden is confirmed in Democritus. The Void clings to the outlines of things, and things are, beneath appearances, discrete entities of matter, impenetrable, unchanging. Change is only a shift of position, a change of configuration. Implicit in atomic dualism, Capek shows, is the complete elimination of movement and time, since movement and time are separable from the objects that move and change.[40]

Zeno, who in so many respects parodied the fundamental concepts of Greek philosophy, made the elimination of movement and time explicit. Most of his paradoxes are well known, and they all involve an infinite regress, the rape of the finite by zero. For a body to move to a goal, it would have to go half the distance to it, and half that distance, and so on ad infinitum; therefore nothing can move. The threat represented by Zeno is implicit in all of Western thought and appears in such contemporary authors as John Barth and Jorge Luis Borges. (Borges has written an essay in which he traces avatars of Zeno's

38. *The Philosophical Impact of Contemporary Physics* (Princeton, N.J., 1961), p. 9.

39. Democritus, in Philip Wheelwright, ed., *The Presocratics* (New York, 1966), p. 183.

40. Capek, *Contemporary Physics*, pp. 123ff.

paradoxes; for example, in Saint Thomas Aquinas' proof of God's existence, and in F. H. Bradley's proof that no logical relationships are possible between concepts.)[41] A world structured by dualisms necessarily contains faults or cracks, miniature Voids, infinite regressions, into each of which the universe is capable of pouring itself. Georges Poulet's comments on Descartes are relevant. When consciousness becomes a discrete entity, sealed off from the body as it was by Descartes, not only is there "a dividing in two of being, but an infinite multiplication of it into innumerable ephemeral personalities which are less and less in rapport among themselves. Then time itself is fragmented."[42] Thus Descartes could say, "From the fact that *I had been* a little while ago, it does not follow that I ought to be *now...*," and "From the fact that *I am now*, it does not follow that *I must be hereafter....*"[43] He consequently inserted God between each instant of time, by claiming that the world was perpetually perishing and being created; but this is God as zero, as the hidden Void between things.

As Capek points out, Descartes' concept of time was really a spatialized time,[44] as in Zeno. Instants of time were conceived of according to the model of points on a line, or atoms in space, and therefore took on the quality of coexistence that points and atoms possess. But this is to destroy time, to eliminate all distinctions between past and future. The universe is reduced to a series of spatial configurations, which is to say that the universe attains the condition of the formal logic that apprehends it. The universe becomes the structure of the mind externalized, the map of the mind, whose function is to channel all material content into separate and manageable units, free from the condition of change that allows them to slip through our fingers.

Aristotle's formal logic is thus the completion and establishment of the flattening out and mapping of the world implied by

41. "Avatars of the Tortoise," trans. James E. Irby, in *Labyrinths* (New York, 1964).

42. Georges Poulet, *Studies in Human Time*, trans. Elliott Coleman (Baltimore, 1959), p. 57.

43. Ibid., p. 58.

44. Capek, *Contemporary Physics*, p. 162.

Adam's fall and by Thales' act of philosophy. As Kenneth Burke says, "a logic is 'flat,' simultaneous, 'chordal.' "[45] With formal logic all aspects of experience unravel and rope themselves off. Change and movement have separate areas to themselves, and nothing is subject to them. They become the lines connecting things, the corridors and streets joining rooms and buildings; as in a map, or as in the cities and houses we build with a map consciousness, change and movement lie outside the essential areas of things. And these essential areas themselves lie outside of each other. This division of the world into reified movement and sealed-off areas is an important structural element of the naturalistic novel. It implies that there can be no free and universal passage from one thing or place to another. Whitehead's remarks about concepts of matter in Einsteinian physics describe this free passage: "In a certain sense, everything is everywhere at all times. For every location involves an aspect of itself in every other location."[46] The structure of formal logic imposes exactly the opposite condition upon the world. It separates identity and contradiction and imposes schizophrenia. The good cannot touch the bad, the living the dead, sanity madness, or black white. And as Marcuse points out, those areas that cannot be organized by logic become particular, incalculable, "subjective."[47]

If the subjective is the refuse area of formal thought, it thus throws into contrast by its very existence the clarity of the "objective." The structure of formal logic enables civilization to confirm its absolute space of reasonableness, cleanliness, freedom, and wealth, precisely by creating equally absolute but sealed-off spaces of madness, dirt, slavery, and poverty: spaces it can politely observe now and then, as the ladies and gentlemen of the eighteenth century observed lunatics in their cells for recreation.[48]

45. *The Philosophy of Literary Form* (New York, 1957), p. 84.
46. Cited in Capek, *Contemporary Physics*, p. 271.
47. *One-Dimensional Man*, p. 138.
48. Michel Foucault, in *Madness and Civilization*, trans. Richard Howard (New York, 1965), has written the history of civilization's creation of a separate space for madness.

In this sense the structure of logic is that of containment. We "grasp" things with logic; we obtain and fix them. Concepts exist *in* logic as matter exists *in* the space that contains it. Logic is formal, and form is "shape," external, a container. Logic defines by delimiting, by channeling objects into smaller and smaller containers, from genus to species to individual. Thus objects themselves lose their internal coherence, their integrity, in the same way the body does. Their structure is externalized, and they contain their essence or use as if they were cages, just as the body contains its subject. Objects become consumer goods, packaged in themselves, to be drained or emptied, like bottles or cans, and thrown away. Objects become instant waste, like the apple in Eden; their relationship to the body is objective and centrifugal rather than sacred and centripetal. The structure of objects in modern literature, especially in the realistic novel and in some contemporary authors such as Kafka, Sartre, and Burroughs, finds its origins in this radical surgery performed upon them by formal logic.

This surgery and its implications for human perception can also be seen in the doctrine of primary and secondary qualities, which literally cuts objects in two. The doctrine is implicit in Aristotle[49] and best known in Locke, but received its first complete formulation in Galileo's *Il Saggiatore:*

> This much I have to say, that as soon as I form a conception of a material or corporeal substance, I simultaneously feel the necessity of conceiving that it has boundaries, and is of some shape or other; that relatively to others it is great or small; that it is in this or that place, in this or that time; that it is in motion or at rest; that it touches, or does not touch another body; that it is unique, rare, or common; nor can I, by any act of imagination, disjoin it from these qualities; but I do not find myself absolutely compelled to apprehend it as necessarily accompanied by such conditions as that it must be white or red, bitter or sweet, sonorous or silent, smelling sweetly or disagreeably; and if the senses had not pointed out these qualities, it is probable that language and imagination alone could never have arrived at

49. *Metaphysics* 1020b 13ff.

them. Therefore I am inclined to think that these tastes, smells, colours, etc, with regard to the object in which they appear to reside, are nothing more than mere names, and exist only in the sensitive body; insomuch that when the living creature is removed, all these qualities are carried off and annihilated, although we have imposed particular names upon them (different from those other and real accidents), and would fain persuade ourselves that they truly and in fact exist. But I do not believe that there exists anything in external bodies for exciting tastes, smells and sounds, but size, shape, quantity, and motion, swift or slow.[50]

I have quoted Galileo at length not only because he clearly states the distinction between primary and secondary qualities, but also because he summarizes most of the assumptions of Greek atomistic thought carried over into Newtonian physics, assumptions upon which our everyday notions of reality are based. Primary qualities are those that contain or are contained; they represent the object in its shape, defined by the clarity of absolute space, with all the layers of our subjectivity peeled off it. Primary qualities refer to the object in total isolation, perhaps as seen by God, but not from a human point of view. Thus Newton appropriately defined space as *Sensorium Dei*. Objects stand forth in their true and naked natures only in the eyesight of God and in the mathematics of the scientist (which becomes a new and more reliable sight); otherwise they are obscured by being divided from themselves. This division is inseparable from the body-mind split in man, for my senses are in a fundamental respect unreliable since I reside inside my body, observing objects as best I can, while tolerating because I have to the blindnesses the walls of my body impose. Newton's expression of this split is still the most pointed: "in philosophical disquisitions, we ought to abstract from our senses, and consider things themselves, distinct from what are only sensible measures of them."[51]

50. Cited by Alfred North Whitehead in Samuel Rapport and Helen Wright, eds., *Physics* (New York, 1965), pp. 11–12.

51. Quoted in J. J. C. Smart, ed., *Problems of Space and Time* (New York, 1964), p. 84.

Essential to the classical modern world, then, is a schizo-phrenic self-body dichotomy, a dichotomy initiated by the Fall and confirmed in the structure of formal logic and modern science. Descartes made this dichotomy explicit in his well-known distinction between *res cogitans* and *res extensa*. The body becomes an object and an annoying one at that. Its structure is not the spontaneous unity of a whole and its parts, but the mechanical one of fragmented parts placed in a series. Vesalius, the founder of modern anatomy, dismembered the body in a series of etchings that placed skeletons, muscle systems, bodily parts, etc., into the exact perspective of seventeenth-century landscapes. McLuhan calls technology an amputation of the self,[52] but it is really an amputation of the body from the self and of bodily parts from each other.

Anatomy, then, is the most fundamental technology: it presupposes that the body exists in objective space, thus presupposes that the parts of the body are mutually independent in both space and time. Erwin Straus has commented on the implications of this for psychology: "Regardless of one's conception of the interrelation of individual senses, they remain parts, separated in space. Their functions are processes separated in time. Since objective psychology interprets experiencing epiphenomenologically, it is bound by its methods to atomistic concepts."[53] Objective psychology systematically excludes the living body from the world, just as it excludes consciousness from the body. As in Pavlov's experiments, "the organism has no relation to its environment except for the fact that its border areas can be excited from outside."[54] The process of sensing thereby becomes a series of referential mappings. When I see, an object is projected upon the retina, a signal or excitation is conducted from the retina to the cerebral cortex, and an image appears in consciousness isomorphous with the cortical motion.[55] Consciousness is not once, but twice, removed from the world.

---

52. *Understanding Media* (New York, 1964), p. 53.
53. *The Primary World of the Senses*, trans. Jacob Needleman (New York, 1963), p. 54.
54. Ibid., p. 45.
55. Ibid., p. 162.

This psychology has produced the traditional descriptions of schizophrenia; yet this psychology itself is based upon a schizophrenic split. As Ronald Laing points out, the basic split in schizophrenia is between an embodied self and an unembodied self.[56] This is precisely the view of the person assumed by classical psychology. The extent to which this view has produced rather than cured schizophrenia can only be guessed at. "The 'cause' of 'schizophrenia,'" says Laing, "is to be found by the examination, not of the prospective diagnosee alone, but of the whole social context in which the psychiatric ceremonial is being conducted."[57] This context is modeled upon that of medical science: the patient is a body whose behavior is noted and recorded from the normative point of view of a detached observer. I say "normative" because this point of view bears the stamp of Western culture. To the extent that we all partake of the assumptions described in this chapter, we participate in this point of view. And to that extent, we are all schizophrenic.

It remains to justify my application of the term "schizophrenic" to this structure, to show that the schizophrenic experience itself reveals affinities with the forms of Western thought. We have seen that the body-self split is a common element in both schizophrenia and the structures of life and thought in the West. In schizophrenia, when this body-self split becomes pronounced, a vacuum often develops inside the body; there are feelings of total impotence, emptiness.[58] This is what Ludwig Binswanger calls "being-a-hole."[59] The body becomes a shell in which a void exists, not unlike the Void of the Greek atomists. In a sense, the void also exists outside for the schizophrenic, since the world becomes the not-me, the Other, an absolute, homogeneous, impersonal space gathered into sharply defined boundaries, which are the edges of the body. There is a complete mapping off of areas of experience in schizophrenia,

---

56. *The Divided Self* (Baltimore, 1965), p. 66.
57. *The Politics of Experience* (London, 1967), p. 103.
58. Laing, *Divided Self*, p. 75.
59. "The Case of Ellen West," trans. Werner M. Mendel and Joseph Lyons, in *Existence*, ed. Rollo May, Ernest Angel, and Henri F. Ellenberger (New York, 1958), p. 319.

a total separation of each thing into its own principle, self, body, and world, as in the structures of Greek and modern scientific thought.

For the schizophrenic it is precisely the objectivity of the world, its total Otherness, that causes that world to exist as a threat. Objectivity takes on life by virtue of its very objectivity, and actively persecutes the schizophrenic. "Everything, everything turns against me," said one of Minkowski's patients. "How clever and infamous their scheme is. All one has to do is continue doing what one has always done—washing, combing one's hair, eating, going to the toilet—and all this will be turned against me."[60] Daniel Paul Schreber, a schizophrenic who has written an account of his illness, put it even more explicitly: "I feel a blow on my head simultaneously with every word spoken around me, with every approaching footstep, with every railway whistle, with every shot fired by a pleasure steamer, etc."[61]

The threat the world presents for the schizophrenic is often a threat of control. In the West, the split of the world into two absolute principles, subject and object, has enabled civilization to control and manipulate nature, as Marcuse has pointed out.[62] The experience of schizophrenia reveals one of the underlying horrors of Western civilization: that to control is always in a sense to be controlled, since splitting the world into subject and object makes the subject into an object, i.e., a discrete entity, as well. Thus Schreber feels that his body is penetrated by the rays of God and that God and his doctor are trying to perform a "soul-murder" upon him.[63] Everything and everyone watches the schizophrenic in order to gain an advantage over him, to seize control over everything he does.[64] Voices urge him to perform actions contrary to his nature. Passages in novels tell him that he should do something, or are indications that the

60. Eugene Minkowski, "Findings in a Case of Schizophrenic Depression," trans. Barbara Bliss, in *Existence*, p. 135.

61. *Memoirs of My Nervous Illness*, trans. Ida Macalpine and Richard A. Hunter (London, 1955), p. 94.

62. *Eros and Civilization* (New York, 1955), p. 100.

63. Schreber, *Memoirs*, pp. 54ff.

64. Laing, *Divided Self*, p. 113.

author knows about the sins of his past and hence has control over him.[65]

The reaction of the schizophrenic to this total threat of the object-world is to cover himself,[66] to develop "false self systems,"[67] roles, parts, masks, as armor against the weight of the Other, against the world's attempt to control him. But to disperse one's personality into roles is to wear one's self away, as Binswanger points out.[68] The schizophrenic's roles and masks are discrete; they atomize his personality. This is one of the central features of schizophrenia, and it displays an obvious affinity with the structures of Western thought, themselves based on discreteness and atomization. In schizophrenia, areas of the personality are fragmented and mutually exclusive; they have nothing to do with each other.

Often this structure takes on the strength of hallucinatory experience. Schreber describes it in these terms: "I felt as if I myself existed for some time also in a second, mentally inferior form," and "souls in nerve-contact with me talked of a plurality of heads (that is several individuals in one and the same skull) which they encountered in me and from which they shrank in alarm crying 'For heaven's sake—that is a human being with several heads.'"[69] As this statement indicates, the fragmentation of the personality in schizophrenia is often accompanied by a system of fantasy. Indeed one of the primary devices the schizophrenic uses to cover himself is to retreat into fantasy. And only in schizophrenia and in Western civilization does fantasy exist in a pure, separate space that can be retreated to, having been siphoned out of the objective, "real" world. Fantasy is such an absolute phenomenon, a total Other, that the schizophrenic loses himself in it and can find no connection with what he has conceived himself to be. This is frightening, and he tries to embody himself in the world again, but he often finds that the

65. See Ludwig Binswanger, "The Case of Ilse," *Existence*, p. 215.

66. Ludwig Binswanger, *Being-in-the-World: Selected Papers*, trans. Jacob Needleman (New York, 1963), p. 258.

67. Laing, *Divided Self*, pp. 196–97.

68. *Being-in-the-World*, p. 259.

69. *Memoirs*, p. 86.

body too has become Other, a thing, and none of its actions have anything to do with each other or with his intentions. One schizophrenic "wanted to drop a shoe, and instead he dropped a big log; he wanted to put something in a drawer and instead he threw a stone away."[70]

This is one of the most striking aspects of the schizophrenic experience, the simultaneous presence but absolute separation of a fantastic space and a real space. And the point is that both of these spaces become fantastic, the real one as well as the fantastic one, since they are equally experienced as unreal. This is why the world and the body in their most real states, as objects, take on the fantastic condition of dismemberment and fragmentation in both schizophrenia and in the classical Western structure of reality. Dismemberment is a common hallucination in schizophrenia—schizophrenics report their noses hanging off or their ears going through the wall[71]—and dismemberment reveals a strong affinity with the surgery performed upon the body by Vesalius as one of the initial acts of modern science. The schizophrenic experiences the absolute objectivity of the space that Vesalius placed the body in and that Newton placed matter in, and reacts by dismembering and thus giving that space its most proper elements—little pieces, atoms, parts.

For the same reason, the schizophrenic sometimes disperses his entire body into the outside world; he merges his own thingness with that of the objects in his environment. For many schizophrenics this feeling of merging is an ultimate and horrible experience. "That's the rain. I could be the rain." "That chair ... that wall. I could be that wall. It's a terrible thing for a girl to be a wall."[72] On the surface, such merging would seem to be a breaking down of the me-not-me structure. But in reality it is due to the absolute nature of that structure. Since the me exists as a void, an empty shell, and the not-me as solidity, the focus of consciousness oscillates between them, in much the same way

70. Cited in Ephraim Rosen and Ian Gregory, *Abnormal Psychology* (Philadelphia, 1965), p. 317.
71. James C. Coleman, *Abnormal Psychology and Modern Life* (Chicago, 1956), p. 272.
72. Quoted in Laing, *Divided Self*, p. 198.

as the parts of a gestalt pattern oscillate between figure and ground. As Laing asserts, an intolerable double bind develops, in which there is either "radical isolation in self-absorption or complete absorption into all,"[73] two absolute polarities with no in-between.

The world as object, as absolute Other, also stains objects themselves with a certain character (or lack of character) for schizophrenics, and this is the same as for objects according to the structures of Western thought. In civilized society, because objects are discrete and because they are objective, that is, without sacred significance, their use-function constitutes their full meaning. This is most true of civilization as it develops into a consumer culture, but such a development is implicit in the subject-object dichotomy of Western society. Waste is created by the structure Western thought gives to objects, for waste is possible only when objects whose full meaning is "use" have become useless. Schizophrenics, Arieti points out, are fascinated by waste, by their own waste deposits and the waste deposits of the object-world, that is, by junk. Some smear themselves with their own feces or even eat their own feces,[74] and many develop what Arieti calls the habit of hoarding. "The objects which, in the course of my investigation, were found to have been hoarded by the patients were papers of any kind—old letters, toilet paper, pages of newspapers, etc.—pieces of wood, stones, leaves, sticks, soap, spoons, strings, rags, hairpins, old tooth-brushes, wires, cups, feathers, cores of fruit, stale food."[75]

Not all schizophrenics simply hoard objects, however. One of Minkowski's patients thought all the objects of the world would be put in his stomach,[76] and Arieti points out that on the autopsy tables of mental institutions "it is a relatively common experience to find spoons, stones, pieces of scrap iron, wood, paper, cores, etc., in the stomachs or intestines of patients who were affected by the most advanced stages of schizophrenia."[77]

73. Ibid., p. 91.
74. Silvano Arieti, *Interpretation of Schizophrenia* (New York, 1955), p. 365.
75. Ibid., p. 352.
76. *Existence*, p. 128.
77. *Schizophrenia*, p. 364.

If the schizophrenic isn't directed outward, toward merging with things, then things are literally directed inward toward him. Direction in one's gestures is polarized in schizophrenia into either totally active or totally passive states, so that the person either disperses himself into the world in a salad of frenzied actions or completely withdraws into an immobility, a catatonia, bringing with him only the ability to incorporate and consume. He incorporates the fragments of his world, its left-over objects.

The schizophrenic's world is fragmented in all ways, spatially, physically, temporally—the world exists in discrete, mutually exclusive units; hence there is no process; the world is immobile. The shattering of time is one of the most significant features of both schizophrenia and Western society. Here is Arieti's description of Sally, a twenty-three-year-old schizophrenic:

> When she was not in a catatonic state, she had the impression that small pieces or corpuscles were falling down on her body or from her body. She preferred not to move, because she was afraid that her movements would cause small pieces to fall. She had to reassure herself constantly that pieces were not falling down, and she had to look around constantly in an obsessive way. If she moved, even if she made the smallest movement, she had to think about the movement, dividing it into small parts to reassure herself that each part of the movement had not been accompanied by the falling of small bodies.[78]

The atomization of time seen in Descartes is here radical enough to be a felt structure, something that entirely infuses Sally's world. All presence, all movement, and all states of consciousness are units, things, and the world is reduced to their static condition. Compare such a world with the one implied by William James when he says that "states of consciousness are *things*, like sensations, desires, emotions, acts of cognition, logical considerations, decisions, volitions, and the like."[79] A world so

78. Ibid., p. 111.
79. Quoted in Straus, *Primary World*, p. 19.

completely spatialized naturally resists any temporal becoming. And as Bergson has shown, all classical philosophical and psychological models of consciousness are spatial ones.[80] The spatialized psyche, the psyche composed of discrete elements that have nothing to do with each other, is a significant feature of schizophrenia, as seen with regard to the atomization of the schizophrenic's personality. This psyche lacks the synthetic strength of temporal becoming, which Western thought also lacks. As Hume said, "the time, as it exists, must be composed of indivisible moments."[81] For Western thought, as for schizophrenia, temporality exists in a dead state, and its units block up the future, so that it piles up around the self in thicker and thicker layers, as Samuel Beckett's Unnamable puts it.[82] This spatialized time is one of the primary structural principles of the realistic and naturalistic novel.

The best summary of the schizophrenic experience and its alliance with the forms of Western thought can be found in Binswanger's phrase "either-or," which he says constitutes the underlying structure of schizophrenia.[83] Either-or is the Principle of Contradiction as a living principle of experience; it is the structure that says one is either this personality or that one, but there is no connection between them; one is either isolated in the self or merges with the world; one is either detached from the body, or one's body is subject to control, torture, and dismemberment; one is either manic or depressive; one either lives in a frenzied world that is always present, always now, or one retreats into complete immobility. Total frenzy and complete immobility are in many respects the same, since both eliminate the temporal dimension of becoming. In this respect, the paradox of either-or is that aspects of experience are so polarized that they are at bottom the same. As Binswanger says about the manic-depressive, "wherever you encounter the phenomena of

80. Henri Bergson, *Time and Free Will*, trans. F. L. Pogson (London, 1910), pp. 176ff.
81. Quoted in Straus, *Primary World*, p. 20.
82. *The Unnamable* (New York, 1958), p. 143.
83. *Being-in-the-World*, p. 254.

mounting life—the blooming, flourishing, gleaming, resounding, the jubilantly soaring lark and the eagle lifting itself drunken with sun into the ether—you will never fail to find the phenomena of deciduous life—the withering, decaying, moribund, deformed or disorganized, the gray, gloomy, hateful, dirty, stinking, the worm crawling in the ground, the death's head."[84] Schreber's experience confirms this: "At the very moment of the height of voluptuousness, headache or toothache is produced by miracle to prevent fully developed voluptuousness."[85]

Similarly, the either-or structure of isolation from the world and merging with it represents such a polarization that the two are the same; both represent an alienation and deadening of consciousness, a total surrender to objectivity. This paradox of either-or, by which things are so polarized that they become the same, lies at the bottom of the structures of Western thought too. Either-or seals aspects of being off from each other, gives them the character of being-sealed-off, of things. Thus the subject-object dichotomy objectifies the subject; the separation of space and time spatializes time; the absolute polarization of atoms and the Void, and later of matter and space, makes space into a thing itself, a condition confirmed by the scientific theory that an ether fills and constitutes space. The thesis of this book is that the absolute separation of reality and unreality, and of sanity and insanity, makes reality something unreal and makes the structures of classical Western thought that instituted that separation insane—that is, schizophrenic.

And either-or, the separation of Being and Nonbeing, makes discreteness and therefore maps possible: either-or doesn't exist in the garden. From a wider perspective, either-or separates the garden and the map themselves; this is because the garden has been subject to the map in our civilization, a situation that is the central theme of Conrad's *Heart of Darkness*. Through this application of the map to the garden, Kurtz contracts his sickness, a sickness most accurately called cultural schizophrenia.

84. "On the Manic Mode of Being-in-the-World," in *Phenomenology: Pure and Applied*, ed. Erwin Straus (Pittsburgh, 1964), p. 137.

85. Schreber, *Memoirs*, p. 239.

3

Heart of Darkness describes the return of civilization to the Garden. "Going up that river was like travelling back to the earliest beginnings of the world, when vegetation rioted on the earth and the big trees were kings." Yet the fluid relationships between the person and his environment that are characteristic of consciousness at the world's beginnings are absent in the world Marlow describes. The structure of consciousness of the Europeans in the story is the opposite of that of the world they confront in the Congo. It is a map consciousness, one that charts and administers, that moves in a world already constituted, with "a butcher round one corner, a policeman round another." The importance of the structure of maps for understanding the forms of civilization is indicated by Marlow at the beginning: "Now when I was a little chap I had a passion for maps. I would look for hours at South America, or Africa, or Australia, and lose myself in all the glories of exploration. At that time there were many blank spaces on the earth, and when I saw one that looked particularly inviting on a map (but they all look that) I would put my finger on it and say 'When I grow up I will go there....' But there was one yet—the biggest, the most blank, so to speak —that I had a hankering after."

The consciousness of young Marlow is a product of five centuries of exploration and map-making, the period in which modern civilization formed itself. In a sense, maps represent the most fundamental language of this civilization. Just as the revolutionary power of words lay in the ability they gave man to carry objects around with him, out of their presence, so the revolutionary power of maps lay in the ability they gave man to carry the world around with him. The truth of this ability cannot be emphasized too much; Marlow doesn't look at representations of South America or Africa but looks at the countries themselves. This is not to say that his map brings these countries closer. Rather it incorporates into its very structure the distance between them and him. The transforming power of maps lies in this structure; maps make the world over into their own image by distancing the world, by disposing of it beforehand as Other. In this sense a map is always complete, even if it has blank spaces. The blank space of the Congo is a space; it is circumscribed and has boundaries. The completion of a map is only a matter of further refinement, of closer inspection and measurement. Until this is done, the unknown simply has an area of its own—just as, in the map of formal logic, those aspects of experience that can't be properly charted are relegated to the space of subjectivity.

The sense that the world was being nailed down, and that it was only a matter of further refinement and measurement before the map of physical life was securely in hand, was particularly strong in the late nineteenth century, when *Heart of Darkness* was written. Laplace's remarks in 1886 are typical of the attitude of scientists: "An intellect which at a given instant knew all the forces acting in nature, and the position of all things of which the world consists—supposing the said intellect were vast enough to subject these data to analysis—would embrace in the same formula the motions of the greatest bodies in the universe and those of the slightest atoms; nothing would be uncertain for it, and the future, like the past would be present to its eyes."[86] By the 1890s, professors of physics were warning their students to pursue other disciplines, since the future of physics was to be only in searching for "one more decimal place."[87] Because map consciousness envisioned all areas of experience as closed and discrete, the entire world itself was about to finish itself, to be sealed off and complete. Its completion would specifically be in reference to the vast intellect mentioned by Laplace, which observes and analyzes it from a distance. But the terms by which the world is known, the structure of the act of mapping the world, enable us all to possess this distance.

In such a world, one mapped off and completing itself at a distance, the imperialism Conrad describes operates. Control lies in the hands of those who work from the greatest distance:

86. Quoted in Capek, *Contemporary Physics*, p. 122.
87. Rapport and Wright, *Physics*, p. 90.

the Council in Europe. Marlow, when he interviews for his job, sees their map on the office wall: "There was a vast amount of red—good to see at any time, because one knows that some real work is done in there, a deuce of a lot of blue, a little green, smears of orange, and, on the East Coast, a purple patch, to show where the jolly pioneers of progress drink the jolly lager-beer." For those who work *in* these areas, the act of distance is achieved by transforming the earth itself into a map: "Paths, paths, everywhere; a stamped-in network of paths spreading over the empty land, through the long grass, through burnt grass, through thickets, down and up chilly ravines, up and down stoney hills ablaze with heat."

The map of the Congo *is* precisely the circulation of ivory: paths of transportation and centers of storage imposed upon its blank space. The map of the Congo is its colonization, its seizure and consequent subjection to control and administration. Since the Congo is predisposed to be Other for the white man, since he is in that space rather than of it, the only act he can perform toward it is "to tear treasure out of the bowels of the land," to map it off for himself as property. The relationship of property enables the European to keep at a distance the only aspect of the Congo he might feel a tie with: its human beings. The bodies of natives are objects for the white man, his property. When he arrives at the first station yard, Marlow observes dying natives strewn beneath a tree, much like the machinery and equipment he had just seen lying haphazardly around the yard. Later the station accountant remarks to Marlow that "the groans of a sick person distract my attention, and without that it is extremely difficult to guard against clerical errors in this climate."

But despite the administrative control imposed by Europeans upon Africa, and despite the need a map consciousness has to complete itself down to the last decimal place, *Heart of Darkness* is also about the violent resistance the world offers to being mapped and controlled. The paths of the ivory trade barely scratch the surface of the Congo. The same sense in which a map is always complete is also the sense in which it is incomplete; its blank space is circumscribed and sealed off because it is blank, because it is unknown and resists being mapped. In circumscribing the Other, civilization hardly touches it; in fact it has made it Other in order to be relieved of the burden of touching it. By "Other" I mean exactly those aspects of experience predisposed by civilization to be mapped, but gathered together in a new alliance, a new blank area, because they cannot be mapped: the life of the body, the condition of the garden, of the fantastic, of the dream.

Conrad's "darkness" contains all these elements, thrown together in an area separated from civilization, in Africa rather than Europe, because their very separation enables civilization to confirm itself. The time when maps were on the verge of completion, when the world was arranging itself into a finished body of knowledge, totally circumscribed, was also the time when the world became implacable, when it gathered its strength to overwhelm the consciousness of someone like Kurtz, precisely because the former needed the latter, because civilization could map itself into its forms only by excluding certain other forms which, due to their exclusion, became the forms of darkness, the absolute collective shadow of civilization. Kurtz's woman sums up these forms of darkness: "the colossal body of the fecund and mysterious life seemed to look at her, pensive, as though it had been looking at the image of its own tenebrous and passionate soul." The fecund life is mysterious and therefore dark, because the civilized man can relate to it only as Other, as a discrete entity separated from himself. Hence the fecund life, the life of the body and of the Garden, is inextricably associated with evil, with "forgotten and brutal instincts" and "monstrous passions." And hence Kurtz's soul is mad, and his words contain "the terrific suggestiveness of words heard in dreams." Civilization's map consciousness creates an either-or situation; it necessitates schizophrenia. If I enter the forms of darkness, I abandon those of civilization, and thus I abandon my identity. My primary roots in the wilderness, the garden, the body, are Other, and as Other they can only assume a terrible aspect when I confront them; they can only consume me.

When the Europeans in *Heart of Darkness* leave their tiny

islands of civilization, they enter the presence of this terrible Other. Its blank appearance on Marlow's map accurately reflects some of its significant qualities: it is homogeneous and absolute, a complete, continuous surrounding Void that either forces each person back exclusively upon himself or, as in the case of Kurtz, swallows him entirely. There is no navigating this Other, as Marlow knows, for it is precisely what navigation has needed to exclude in order to exist:

> You lost your way on that river as you would in a desert, and butted all day long against the shoals, trying to find the channel, till you thought yourself bewitched and cut off for ever from everything you had known once—somewhere—far away in another existence perhaps. There were moments when one's past came back to one, as it will sometimes when you have not a moment to spare to yourself; but it came in the shape of an unrestful and noisy dream, remembered with wonder amongst the overwhelming realities of this strange world of plants, and water, and silence. And this stillness of life did not in the least resemble a peace. It was the stillness of an implacable force brooding over an inscrutable intention.

There is no apprehension of the wilderness as an organic form, a fluid unity of whole and parts, as in the Garden. The wilderness is a collective, massive, indiscriminate whole: "Sometimes I would pick out a tree a little way ahead to measure our progress towards Kurtz by, but I lost it invariably before we got abreast. To keep the eyes so long on one thing was too much for human patience." At times in the novel this whole achieves such density that it becomes the actual space in which the characters move, clinging to their skins. Of the fog near Kurtz's station, Marlow says: "Were we to let go our hold of the bottom, we would be absolutely in the air—in space. We wouldn't be able to tell where we were going to—whether up or down stream, or across—till we fetched against one bank or the other—and then we wouldn't know at first which it was." This is the antithesis of living in a map space, for it is the pure act of being lost. And yet it is not the space of the garden, since in this fog, a Void really, there is no possibility for even the illusion that I project myself into the world, that I organize myself with the things around me, because there are no things, not even outlines; there is no *there*, no foreground or background. All orientation has dissolved. The Other has achieved a total homogeneous unity and thereby forced me radically and unmercifully into my body, just as the Void of the Greek atomists forced matter into its own impenetrable walls.

In fact the space the Europeans in *Heart of Darkness* encounter is the space of the garden as Other, the garden distanced by the application of map consciousness. It is homogeneous and absolute because it is Other, and thus its ability as a garden to suck Kurtz out of himself, to evict him from himself by the force of its fluidity, is absolute also. Hence, although Kurtz is lost just as the other Europeans are, his quality of being lost, of being isolated, takes on the condition of its own opposite, of mergence. Kurtz's consciousness, or lack of it, is a schizophrenic one, and it is made possible by the either-or polarities of garden and map, polarities created by imposing the latter upon the former. Thus Kurtz is either utterly lost or totally found, and both situations are deplorable. He is lost by virtue of the total isolation his imperialism imposes upon him, the isolation one is left with after consuming the world.[88] But he is found because the garden surrounds him, and he disperses totally into it, merges with it, and it consumes him: "It had caressed him, and—lo!—he had withered; it had taken him, loved him, embraced him, got into his veins, consumed his flesh."

This is what the great shadow of the night eventually does to Decoud in *Nostromo*, and what it threatens to do to the narrators of *The Secret Sharer* and *The Shadow-Line*. The image of total Otherness occurs frequently in Melville also, particularly in *Moby Dick* when Pip falls overboard and finds himself alone on a formless, infinite ocean, an experience that drives him insane. The blank space on Marlow's map is of the same structure as this infinite ocean. It has a line around it, like the horizon for Pip, or like the line around zero, but its hollowness

88. J. Hillis Miller makes this point in *Poets of Reality* (Cambridge, Mass., 1965), pp. 6–7.

is absolute and extends to its center, its heart, just as Kurtz himself is described by Marlow as "hollow at the core." The imagery of holes in the story is an expression of this schizophrenic insertion of zero into the world, of the way in which gaps open up between the body and the world, and the self and the body. Marlow looks at Kurtz "as you peer down at a man who is lying at the bottom of a precipice," and later has a vision of him "opening his mouth voraciously, as if to devour all the earth with all its mankind." Kurtz resides in the hollow container that his mouth opens into. He is like Mrs. Moore in the Marabar Caves in Forster's novel; he lives in the echo that reduces everything to "boum," the echo of his own eloquence and of his greed. The only way he can embody himself is to obliterate himself, to merge totally with his environment.

I should emphasize that this merging is very different from the original condition of the Garden, in which there is free passage between self and other. The experience of total merging is possible only when the Garden has been violently transformed by the application of a map space. Merging is the polar opposite of being trapped, of being limited to one's own location, to the extent that either one of these conditions when pushed far enough becomes the other. Instead of free passage there is complete confinement, either in the immobility of isolation or in the complete mobility of dismemberment and merging, which is still immobility. A novel that is similar to *Heart of Darkness*, but describes an entirely different alternative, is Faulkner's *The Bear*. Ike McCaslin leaves his compass behind and enters the wilderness, but instead of merging with the wilderness, the wilderness organizes itself around him, and he becomes *of* it, much like Adam in the Garden. Ike is one of the few characters in modern literature who achieves a wholeness of consciousness. Most of the others are descendants of Kurtz or, more exactly, of the map consciousness that makes Kurtz possible.

Map consciousness reflects the general subject-object split that informs most of modern sensibility. It is no coincidence that Descartes, who formulated the subject-object dichotomy, also invented coordinate geometry, which made the theory of functions and accurate, scientific map-making possible. The structures of the subject-object split and mapping depend equally upon a sense of location, of isolated entities existing in a space oriented by absolute coordinates. This vision of the world makes the colonization of the Garden possible, and this vision suffers the revenge the Garden takes. Schizophrenia, as *Heart of Darkness* shows, is the white man's disease, the price he pays for draining the blackness out of his own being and attempting to enslave it; for that blackness, because it has been enslaved, rises up to overwhelm Kurtz.

The one person in *Heart of Darkness* who begins to break down this schizophrenia is Marlow. The heart of the story's title exists in him and in the Congo too, but not in a way that is spatially limited to either one. The breakdown of a strict sense of location in the story is clearest with regard to the structure of Marlow's journey. His trip is not simply an external movement toward a preexisting goal; it is a transformational journey that is interior also, in a way that destroys the distinction between interior and exterior. Marlow, in a sense, becomes his movement, just as the metaphor of the story's title becomes a metamorphosis. This is evident at the story's end, when Marlow's darkness invades the external space of civilization: "The vision seemed to enter the house with me—the stretcher, the phantom-bearers, the wild crowd of obedient worshippers, the gloom of the forests, the glitter of the reach between the murky bends, the beat of the drum, regular and muffled like the beating of a heart—the heart of a conquering darkness." The point of view here is a constituting one, one that participates. That participation is frightening, because Marlow participates in what he had previously disposed of as separate from him. But at least those barriers have been destroyed. In this passage there is not posited a preexisting reality into which Marlow's consciousness enters and over which it takes control. Rather there is a mutual penetration between Marlow and his world.

In this sense *Heart of Darkness* tentatively overcomes the map structure it is about. Marlow's experience in the Congo, while very similar to Kurtz's, is in an important respect the opposite of his. Kurtz's consciousness is structured to such a complete extent by the map of civilization ("All Europe contributed to the making of Kurtz") that when confronted by the antithesis of that map, he can only split in two. Marlow, however, proves fluid enough to find the connection between the darkness and himself, so he doesn't confront it as complete Other. "It was unearthly, and the men were—No, they were not inhuman. Well, you know, that was the worst of it—this suspicion of their not being inhuman. It would come slowly to one. They howled and leaped, and spun, and made horrid faces; but what thrilled you was just the thought of their humanity—like yours." Marlow's fluidity is indicated at the beginning of the novel too, when the blank area of his map draws him like a mirror into its own incompletion. Marlow is an active witness to the Other, not an objective observer of it. The very act of telling his story is part of that witness, for he creates the darkness of the Other in its telling, just as he creates his actual journey into the Congo rather than following a map. The story thus becomes the act of destroying the walls a map space imposes between his heart and the heart of darkness.

Conrad's departure through Marlow from the novelist's traditional role of being an objective observer is an important comment upon the schizophrenia of the traditional novel. Before Conrad, and before James, Woolf, Joyce, Proust, Kafka, and others, the novel was preeminently the genre of location and property, the literature whose form was primarily spatial and whose space was that of a map. The degree to which the novel has preserved its map structure, despite the experiments of Conrad and others at the beginning of the century, can be measured by the second wave of experiment in fictional forms, that being conducted by such writers as Barth, Pynchon, Barthelme, Borges, Beckett, Robbe-Grillet, and Burroughs. All these writers are reacting against a strong tendency in the structure of the novel to assume an already constituted world in which man is strictly limited to his location in a map space. One of them, Burroughs, uncovers the latent schizophrenia in this structure by basing his images and the rhythm of his writing upon the same polarity of isolation and merging that is Kurtz's schizophrenia. These topics, the novel, the exhaustion of the novel in Burroughs, and the relationship of both to schizophrenia, are the subject of the next two chapters.

2 / Objectivity, the Novel, and Schizophrenia

In addition to its literary meaning, "plot" means a small area of property, and, as a verb, the action of locating and marking a point on a plane by means of the coordinates of the point. Both of these meanings indicate the spatial bias of the concept "plot." In the realistic novel, plot is the floor plan, the map of the actions and interactions of the characters. Plot is the property which unfolds in front of the reader and upon which he trespasses, the map by which his attention is delimited and channeled, located and fixed. Robert Louis Stevenson asserted that the plot of *Treasure Island* literally exists as a map, and went on to generalize about the necessity for novelists to map their property:

> It is, perhaps, not often that a map figures so largely in a tale, yet it is always important. The author must know his countryside, whether real or imaginary, like his hand; the distances, the points of the compass, the place of the sun's rising, the behavior of the moon, should all be beyond cavil. . . . I never write now without an almanack. With an almanack, and the map of the country, and the plan of every house, either actually plotted on paper or already and immediately apprehended in the mind, a man may hope to avoid some of the grossest possible blunders.[1]

Stevenson has shown why it is not necessary for realistic novels to occur in actual, familiar places. Not the fact of reality but the

1. Miriam Allott, ed., *Novelists on the Novel* (New York, 1959), pp. 303–4.

structure of "reality" is important in the novel. One important aspect of this structure is "plot" in the widest sense, not simply the pattern of actions of the characters but the pattern of the world of the novel itself.

Plot is the structure made possible by the formal logic of the West and the application of that logic to objective space. It is no coincidence that the novel arose in the great age of classical physics, when the earth was being perceived as a map and therefore was being transformed into one. The greater the distance an artist stands from his materials, the greater his need for a maplike structure. And the novel is the form in which the greatest amount of distance is incorporated, the form whose space is an unbounded container, a theater with the horizon for its walls. The novelist looks down from a distance upon his materials. He is, as Forster says, "poised above his work, throwing a beam of light here, popping on a cap of invisibility there, and (*qua* plot-maker) continually negotiating with himself *qua* character-monger as to the best effect to be produced."[2] From the early stages of the genre, novelists have been aware of this objective distance and have asked their readers to achieve the same point of view. "This work may, indeed, be considered a great creation of our own," says Fielding in *Tom Jones*, "and for a little reptile of a critic to presume to find fault with any of its parts without knowing the manner in which the whole is connected, and before he comes to the final catastrophe, is a most presumptuous absurdity." The "ideal spectator" of the novel, says Forster, cannot expect to view the "cross-correspondences" of its action "until he is sitting up on a hill at the end."[3]

The world is obviously experienced in a radically different manner when it is there, below me or facing me, rather than here, enveloping me. There, at a distance, it becomes objective; it is given a framework, its structure and contours become more apparent, and its ribs begin to show. The tendency in realism and naturalism is for plot to emerge from the novel and become a structure for itself, that is, external and delimiting rather than

2. E. M. Forster, *Aspects of the Novel* (New York, 1927), p. 145.
3. Ibid., p. 132.

internal and synthesizing. I do not deny the possibility that plot, in the traditional sense of a pattern of action, can be the synthesizing agent of the novel, as R. S. Crane asserts;[4] nor do I deny the ability of the novel to plunge me into its world. But this is only one aspect of the novel, one polarity, upon which the novel constructs itself. Sartre says the novel is "a great form in motion, in other words, the act of reading,"[5] but the novel is also a great form in stasis, in other words, the state of having been read. In fact, by emphasizing the referential function of language and almost totally minimizing its surface textures, the realistic novel hollows out language, makes it transparent, and thus neutralizes as much as possible the act of reading. The classical Newtonian and Cartesian consciousness of the world, in which change and process are neutralized, gave birth to this aspect of the novel.

In many respects the frozen space, the map structure of the novel, is its most significant feature. The novel grew toward it in the nineteenth century, and it accounts for visual realism. It is the defining characteristic of naturalism, to the extent that naturalism becomes the purest form of the novel, the form that neutralizes temporal process to the greatest degree and schematizes the world in ways that can only be called schizophrenic. This aspect of the novel, through naturalism, accounts for the contemporary exhaustion of fictional modes in such writers as Barth, Pynchon, Robbe-Grillet, Beckett, Sartre, and Burroughs. Unlike most writers, these novelists have reacted not to the literary generation immediately preceding them but to one much earlier. Roquentin, in Sartre's *La Nausée*, does not read Proust or Gide but Balzac and Stendhal. *The Sot-Weed Factor* is a parody not of *Ulysses* or *Lord Jim* but of *Tom Jones*. Sartre, Beckett, Robbe-Grillet, Barth, and others react not against the writers of the generation of Proust, Gide, Conrad, and Joyce, but against the same literature that the latter reacted to. In fact they react more obviously against that literature, for rather than

4. R. S. Crane, ed., *Critics and Criticism* (Chicago, 1952), p. 620.
5. Jean-Paul Sartre, *Literary and Philosophical Essays*, trans. Annette Michelson (New York, 1962), p. 7.

offering alternatives to realism and naturalism, as Proust and company did, they incorporate the structures of realism and naturalism and carry them to their logical extreme; they use realistic and naturalistic forms to parody themselves, and thereby bring the novel to strangle itself.

For example, the soldier in Robbe-Grillet's *Dans le Labyrinthe* wanders around in a setting similar to the street settings of novels by Zola, Crane, or Dreiser. But the streets of the town in Robbe-Grillet's novel have taken on an added dimension. Their maplike structure turns upon itself, reproduces itself, leads to everywhere, to nowhere. The structure of naturalism has, by being pushed to its extreme, become its opposite, a fantastic structure. The world has retained the organization required of it by the distance of the naturalistic novelist, but it has retained it close up. Robbe-Grillet's soldier wanders around in a map; it is a map-world that envelops him, not a world that is a map only at a distance. The frozen space of the realistic novel has swallowed its temporal dimension; its structure has externalized itself and overwhelmed all other aspects of it. This means, for many contemporary writers, that reality or objectivity is simply one organization of our being-in-the-world among many possible organizations. From this realization it is only a short step to the knowledge that reality itself is fantastic and dreamlike.

1. The Early Novel

The objective space of classical physics, as Bergson and others have pointed out, can exist only if time itself is spatialized, that is, eliminated.[6] The neutralization of the temporal dimension is implicit in the novel from the beginning. Theorists of the novel, such as Ian Watt, Frank Kermode, or Northrop Frye, typically assert that the novel represents the "alliance of time and Western man,"[7] but such an assertion represents a naive

6. Bergson, *Time and Free Will*, pp. 98ff. See also Capek, *Contemporary Physics*, pp. 121ff.

7. Northrop Frye, *Anatomy of Criticism* (Princeton, N.J., 1957), p. 307. See also Ian Watt, "Realism and the Novel Form," in Robert Scholes, ed., *Approaches*

acquaintance with the significance of time in the classical Newtonian world picture. "All things," said Newton, "are placed
in time as to order of succession; and in space as to order of
situation."[8] The important factor is that for both space and
time, things are placed. What we call a sense of time consists
of the ability to imagine positions in time, locations or goals.
The term "succession" itself is based upon a geometrical model,
by which seconds or instants are conceived of as points and the
passage of time as a line. As Capek shows, such a model destroys the asymmetrical nature of time, and juxtaposes the past
and the future in the same space.[9]

The particular sense of time that civilized man calls history,
as G. L. S. Shackle points out, is a spatialized time, like the
"Bayeux Tapestry brought to life."[10] It depends on the relationship of juxtaposition that defines space, and this relationship is specifically a timeless one. When the concepts of distance
and succession are defined as mutually exclusive, when space
and time are separated, any distance between two points in
space is instantaneous, that is, a particle could travel from one
point to the other with infinite velocity, and thus space is a
timeless, frozen juxtaposition of points.[11] The only possible
way to preserve a sense of time is to make time spaceless, to
make time "subjective" as Kant did, while space remains "objective." But in the end this amounts to a spatialization of time,
since the only way to plug time back into the objective world
is to spatialize it, with lines, with clocks and calendars, with history, with the novel.

The novel, at least the realistic and naturalistic novel, partakes of a virtual subject-object schizophrenia, and expresses
this schizophrenia through the framework of objective space.
The temporal dimension exists in the world of the novel encap-

to the Novel (San Francisco, 1961), pp. 68–69, and Frank Kermode, *The Sense
of an Ending* (New York, 1967), p. 167.

8. Isaac Newton, "Absolute Space and Time" (from the *Principia*), in Smart,
Problems of Space and Time, p. 83.

9. Capek, *Contemporary Physics*, p. 162.

10. G. L. S. Shackle, *Decision, Order, and Time in Human Affairs* (Cambridge, 1961), p. 16.

11. Capek, *Contemporary Physics*, p. 169.

sulated in individual consciousness, and these capsules move in a frozen, unchanging space, as Pamela's letters move across the English countryside. Not only temporality but all aspects of experience that will not remain inert and measurable are siphoned out of the external world. "Qualitative variety as well as qualitative transformation are *psychic additions* of the perceiving human mind; they do not belong to the nature of things."[12] Hence all apparent qualitative changes of characters in the novel are changes in spatial configuration, changes in alliance and position, including social position. Pamela, Joseph Andrews, and Tom Jones at the end of their respective novels occupy new places, physically, economically, and socially, which were waiting to receive them. In this objectivity of place the novel finds the strength of its structure. The world of realistic and naturalistic fiction is an already constituted one, a preexisting framework of spatial configurations and juxtapositions in which characters, with their sealed-off subjectivities, move. This sense of being already constituted is true of the language of the realistic novel also. As mentioned earlier, realism emphasizes exclusively the referential or map function of language, while ignoring its surface textures, its function as speech. Consequently it hollows out the act of reading, and neutralizes even the temporal dimension built into the form of narrative.

The world of the novel is an already constituted, timeless place for the author too. He appears before it and sets up his recording apparatus. This is the presupposition of all theories of art based on the concept of imitation, on mimesis, from Aristotle to Erich Auerbach. The artist copies reality; he holds a mirror up to the world. This kind of metaphor was particularly strong in the seventeenth and eighteenth centuries, when the novel was being born. Not only art but all knowledge was thought of as a copy of the external world; the mind was often conceived of, one epistemologist has pointed out, as a camera. "Just as there are images on the back of the camera so there are *ideas in the mind.* Just as there are obscure and confused, clear and distinct images so there are *obscure and confused, clear and*

12. Ibid., p. 79.

distinct ideas. Just as we inspect the images on the screen, so we *introspect ideas* in the mind. Just as images are reflected light, so there are *ideas of reflection.*"[13]

As Ortega y Gasset shows, the theory that thought is a copy or image of reality is based on a notion of the real that originated in Greek philosophy. "Ever since Parmenides, the orthodox thinker in search of an object's being holds that he is searching for a fixed, static consistency, hence something that *already* is, which already composes or constitutes it."[14] The very act of philosophy establishes this static consistency, the act, as in Thales, of searching from a distance for the homogeneous reality beneath appearances. If change in the novel is change only of place or position, it is because the real is conceived of as a homogeneous thing beneath appearances—in Capek's words, "a constant, substantial quantity persisting through time."[15] Motion and change are simply the displacement of immutable quantities of matter in space. In physics this view is expressed primarily through the conservation laws (energy, matter, momentum). In the novel it is built into the strict objectivity and homogeneity of nature that every realistic and naturalistic novelist presupposes.

In this respect, the assertion that realism is the literary form that admits no presuppositions and adheres to no philosophical tenets, an assertion made, for example, by Zola,[16] is naive in the extreme. The realist assumes not only that nature is a thing, a persistent, unchanging, objective body of matter, but also that there is a homogeneous continuity of space that connects the world around him to the world of his novel, the same kind of continuity of space that exists between a mirror and the space outside it. Although the realistic novelist works through the medium of signs and symbols, that is, language, this medium is essentially invisible, and the world the novelist reveals through

13. Colin Turbayne, *The Myth of Metaphor* (New Haven, 1962), p. 205.

14. José Ortega y Gasset, *History as a System*, trans. Helene Weyl (New York, 1961), p. 192.

15. Capek, *Contemporary Physics*, p. 326.

16. Emile Zola, *The Experimental Novel*, trans. Belle M. Sherman (New York, 1893), p. 4.

its lens, even if it is a world in miniature, partakes for him of the same objective structure as the real world.

As Capek shows, the objective, timeless consistency of the natural world is inseparable, logically, from the homogeneity of space, and both are intimately involved with what physicists call the "Gulliver theme" in classical physics. "Lilliput is exactly like our human world except for size; all proportions are exactly preserved. Similarly, Brobdingnag is basically nothing but our world constructed on a larger scale. This idea of geometrical similarity between various layers of spatial magnitudes is one of the most characteristic themes of classical thought."[17] In the seventeenth and eighteenth centuries, the discoveries made with the microscope and telescope seemed to confirm this concept; thus Pascal could see in the atom "an infinity of universes, each with its firmament, its planets, its earth in the same proportions as the visible world."[18] For the realistic novelist, the novel is the genre that incorporates this "infinity of universes"; it is the world within a world whose space, no matter how small or distant, mirrors the objective homogeneity of our own visual dimension. The space of the novel is homogeneous because it contains the very small and the very distant as reproductions of the nature around us—that is, because it is infinitely divisible, which is the mathematical definition of homogeneity.

Einstein's physics has dissolved these fundamental tenets of the classical world. Space does not exist for the very small or very large as it does for our dimensions, and matter does not partake of a continuous, unchanging integrity of identity. The distinction between matter and space upon which these principles depend is blurred for subatomic particles, as Heisenberg's Indeterminacy Principle shows.[19] We cannot begin to understand the structure of the realistic novel until we realize that the novelist does not mirror objective, homogeneous space, but creates that space through the act of mirroring, with the attitude of realism. Far from being the neutral form that copies the

17. Capek, *Contemporary Physics*, p. 22.
18. Blaise Pascal, *The Pensées*, trans. J. M. Cohen (Baltimore, 1961), p. 52.
19. Capek, *Contemporary Physics*, pp. 289ff.

objective world, realism creates the objectivity of that world by approaching it with the mental and aesthetic structure of "copying," whether the act of copying lies in mirroring or in mapping, that is, mirroring from a distance. Upon this structure classical physics is based; our thought processes copy the real world, so we can assume that reality reproduces itself everywhere as it does for our visual dimension. On this basis, for example, the homunculus theory of reproduction was formed, the theory that the human animal exists in the original embryo fully formed, although on a small scale.[20] But this kind of mirror reality is a fiction established by the very structure of mirrors. Objective space does not exist for my body in its everyday experience, but it does exist when my body is thrust out there, in a mirror, when my body is copied. A mirror cuts the world off from its reference to me, and thus preconditions space to receive me only as an indifferent container receives its contents, that is, objectively.

This is the basis of the objective nature that every realistic and naturalistic novelist presupposes. Consider the notion of "character," for example. Since the realistic novel mirrors the world, people can exist in it only objectively, as timeless, consistent identities. The foundling theme in Fielding is the clearest example. Both Joseph Andrews and Tom Jones are apparently foundlings, although objectively, beneath appearances, they are of noble blood. Plot in these novels becomes the representation of a passage from potency to act. The illusion of time is achieved through the drag that the bulkiness of Tom's and Joseph's disguises as foundlings imposes on the revelation of their true natures. For each, the arrival at a final destination, London or Booby Hall, means the stripping away of all disguise and the disclosure of the true social position that was there all the time. The final objectivity of place in the novel pierces apparent change and apparent form in order to, like a mirror, contain only objective nature.

This sense of character is a basic component of realism. In its pure form, it makes the immobile characters of Beckett possible, since underlying all the apparent movement and change

20. See ibid., pp. 23–24.

in the novel is an absolute stasis, a Parmenidian, consistent, unchanging Being, a catatonia. In Beckett all motion is a parody of motion, referred, as Watt's movement is, to "the frigid machinery of a time-space relation." The most significant movement in Beckett is waiting, or simply being there, as in *Waiting for Godot* and in the novels *Malone Dies* and *The Unnamable*. All of Beckett's characters exist as Malone does, in an objective space that contains and mirrors their own timeless objectivity, in a world, a house, a room, an urn, a garbage can, or as the Unnamable does, in simply a void. In all cases, Beckett's characters are immutable, changeless; either they don't move or they move without moving, since, as the Unnamable says, time "piles up all about you, instant on instant, on all sides, thicker and thicker." Saul Bellow alludes to this kind of unchanging nature when he has Augie March say that "a man's character is his fate," and John Barth parodies it when characters like Burlingame in *The Sot-Weed Factor* and Bray in *Giles Goat-Boy* metamorphose their personal appearance, and seemingly their very identity, at will.

The structure of mirroring or copying makes plot as well as character more understandable. The space of a plot can only be objective, and characters can only be *in* it (rather than *of* it) like contents in a container, like my body in a mirror. A mirror creates the illusion of three dimensions, but there is an implicit flatness to it, and the same is true of the novel and its plot. The novelist creates space by juxtaposing events, by presenting us with instantaneous cross-sections of his world. While one character is in one location, another character is in a different location, and both are oriented toward a common goal. Every time Joseph and Adams part in *Joseph Andrews*, Fielding follows one to an intermediary goal, at which the other either already has arrived or soon arrives and from which they separately depart. Often Fielding backtracks after one character has arrived, and follows the path of the other; so not only is there a consciousness of the simultaneous movement of the other when we are following one, but also there is an actual simultaneity, a juxtaposition of their actions side by side in the novel's pages. This simultaneity of the existence and actions of the characters generates the space of the novel. And this space is two-dimensional, since the relationship between the two characters is always instantaneous, that is, the characters are always beside each other in relation to a common goal, no matter how far apart they are. As in Newton's universe, the distance between them excludes the time it would take to get from one to the other.

Only this kind of flat, geometrical, rather than temporal, distance would permit the convergences and fortunate encounters the realistic novel depends on. Chance encounters in the novel are always spatial; characters converge and diverge at particular intermediary places, the inn, for example. The rhythm of convergence and divergence creates the plots of most realistic novels. This frozen rhythm requires a map space that channels movement in highly organized ways, a space of roads on the one hand and already existing places for storage, inns or homes, on the other. Adams' tendency to lose his way in *Joseph Andrews* is humorous precisely because it is set against such a map space. A map organization splits motion into areas of absolute movement and absolute rest and thus reifies motion, makes it a thing in itself, apart from entities that move. When this organization becomes fully realized in the novel, as in naturalism, it is impossible to get lost; it is possible only to be trapped.

The map organization, as I pointed out in Chapter One, makes the distribution of economic goods possible. In the novel this organization makes possible the distribution of "objective nature," the timeless persisting material of the novel's characters. In *Tom Jones* and *Joseph Andrews,* characters are able to reaffirm their timelessness in resting places that wait for them along the road. Disclosure scenes often occur at these resting places, as prefigurations of the final disclosure of the central character's true nature. For example, in *Joseph Andrews* Mrs. Tow-wouse walks in on Mr. Tow-wouse and Betty making love. The importance of such a scene is that the space Betty and Mr. Tow-wouse are in preexists for Mrs. Tow-wouse; she intrudes upon it, arrives there. The novel is the genre of timeless arrivals and departures, at and from places that previously exist for the purpose of to-be-arrived-at or to-be-departed-from.

Fielding's awareness of this with regard to the actual form of the novel can be seen in *Joseph Andrews* when he compares his chapters to inns, and the account of the contents prefixed to the chapters with inscriptions over the gates of inns, so that the reader may enter them at will, as if they were all equidistant from him, like locations on a map. "As we are not tied down to an exact concatenation equally with other historians, so a chapter or two (for instance, this I am now writing) may be often passed over without any injury to the whole." This is very different from Henry James's assertion that each part of a novel contains all other parts.[21] James was talking about an alternative to the realistic novel that doesn't separate locations on a map space and make them mutually exclusive, as realism does. For the characters of a realistic novel and for its readers, its various locations are there, are situated and contained, and await one's arrival. The temporal act of reading becomes the spatial act of entering and exiting, of opening and closing the door of the book. To go forward in the novel means to move on with the characters to occupy another space, not to evolve or become in time.

In this respect, the significance of actions in a realistic novel is other than the actions themselves; their completion lies at a distance, lies not in unfolding and gesturing but in collapsing in lieu of the imminent future, the outcome, the catastrophe. The rhythm of convergence and divergence in the novel is patterned overall by a final convergence, an arrival in a place that will mirror the central character's objective nature. In the realistic novel, it is not the act of moving that effects a change (as it is for Marlow in *Heart of Darkness*), but the state of having moved, the arrival. Movement itself is illusory because it contains an unchanging core, a core that implicitly rests in its goal, the social position of the protagonist, right from the beginning.

21. Henry James, "The Art of Fiction," in Scholes, *Approaches to the Novel*, p. 302.

Other forms of literature, such as lyric poetry, establish centers, but the novel establishes destinations, teleologies, and to do this breaks up centers into left and right, up and down, into a timeless map space. The exact timing of Wilson's arrival at Booby Hall at the end of *Joseph Andrews*, or of Tom's rescue at the end of *Tom Jones*, is possible only when time is given a teleology, when time is spatialized, when its significance lies in a location outside of movement itself. Aristotle defined the nature of the various elements according to the destination of their movements (fire and air up, water and earth down). The built-in imperfections of the world, its clutter, its obstructions and hindrances, prevent these elements from fully becoming what they already are, from arriving at their destinations. The realistic and naturalistic novel is the form that carefully places such obstructions along the map of its character's movements, and then collapses them toward a goal, a final position, which allows that character to become what he already is.[22]

Sartre's remarks about Mauriac's *La Fin de la Nuit* are relevant to this point. The "graph" of Thérèse's ups and downs in the novel represents "dead time, since the future is spread out like the past and simply repeats it."[23] This graph is made possible by the author's omniscient viewpoint, the vantage point he assumes that is similar to that of God. "God sees the inside and outside, the depths of body and soul, the whole universe at once. In like manner, M. Mauriac is omniscient about everything relating to his little world."[24] The true human relationship to

---

22. Frank Kermode, in *The Sense of an Ending*, argues that the teleology of the novel is precisely what provides it with a human and significant time, a time that is not simply quantitative but charged with a meaning derived from its relationship to the end and to endings in general, to death (see especially pp. 35ff.). My disagreement with Kermode can be summarized as follows. Although the sense of an ending is certainly immanent in the true sense of time, so is the sense of a beginning. And the lack of the latter accounts for the lack of a sense of becoming in realistic fiction. Endings are consequently not arrived at organically, in the process of growth, so they always and only preexist. Time is thus spatialized and is not significant. For a full discussion of what I mean by "becoming" and "growth" in relation to time, see Chapters Four and Five.

23. *Literary and Philosophical Essays*, p. 20.

24. Ibid., p. 15.

COLLEGE OF THE SEQUOIAS
LIBRARY

"inside and outside," as Straus shows, is a temporal one: "Within and without are separated by a limit of possible action."[25] Thus to see the inside and outside simultaneously is to spatialize time, to freeze it into a map of the world. Sartre specifically calls this elimination of time in the novel an elimination of freedom. For a novel to incorporate true human freedom, the future cannot preexist for any of its characters.[26]

Because of this lack of freedom in realistic novels, many of the actions of characters seem mechanical. This includes not only overall actions, plots, but immediate actions and movements, gestures. Fielding often exploits the mechanical movements of his characters for purposes of humor, but one often feels in reading certain passages that he had no other choice.

> Not conceiving any extraordinary affection for the beauty of Joseph's person, nor being extremely pleased with this method of salutation, he collected all his force, and aimed a blow at Joseph's breast, which he artfully parried with one fist, so that it lost its force entirely in air; and, stepping one foot backward, he darted his fist so fiercely at his enemy, that, had he not caught it in his hand (for he was a boxer of no inferior fame), it must have tumbled him on the ground. And now the ravisher meditated another blow, which he aimed at that part of the breast where the heart is lodged; Joseph did not catch it as before, yet so prevented its aim that it fell directly on his nose, but with abated force. Joseph then, moving both fist and foot forwards at the same time, threw his head so dexterously into the stomach of the ravisher that he fell a lifeless lump on the field, where he lay many minutes breathless and motionless.

Fielding's description consists of a series of discrete tableaus, snapshots of frozen positions placed in a series and arranged according to outcome. There is a stop-start motion to the description as a whole, like the jump of the minute hand on a clock registering the time that already has passed. Objective space in the novel receives the body as an object, and thus establishes beforehand that its actions will be those of an object, that is,

25. Straus, *Primary World*, p. 244.
26. Sartre, *Literary and Philosophical Essays*, p. 7.

mechanical. The mechanical nature of overall actions, of plots, is disguised by a map structure; a plot has the continuity of its roads, its channels, even if that continuity is reified, separated from the subject who belongs to it. Actions and gestures of the body lack even this reified continuity. Each character in Fielding's description brings together one by one the actions of his body; he seemingly makes a separate decision for each stage of his overall motions, so there is no organic synthesis and no continuity to those motions.

The objectivity of the body in realistic fiction is a direct expression of the schizophrenia implicit in realism. By copying, by mirroring, realism places the body in the two-dimensional framework of objective space, and thus divides the body from the self. Mirrors, echoes, and shadows, as Laing shows, are common schizophrenic images.[27] The mirror makes the body into the object of someone else's observation, whether that someone else is actually another person or the disembodied self. In Pynchon's *V.*, a novel that parodies realistic structures, two of the characters, V. and Mélanie, are lovers and arouse each other sexually by looking at each other in a mirror. Realistic fiction reduces the body to a fetish, an object, of the same nature and significance as a shoe, say, for a fetishist. For this reason there is an implicit threat of dismemberment in the realistic novel. When the body is an object, there is no interpenetrating subjective synthesis to parts of the body, and hence those parts are potentially detachable, as they are for the schizophrenic.

Many of Fielding's descriptions of the actions of characters convey the impression that members of the body have separated from it and are being used as autonomous objects. "He clenched his fist and presently darted it at that part of Adam's breast where the heart is lodged." Or "having planted her right eye sideways against Mr. Jones, she shot from its corner a most penetrating glance." The objective space of the novel creates the same condition as does the space of Vesalius' woodcuts, a schizophrenia whereby the actions of the body become discrete movements of discrete entities, entities whose relation to the

27. See Laing, *Divided Self*, pp. 115ff., 169.

body as a whole is mathematical rather than organic. The dismemberment that is virtual in Fielding becomes actual in *V.*, as when V.'s hair, feet, and one eye are removed by the children of Valleta. Similarly Burroughs' characters are frequently subjected to violent dismemberment.

The objectivity and potential fragmentation of the body in realistic fiction go hand in hand with a world of fragmented objects. The novel is the form in which objects as such are first described in detail, and this is because the novel is an expression of that same schizophrenic consciousness, solidified in Newton's science, that divided subject and object and emptied objects totally of human and sacred significance, rendering them merely objective. Released from the synthetic organization of the human, objects fall apart and become discrete, mutually exclusive; they become fragmented and movable, and the only organization that can then handle them is an administrative map organization, a mechanical distribution of goods.

The novel, as several critics have pointed out,[28] is a middle-class phenomenon, a form born into a capitalistic world of movable objects for sale and consumption. The plot of much of *Moll Flanders* is the map of London, particularly when Moll, in the second half of the novel, follows the economic distribution of the city into those areas most ripe for theft. *Moll Flanders* shows the way in which the objectivity of the body is inseparable from the sudden visibility and objectivity of objects in realism. The turning point of the novel occurs when Moll loses the sexual power of her body and, it is implied, enters menopause. It is then that her stealing becomes its own justification and she accumulates objects, linen and gold, not out of necessity but out of a displaced sexuality, an obsessive consumption of objects and goods that feed the body's new-found objectivity.

The same kind of displaced sexuality underlies Richardson's lavish descriptions of Pamela's clothes and the costume fetish Mr. B—— displays in his attempt to seduce Pamela. Pamela's own eventual success, her attainment of wealth and the objects

---

28. Lionel Trilling, *The Liberal Imagination* (New York, 1953), pp. 204–5; Harry Levin, *Contexts of Criticism* (Cambridge, Mass., 1957), p. 71.

of the upper class, is her reward for displacing her sexuality and objectifying her body. When the body has become an object and objects have fled to the furthest remove from the self, incorporation and consumption, the acquisition of goods, are the only connection the body can make with the world. The recurrence of novels of success and property over the last three centuries is an indication that the theme of consumption of objects is built into the structure of realism and naturalism, from *Moll Flanders* and *Pamela* to *La Terre, Le Rouge et le Noir, The Rise of Silas Lapham, McTeague, Sister Carrie, The Old Wives' Tale, The Man of Property*, and *Babbitt*.

2. Naturalism

To summarize: the realistic novel is the literary form that occurs when the world, objects, and the body are all defined as entities sufficient unto themselves, separate from the self. In this schizophrenic arrangement the space of the world is laid out like a map, and objects and bodies circulate in it as shells that encapsulate unchanging identities. This structure is implicit in all realistic novels. There is no need to go into all I have neglected, the comic dimension of the novel, the act of reading, and so on. All this is certainly present, but it does not explain the further development of realism into naturalism, and into the parodies of the novel form that exist today.

In naturalism, the point of view that creates the map space of the novel institutionalizes itself in a theory of the novelist as scientist. The novelist is an observer and recorder, and he stands at a distance without manipulating his materials; he is objective.[29] Of course there are many internal contradictions to this aesthetic, as there are for any theory that considers itself not a theory but a slave to facts and "the way things are." Although the novelist is an observer and proposes not to interfere with his materials, he carefully places his subject in certain controlled conditions, as the experimental scientist does, and then alters those conditions to see what will happen. The division

29. Zola, *Experimental Novel*, pp. 124–25.

of Fouan's land in the first book of Zola's *La Terre* is an example. Fouan's doom is sealed from the beginning with this alteration of his environment, as his relatives try to tell him. Because Fouan is of a certain nature and behaves in certain ways according to that nature, and because his environment is of a certain nature, this can only be so. The naturalist carries to its logical conclusion the assumption of realism that there is a static, consistent nature to things, and insists on an absolute determinism.[30]

It is only appropriate that mechanical models come to characterize the naturalist's view of nature; as Zola says, the object of experiment is to reduce things to the condition of "subservient machinery."[31] The distance of a map perspective thus becomes a perfect tool for this view of the world. From a distance, a man's actions and gestures look like those of a puppet or automaton, men in groups look like ants, the world of existence is mere earth, and the earth itself is a map, the inert unchanging background against which men play out their petty differences, their comic games. *La Terre* is typical of naturalistic novels in the way in which it opens and closes with a maplike survey of the novel's terrain. The point of view of these surveys is an overhead one, usually obtained by perching a character on top of a hill. "Under the enormous sky, an overcast sky of late October, the ten leagues of arable land at this time of the year were broken into great ploughed squares of bare rich yellow earth alternating with green expanses of lucerne and clover—the whole scene, without a single hillock, without a single tree, blurring away and sinking down to a horizon-line as clear and rounded as the sea."[32] Such an overview is the underlying structural principle of naturalism. In it, men are always "dwarfed by distance," as the narrator of *La Terre* says, and the individuality of man is overwhelmed by the flow of humanity, as in the street scenes in *Sister Carrie,* where Carrie is literally "carried" by

30. Ibid., p. 29.
31. Ibid., pp. 24–25.
32. Emile Zola, *The Earth,* trans. Ann Lindsay (New York, 1954).

the traffic of people channeling through the network of streets in Chicago.

Zola's plan for an interlocking series of novels about the same family and branches of that family participates in this overhead structure, as does Balzac's plan for a panoramic Comédie Humaine, which, as he said, "will represent all social effects, without forgetting a single situation in life, a physiognomy, a way of life, a profession, a social zone, a part of, or anything of childhood, old age, maturity, politics, law, war."[33] The overview is a characteristic sign of nineteenth-century thought in all spheres, science, philosophy, economics, etc., from Darwin and Spencer to Marx, Hegel, and Laplace. Its spatial contours adhere to the principle of juxtaposition, whether it be of the rich and the exploited poor in Marx or of the great contrasting variety of human and animal life in Darwin. In the novel, this spatial juxtaposition becomes the common theme of naturalism. Carrie and Hurstwood at the end of *Sister Carrie* live in two proximate but completely different social contexts; one is rich, the other poor.

Such juxtaposition depends heavily upon a map space, for only in a map are pure proximity and strict, rigid lines of demarcation combined. The naturalistic novelist writes as if his terrain were literally a blueprint, as if he had snipped all the tops off houses and rooms and could attain the supreme, even if supremely simple, ironic vision. At the end of *The Octopus*, Presley dines with the upper class, while Mrs. Hooven and her daughter die of starvation outside; Père Goriot dies while his daughters are dancing. The literature of the small town in America—*Winesburg, Ohio, Main Street*, and *Our Town*, for example—derives both its form and its major theme from the structure of ironic overviews in naturalistic fiction.

The overview reifies the world, makes it a thing in itself, strictly separated from the people who occupy it. The irony of Zola's remark that "man cannot be separated from his surround-

33. Quoted by Erich Auerbach in *Mimesis*, trans. Willard Trask (New York, 1957), p. 423.

ings"[34] is that it describes a world in which man is trapped by his surroundings, isolated in the world, as Pavlov's dogs were isolated in the carefully constructed environment of his laboratory. In naturalism the world becomes its own organization, and this organization is an external one; it contains experience rather than informs it. Such an organization precedes the stuff it organizes. In *Sister Carrie*, "the city had laid miles and miles of streets and sewers through regions where, perhaps, one solitary house stood out alone—a pioneer of the populous ways to be. There were regions open to the sweeping winds and rain, which were yet lighted throughout the night with long, blinking lines of gas-lamps, fluttering in the wind. Narrow board walks extended out, passing here a house, and there a store, at far intervals, eventually ending on the open prairie."

The land has become a thing, a map, its own map, the "subservient machinery" that Zola talks about. "J'ever stop to consider, Myra," says Babbitt, "that before a town can have buildings or prosperity or any of those things, some realtor has got to sell 'em the land? All civilization starts with him." Thus one of Babbitt's developments is described as a once dipping meadow, ironed out into a flat plain "with small boards displaying the names of imaginary streets." Zola's *La Terre* examines the alienation of men from the world that this transformation of it into mere earth and subsequently into the map of property has caused. As property, as a thing, the earth is fragmented, split, weakened, drained.

When the earth has become total Other, it is used like an object, emptied of its fertility, cut up and sold. Ownership, what Zola calls "the ferment of mine and thine," alienates the earth and, reciprocally, those who own and use it. Old Fouan's division of his land, the central motivating incident of the novel, results in an atomized earth, each piece of which tightly clings to its own boundaries: "Up on the plateau were still ten more acres of arable land, but these were already divided into a dozen strips, each one not much more than an acre in size. One parcel indeed was only about a rood; and when the

34. *Experimental Novel*, p. 232.

surveyor sarcastically asked if he were to start cutting it up, the argument started again. . . . Yes, yes, a third of a rood each, it was only fair. So all the strips were divided and everyone was quite certain that neither of the others had anything he didn't have." The increasing impoverishment of the earth mentioned several times during the course of the novel is the result of this radically refined organization of it, which in turn is the result of its absolute objectivity.

In naturalism all aspects of human experience eventually are reduced to this objectivity. Not only are space and time separated from each other and frozen, but from an overview they are dissolved into the same organization, which is the earth. "The earth, the sustainer, would always remain," says Zola at the end of *La Terre*. "She contained space and time." Projected onto its two-dimensional surface, all modulations of experience are contained and organized by the earth, each in its separate area. The ultimate irony of naturalism is that Life itself is capitalized, objectified and separated from living beings. At the end of *La Terre*, Jean sees from a hill "the sowers in the ploughed fields, their ceaseless movement producing an infinite living wave of fertility, the seeds falling in a rain over the open furrows." In a less subtle but similar passage, Presley mounts a hill at the end of *The Octopus* and reflects: "Men were naught, death was naught, life was naught; FORCE only existed—FORCE that brought men into the world, FORCE that crowded them out of it to make way for the succeeding generation, FORCE that made the wheat grow, FORCE that garnered it from the soil to give place to the succeeding crop."

The implicit assumption of realism, that nature is an objective consistent identity, is here carried to its naive but inevitable conclusion. Life, History, Force, People, all are reified by the naturalist; they are identities separated from those who are people or have life; they are Other. This is why the map organization plays such an important role in the structures of naturalism. If force is to be a thing, the accumulated energy of entities that have force, but stripped of those entities in order to become an entity for itself, its structure has to be externalized, lifted out of its skin and used to delimit and channel its substance. Its structure has to become negative and preventive, not informing and synthesizing, repressive not expressive, mechanical not organic. In *The Octopus* this structure is represented by the novel's two central images, both of which are images of the world itself as a map: the elevators and chutes that channel wheat, explicitly identified with "Force" and "Life," into the hold of a ship at the novel's end; and the railroad tracks that spread the mechanical "Force" of the novel's title across the flat San Joaquin Valley. The connection between the two is made explicit by the railroad company's president when Presley visits him: "Try to believe this—to begin with—*that railroads build themselves.* Where there is a demand sooner or later there will be a supply. Mr. Derrick, does he grow his wheat? The Wheat grows itself. What does he count for? Do I build the Railroad? You are dealing with forces, young man, when you speak of wheat and the Railroads, not with men."

The concept that railroads build themselves seems to imply that the forces the novel describes are all, like wheat, organic, spontaneous, and natural. But the irony of the novel, and in a sense of naturalism as a whole, naturalism as an extensive system of thought in the nineteenth century as well as a literary movement, is that the organic is always mechanical, rather than vice versa. Consider this passage: "The whole map was gridironed by a vast complicated network of red lines marked P. and S.W.R.R. These centralized at San Francisco and thence ramified and spread north, east, and south, to every quarter of the state, from Coles, in the topmost corner of the map, to Yuma in the lowest, from Reno on one side to San Francisco on the other, ran the plexus of red, a veritable system of blood circulation, complicated, dividing, and reuniting, branching, splitting, extending, throwing out feelers, off-shoots, tap roots, feeders." The reduction here is clearly from the organic to the mechanical, since both terms of the metaphor (the tree and the railroad) are contained within the framework of a map, that is, both are viewed from the overhead distance that accompanies mechanical manipulation and control. The naturalistic viewpoint reduces the garden to the map by mechanically channeling experience into sealed-off spaces. The wheat chutes and railroad tracks in *The Octopus* are the Tree of Life turned inside out, its life contained and distributed by a mechanical structure rather than self-proliferating and expressive.

Naturalism has no choice but to separate life from structure, and thus determines beforehand that all structure will be external and delimiting. Naturalism can see aspects of experience only as juxtaposed, as existing beside each other. The naturalist creates the schism of vitalism and mechanism in biology, and the naturalist drains the spiritual, irrational, and supernatural out of the world of experience and siphons them off into a pure space that circumscribes and consequently disposes of them.[35] (Vanamee represents this pure space in *The Octopus*.) When aspects of experience are projected onto a flat plane from overhead, they have to arrange themselves into discrete entities, like the homolographic map of the earth that splits the spherical surface of the earth apart like an orange peel and flattens it out. The two-dimensional condition of a map, its structural schizophrenia, becomes the unreal condition of experience in naturalism. There are two McTeagues, a bestial, Darwinian, inner McTeague and a placid, dumb, outer McTeague, and they exist beside each other, as inner and outer exist beside each other on a floor plan. There is no evil or good in the flat world of naturalism, because from overhead there are no shadows, no other sides to things that cause them to throw their sides at me, that cause them to have a reference to me, to be moral.

If the naturalistic viewpoint is neutral, as its proponents claim it to be, it is because things have a relation only to themselves as things. But in this respect, neutrality is a particular viewpoint, an overhead and consequently two-dimensional one. This is why the only quality that actions finally have in naturalism is that of quantity, up or down, left or right. The melodramatic simplicity of many naturalistic novels stems from such a reduction to the two-dimensional and quantitative. Characters rise

35. Zola does this continually in *The Experimental Novel*; see p. 54, for example.

or fall; they assume a higher or lower social position, period. Movement is either progress or decline, and either way the movement always preexists, since it is a thing in itself, a force. Given this force, plot in naturalism is necessarily mechanical, since it guides actions by blocking off certain possibilities and opening up others. This is the natural development of the spatialized plot of realism, both structurally and thematically—it is plot as a trap. In *The Octopus*, the wheat elevators and chutes lead to a bin into which S. Behrman falls, to be buried alive by Wheat, Force. In O'Neill's play *The Hairy Ape*, Yank bounces around from organization to organization, from wall to wall in the map of New York's streets, until he finally winds up in a cage, the container for which all the channels existed, to which all the streets led.

Naturalism, in this sense, is the inevitable completion of the realistic viewpoint. Men are "motes," as Norris calls them, because all of their identity, their timeless consistent reality, has been squeezed out of them by the spatial pressure of objectivity; it has become Force, Life, Wheat, People. Men themselves have become nonentities, husks left behind by the reality that once composed them and filled them out, a reality that the relentless map consciousness of naturalism can see only as Other, as there, pure and distant, channeling into itself, like wheat. In realism, the objective identity of place and social position mirrored and defined the objective identity of character, and allowed character to achieve itself. In naturalism, the objective identity of place has been inflated into the condition of *all* objective identity, an environment that determines the motes of human beings in it, by drowning them and assimilating them, as New York drowns and assimilates Yank, as the wheat drowns S. Behrman. In realism, plot arises out of a rhythm of convergence and divergence made possible by roads on the one hand and inns or homes on the other. In naturalism, the mechanism implicit in this structure becomes explicit, and plot thus becomes simply the completion of a map that can be completed in only one way, that has always been completed, the map of New York, the railroad, the chutes and elevators that channel the wheat.

3. Realism and Fantasy

From a map that can be completed in only one way, it is a natural step to a labyrinth that can be completed in all ways, that, in other words, cannot be completed. Naturalism finds its logical final step in what Barth calls the literature of exhaustion, the literature whose most common image is the labyrinth, as in Barth himself, Pynchon, Borges, or Robbe-Grillet. The image of the labyrinth is an image of the objective world teetering on the brink of its opposite, of subjectivity; it is the real organization of the world become fantastic. I conclude this discussion of the novel by examining some of the parodies of realism that carry it over into fantasy, then looking closely at two novels, Robbe-Grillet's *Dans le Labyrinthe* and Sartre's *La Nausée*, as the most representative examples of this reversal.

Realism as an organization of the world, rather than a neutral record of what the world actually is, is one of Barth's major themes. In *The Sot-Weed Factor*, Mary Mungummory says of Charley Mattasin: "Read him half a tale or half a chapter out o' Euclid, he could spin ye the balance from his head; and if it differed from the text, 'twas the author, like as not, that came off badly. Ofttimes I felt his fancy bore a clutch of worlds, all various, of which the world these books described was one." Mary is describing *The Sot-Weed Factor* itself, a book about the world of Euclid and Newton (who appears briefly in it), about reality as the Western world has devised it, but also about how this reality is only one of many possible organizations of the world.

The irony of the novel consists in the fact that it is based on the model of *Tom Jones*, and on all the assumptions the world of *Tom Jones* makes, but that its hero, Ebenezer Cooke, achieves disillusionment, not identity, at the end. The very concept of "identity" is called into question by the novel. No one in the novel is what he appears to be; Bertrand, Ebenezer's valet, poses as Ebenezer aboard ship; Burlingame poses as Lord Baltimore, Colonel Peter Sayer, Timothy Mitchell, and Nicholas Lowe. The overwhelming complexity and richness of the novel derive partly from this substitution of illusion for identity. All of the complicated, shifting interconnections of the plot and the political intrigues it involves are brought a step beyond *Tom Jones:* the threads of the plot never are tied up neatly in *The Sot-Weed Factor,* and facts never do dovetail. The maze of the plot, from the overview of the reader, verges on the condition of a labyrinth, the condition in which the consistent identity of the world exists in a shattered state. The space of *The Sot-Weed Factor* is apparently the same kind of map space as in *Tom Jones,* but cracks in this space are always opening up, and they open into voids.

When Burlingame tells Ebenezer that heaven is no "dome," that stars do not exist in the sky as they do on flat navigation charts, Ebenezer's orientation in the world disappears from his vision as if it had been a film over his eyes.

> Viewed in this manner, the constellations lost their sense entirely; their spurious character revealed itself, as did the false presupposition of the celestial navigator, and Ebenezer felt bereft of orientation. He could no longer think of up and down: the stars were simply *out there,* as well below him as above, and the wind appeared to howl not from the Bay but from the firmament itself, from the endless corridors of space.
>
> "Madness!" Henry whispered.

Ebenezer's education in disillusionment is a process of learning to live with this madness, in a world that lacks identity and neat plots. When Timothy Mitchell turns out to be Burlingame, he tells the puzzled Ebenezer: " 'Tis but to say what oft I've said to you ere now, Eben: your true and constant Burlingame lives only in your fancy, as does the pointed order of the world. In fact you see a Heraclitean flux: whether 'tis we who shift and alter and dissolve; or you whose lens changes color, field, and focus; or both together. The upshot is the same, and you may take it or reject it."

Burlingame's comments are an accurate description of that modern fiction which uses the "true and constant" structures of realism to undercut themselves. What is most true and constant in the real world, its identity, is shown to be the least verifiable aspect of it. The peculiar combination of necessity and arbitrariness in *The Sot-Weed Factor, V.*, or *The Crying of Lot 49* is an expression of this lack of substance in the real world, of gaps opening up out of which reality drains. Chance meetings in Pynchon's novels are exploited as parodies of realism by being accepted as part of the normal, necessary order of events. A line of action that is entirely arbitrary, that is taken by chance, links perfectly with others that are stumbled upon, and all of them lead somehow to the right place. Yet this right place, whether it be V. or a full disclosure of the Tristero system, is never finally reached. The clues that Oedipa Maas assembles about the Tristero in *Lot 49* are all happened upon accidentally, through a Jacobean play, a lavatory wall, a chance meeting with another character in a labyrinthine munitions plant, and so on. The atmosphere of a multitude of possibilities is created, an infinite proliferation of plot lines; yet the one that is followed is the only one, the right one, the way out; and yet again, it brings us no closer to an answer, an identity, a V., a meaningful pattern, than we were to begin with.

In the novels of Pynchon and Barth, the labyrinth of possibilities always, finally, outstrips the pattern of actions of the characters. The overview of realism and naturalism that produces a map, an organization of historical links and events, upon close examination inevitably produces a map of a map, an overorganization, a proliferation of choices on the verge of a pattern, but always on the verge. In *Lot 49* the Tristero itself is an image of this: a mail delivery system superimposed on the everyday map of the country, a complicated network whose proximate manifestations we can see (a mailbox marked Waste under a freeway bridge), but whose overall pattern will always, by definition, escape us. In realism the significance of actions always lies outside of them, ahead of them, in a goal, a teleology. A "goal" is the final organization of the variety and plenitude of the novel, the expression of a consistent timeless identity that infuses that plenitude and causes it to cohere, to be a recognizable pattern, a plot.

In Barth and Pynchon, this organizing goal exists only as a possibility, such a distant possibility that the links between it and the plenitude of the novel's world have snapped, allowing that plenitude to fall apart into multiplicity, a labyrinth, with all its parts equal to each other. The clues that a Pynchon character is inevitably able to find are always reflections of themselves in a maze of mirrors, not indications of anything behind them. The dichotomy of appearance and reality, upon which the classical sense of the real is based, and consequently upon which the novel is based, becomes the dichotomy of appearance and appearance in Barth and Pynchon. In *Giles Goat-Boy*, Bray's identity turns out to be nonexistent; he is his shifting disguises, and nothing else. There is no timeless, consistent identity behind appearances; there are only appearances behind appearances, an infinite proliferation of them.

The theme of appearances is important in modern literature, and is carried over from the nineteenth century by the figure of the dandy.[36] The dandy is the final product of the concept of "character" fostered by realism; he is a copy of himself, the man of appearances and many faces who prevents his pure subjectivity from being violated by erecting an armor of multiple external attachments. Wylie Sypher gives Frederick Moreau in Flaubert's *L'Education Sentimentale* as an example of the dandy, but perhaps a better example, because it is a more radical one, is Melville's Confidence Man in the novel of that title, a novel that prefigures a great deal of Barth's and Pynchon's work. By extending himself into his roles, the Confidence Man is everything, and hence nothing, no one; he sustains himself in the vacant air of his identity with no support but style. With the breakdown of a natural participation in the world, that is, with the breakdown of an organic community, roles are the structure by which we attempt to orient ourselves to each other, since only then is orientation as such necessary. A role is a face, a facing, an act of encountering the Other when that Other

36. Wylie Sypher, in *Loss of the Self in Modern Literature* (New York, 1962), discusses the importance of the dandy in the transition from the nineteenth century to the twentieth; see pp. 36–41.

is absolute. A role is necessary when there is a split between inside and outside, when pure subjectivity has to face the world and construct an outside.

The dandy represents the beginning stages of the schizophrenic personality in modern literature; like the schizophrenic, he constructs roles, what Laing calls "false self systems," and like the schizophrenic, his split is between an outward compliance and an inner withholding of compliance.[37] For the dandy, as for the schizophrenic, freedom consists in being inaccessible.[38] The dandy "lives and sleeps in front of a mirror," as Baudelaire says,[39] and yet he is disinterested and feels nothing. He creates himself and distributes his creation among a labyrinth of personalities: lover, aesthete, soldier, poet, saint. He maintains perfect control over these personalities; he uses them, and they obey him. And yet, inside he is nothing, demands to be nothing, since everything he is, is outside. The dandy is the literary figure born out of realism, who extends realism out of itself into the world of appearances that Barth, Pynchon, and others write about. He is a parody of the traditional notion of character in the novel, the man who is not what he appears to be, whose disguise, like Tom Jones's, hides his true nature.

The true nature of the dandy, of course, does not exist; he manufactures it out of the world of changing appearances. The dandy is the first to uncover the actual structure of mimesis: the mirror does not reproduce objective reality, but creates it. Hence the dandy looks in his mirror and creates his roles, his appearances, and then thrusts them into the world of social intercourse. In *The Sot-Weed Factor,* Burlingame is the supreme dandy, able to create and assume any number of roles, to the extent that his body itself becomes the plastic mirror of his imagination:

> "Aye, gentlemen." Burlingame smiled. "Captain Billy's pride and pleasure, till his real son came along." His hands were busy as he spoke, and his appearance changed magically. Off came

37. Laing, *Divided Self*, p. 99.
38. Ibid., p. 113.
39. *Intimate Journals*, trans. Christopher Isherwood (Boston, 1957), p. xviii.

the powdered periwig, to be replaced by a short black hairpiece; from his mouth he removed a curious device which, it turned out, had held three artificial teeth in position. Most uncannily of all, he seemed able to alter at will the set of his facial muscles: the curve of his cheeks and the flare of his nose changed shape before their eyes; his habitually furrowed brow grew smooth, but crow's-feet appeared where before there were none. Finally, his voice deepened and coarsened; he drew in upon himself so as to seem at least two inches shorter; his eyes took on a craftier cast—Nicholas Lowe, in a few miraculous seconds, had become Timothy Mitchell.

Burlingame is his own novel, written by himself. Like the realistic novelist, he thrusts his material into objective space and manipulates it; but his material is not nature or reality—it is the image of himself. Thus Burlingame infuses objective space with the condition of appearances; he infuses reality with fantasy, with hallucination, in such a way that the act of creation collapses the structure of copying upon which it is based. Burlingame is the dandy from the dandy's point of view, the schizophrenic from the schizophrenic's point of view, the point of view that makes no distinction between hallucination and reality and sees all fantasies as real.

Not only in literary figures such as Burlingame or the dandy, but in literature itself this new point of view is born out of the very structure of realism. The illusion that the novel is a copy of reality is replaced by the knowledge that copying creates reality, and that the reality it creates is the novelist himself and his act of copying. The dandy is the literary character who solves ahead of time his creator's problem of what to do when there is no objective, consistent reality to write about. In the twentieth century the novelist's world, like the dandy's, is infused with himself, and the novelist becomes a dandy. The concept of the dandy makes the *bildungsroman*, the artist as his own material, possible. And as the diary sections at the end of Joyce's *Portrait* make clear, the *bildungsroman* represents a convergence of the act of writing and its subject. This is the irony of realism that modern writers such as Joyce, Beckett, or Robbe-Grillet have exploited. In the last analysis, all realism can ever copy is itself, since all I can hold a mirror to is my own act of holding a mirror.

This fact is one of the most important aspects of Western thought structures, and the reason why those structures are exhausting themselves today. If I place myself at a distance from the world, as Thales did, if I objectify it, calling my knowledge a copy of it, that knowledge is bound to possess the structure of my act, that is, it is bound to be about itself. Newton's physics, as Einstein's physics has shown, is valid only for the visual space it creates by its own epistemology. From a view of the mind as mirror and of art as mirror, realism results in its own opposite, reality as a mirror of the mind, i.e., fantasy. This brings us to Robbe-Grillet's *Dans le Labyrinthe*, for the labyrinth is created by holding a mirror to a mirror, by undercutting the structures of realism with realism itself. Robbe-Grillet's novels converge through their structure on their own act of realism, and thus realism becomes what it always implicitly was, fantastic.

The most obvious fact about Robbe-Grillet's world is that everything is proximate; there is, in other words, no world for Robbe-Grillet, no context in which the objects of immediate perception exist. There is only a presence, specifically a visual presence, whittled down in the most radical way to itself. A character in *Dans le Labyrinthe* appears behind a half-open door, or rather "a vertical strip of him"[40] appears, implying that only the visual image I find in front of me is worthy of reporting, and that the rest is suspect, including the rest of his body. There can be no inference to perception, because there is no context to perception; there can be no intentionality to perception, because perception is limited to visual geometry. "Under his right arm he has a brown paper parcel, something like a shoebox, with a piece of white string tied no doubt in a cross; but the only part of the string that is visible goes round the box lengthwise, the other part, if it exists, being hidden by the coat sleeve." The important words here are "if it exists," for not only is the existence of the string on the other side of the package called into

40. Alain Robbe-Grillet, *In the Labyrinth*, trans. Christine Brook-Rose (London, 1968).

question, but so is the existence of the whole other side of the package.

This is a radical and fantastic application of the premise of realism and naturalism that our sense of reality is based on our visual sense. As Zola put it, "it seems at first that, as all the world have two eyes to see with, nothing ought to be more common than the sense of reality."[41] Zola's account of differences between people's senses of reality is the same as Robbe-Grillet's. Zola says that "each eye has a particular way of seeing. Then again, there are eyes which see nothing at all. There is doubtless some lesion, the nerve connecting them with the brain has become paralyzed in some way that science has not been able to determine yet."[42] Similarly, Robbe-Grillet accounts for the fantasy in his novels by asserting that the vision of the subjects he presents to us is often distorted.[43] This is the novelist as pathologist, a fact evident in Zola's choice of Claude Bernard's Introduction à l'Etude de la Médecine Experimentale as the theoretical basis for his assertions about the "experimental novel." In Robbe-Grillet, however, it is an extreme kind of pathology, a cultural rather than individual one, which accounts for the fantastic nature of his work. And this is, specifically, the reduction of a world to its purely visual presence, and behind this reduction, the classical distinction between primary and secondary qualities upon which so many of our notions of the real are based. Robbe-Grillet says that "things are there and they are nothing but things, each limited to itself,"[44] and he deplores any organization of the world that would infuse objects with subjective significance. He is a new Ruskin, denouncing the pathetic fallacy, even to the extent of calling for an elimination of metaphor in literature.[45]

Such an absolute split between subject and object, an absolute insistence upon reality in the classical sense, can result only in schizophrenia, and hallucination, which is the quality that most

41. Experimental Novel, p. 212.
42. Ibid.
43. For a New Novel, trans. Richard Howard (New York, 1966), p. 138.
44. Ibid., p. 72.
45. Ibid., pp. 56–57.

of Robbe-Grillet's novels have. It is as if Robbe-Grillet actually places us in that world of Galileo and Locke, where the only cohesive identity to things consists in their geometrical fixity:

> Still further to the left following the direction of the flower's tail or the dagger's point, a circle, hardly blurred at all, is just broached on one side by a second circle of the same size, but consisting of more than just a projection on the table: the glass ashtray. Then come a few uncertain lines, criss-crossing, left no doubt by various papers, moved several times in such a way as to blur the pattern, very clear in places or on the contrary veiled by the grizzled film, and elsewhere more than half erased as if by the flick of a rag.

Objects in Robbe-Grillet's world are always collapsed into their outlines; they are concrete abstractions, as they are for Locke, real only when they have left their footprints behind: circles on a tavern table, lines in the dust on a mantel, tracks in the snow, the areas of clean cloth where the soldier's emblems have recently been removed. The overlapping geometrical figures in Robbe-Grillet's world would confuse even a Gestalt psychologist. If objects are everywhere collapsed into their surfaces, and these surfaces are flat, that is, they face us and we do not walk around them, then there is finally no way of distinguishing figure from ground, because there is nothing behind things that sets them off. "The doors are shut. The windows are empty of silhouettes, whether glued to the panes or outlined in the background in the depths of the rooms. In any case it would appear from this whole decor that there is nothing behind these window-panes, behind these doors, behind these walls. And the whole scene remains empty: not a man, not a woman, not even a child."

The labyrinth of *Dans le Labyrinthe* consists precisely in this inability to distinguish figure from ground, in the lack of a context for our perception of proximate things. If there is no world enveloping the immediate things we see, then the world is simply a reproduction, a mirroring, of those things that exist before us, in the same way they exist there, everywhere. The absence of a synthesizing goal creates labyrinths for Barth and Pynchon; in Robbe-Grillet this synthesizing goal is seen to be the wholeness that gives the things we face coherence, that is, the world itself. The labyrinth is the repetition of visual presences, city streets and building facades outside, corridors and walls inside; it is the repetition of *here* and the elimination of *there*.

More precisely, it is the repetition of here-now and the elimination of there-then, for the labyrinth consists also in the neutralization of the temporal dimension. Time is flattened out just as objects are, so successive aspects of time are peeled apart and laid out on a plane. In this respect Robbe-Grillet accomplishes what even realism, despite its implicit elimination of time, could not accomplish: he dissolves the temporal act of reading by creating a style that spirals back and forth between certain repeated actions and gestures. If the labyrinth of the novel depends upon repetition, it is established by a syntax of repetition that fragments the past and the future and arranges them spatially, so the act of reading itself becomes a labyrinth. When I turn a corner reading *Dans le Labyrinthe*, I meet either another corner or a place I have been before, so often that "before" ceases to have meaning. The spatialization of time established by the map organization of realism overwhelms Robbe-Grillet's fiction to the extent that it drags explicitly upon the temporality of the reader, creating the studied boredom that characterizes all of his writing. Like the objects in Robbe-Grillet's world, time collapses into its surface, which is the present tense, and remains there, flat.

Flatness is the basic structural principle of Robbe-Grillet's world. Objects are flat, time is flat, and space is flat. This is the realistic novel become what it always was on the verge of being. Robbe-Grillet's characters never walk around objects but face them, as if they were paintings in a gallery; they never walk through the world but face it, as if it were a painting, or a mirror. The reader himself is often made to face an engraving of the inside of a tavern in *Dans le Labyrinthe*, and the distinction between this engraving and the actual tavern in which parts of the novel occur is carefully blurred by the flatness of both. The labyrinth of the town itself is in a sense an illusion, a real illusion created by the flatness of perception: "But the daylight is without brightness, making everything look flat and dull. Instead of the spectacular perspectives which these rows of houses ought to display, there is only a meaningless criss-crossing of lines, and the snow that falls continuously, removing all depth from the landscape as if this blurred view were a badly painted *trompe l'œil* on a flat wall."

The flatness of realism and naturalism depended upon an overview, a structure of distance, whether it was of the author from his materials, of a perceiving character glancing over the terrain of the novel, or of the reader contemplating the novel's plot. Space in the realistic novel is broken down into discrete locations; there is a consciousness of there while I am here, and what makes this possible is an implicit distance that infuses the world with the structure of a map. Robbe-Grillet removes this distance and thrusts the perceiving consciousness of the author-character-reader into that map, into a world structured by distance but experienced close up. Robbe-Grillet's world is one of pure locations laid out beside each other, but we are in that world, not above it. This is the further significance of the repetition of the here and the elimination of there that creates the labyrinth in *Dans le Labyrinthe*. In Robbe-Grillet, the there collapses totally into here, repeats itself around me and in front of me rather than simply beneath me or beyond me. The there is eliminated, distance is eliminated, because the here has assumed its structure, has become a map. And since we are deprived of the distance by which we can compare one here with another and achieve orientation, the map, lived in, becomes a labyrinth.

This is reality pushed into fantasy; it is the condition by which the real, the more real it becomes, is less and less real. The apparent contradictions of Robbe-Grillet's epistemology in *For a New Novel* are expressions of the fantastic nature of this real world. He insists that objects are there, "out of reach,"[46] and thus allies himself with the subject-object dichotomy that

46. Ibid., p. 70.

produced the flat world of realism. Yet he also insists that the world of objects depends for its structure upon the point of view from which it is apprehended,[47] and thus rejects the illusion of objectivity created by realism. Added together, these two assertions constitute Robbe-Grillet's main point: reality, especially as exemplified in literary realism, is simply one organization of the world, one point of view, and is consequently subjective. The reader of Robbe-Grillet is thus placed in the position of exploring the flat, abstract structure of realism close up, of living in the mind of realism, the very doctrine that purported to describe a world outside and previous to the mind.

In this sense Robbe-Grillet's novels converge with their content. The walls, streets, and corridors of *Dans le Labyrinthe* are the structure of the novel, the externalized mental structure of Robbe-Grillet's world; his world is a realistic one that has become its structure. Hence the labyrinth of *Dans le Labyrinthe* is the novel itself as well as its subject matter, is the perceiving mind of the novel as well as what it perceives, is the subject as well as the object. By separating subject and object as radically as he does, by flattening out the objective world and shattering it into a labyrinth, Robbe-Grillet shows the inseparability of subject and object. Robbe-Grillet's world is real in that his characters always intrude upon it, as one always intrudes upon a painting; yet, paradoxically, that world is not already constituted, as the world of realistic novels is. It changes with a character's perception of it. This is true for the reader too; as Robbe-Grillet asserts, the world of his novels begins on the first page and ends on the last, and it doesn't exist previous to those pages.[48] The lesson of *Dans le Labyrinthe* is that all worlds, including the objective world, are creations of a mind in the world, of a mind inseparable from the world, so there can be no epistemology that separates subject and object, least of all one that explicitly does.

The labyrinthian world of Robbe-Grillet returns us to Barth

47. Ibid., p. 147.
48. Ibid., p. 154.

and Pynchon and the labyrinthian plots that structure their novels. The image of the labyrinth should be clear by now: it is an image of the objective world carried to the brink of its opposite, an objective world that is wearing out and beginning to show, like a glove, the subjectivity that has always animated it, like a hand. The labyrinth is a mental structure. The maze of the funhouse in Barth's story "Lost in the Funhouse" exists in the narrator's mind before it exists in the external world. The Library of Babel in Borges' story of that title is a world transformed into the labyrinth of mathematics, of the mind, for it houses every combination of letters and words mathematically possible, including this sentence and all refutations of it, the card catalog of the library and of all libraries, each of those catalogs with one false entry or two false entries, and so on.

The mathematical nature of Borges' labyrinth, and Borges' interest in Zeno, reminds us that the first labyrinths to parody the forms of realism were the infinite regressions of Zeno. In Zeno the infinite regression is the image of Western structures of thought taking their own inadequacy into account with that very inadequacy. Zeno's infinite regressions are like the problem suffered by the most completely realistic painter, the one who paints the scene before him but knows his painting can't be realistic unless he includes himself in it painting the scene, and so steps back and sets up another canvas to paint himself painting the scene, but knows that this, too, cannot be real unless he includes himself painting himself painting the scene, etc. This is the impasse to which the act of copying, which is the basis of realism, brings one. For a subjectivity separated from the objective world to copy that objective world with the structure of objectivity, with the act of "stepping back," is to invite labyrinths to open up. And the irony, of course, is that these labyrinths are subjective.

The paradox of the labyrinth, that the most objective of worlds is subjective, is a theme first consciously dealt with in modern literature by Sartre, in *La Nausée*. It is no coincidence that *La Nausée* is also a polemic for a philosophy which explicitly refutes the major tenet of realism, that reality has an underlying timeless consistency to it, for this tenet, or more precisely the concept of "thing" or "substance" underlying it, makes the subject-object division possible. "All these changes concern objects," says Roquentin about his experience in the course of the novel, but he learns that this means the changes concern him, since "I *was* the root of the chestnut tree."[49] But he learns this only by living in the most real world, the most ordinary one. The strength of the novel lies in Sartre's ability to establish convincingly the coating of commonplace nature that everything wears, and then, out of the heart of that commonplace nature, to reveal it as only a coating. The point of the novel is that "ordinariness" is precisely that subjective structure we create to hold the world at a distance, to keep it objective; it is disguised subjectivity, the excuse for the flabbiness of our own subjectivities; it hides ourselves. This is what Roquentin finds: behind the commonplace film he lays over objects, the film that for most people is a shroud, is himself.

Roquentin's isolation in the world is established by Sartre from the beginning with the novel's diary form. Roquentin has only a few daily acts to perform, all of them self-enclosed: research in the library for his book, dinner at the café, the writing of entries in the diary in his room. In everything he does, Roquentin is, he says, "confined within the limits of my body," and is thus inaccessible. The world for Roquentin is out there, an object, and it is sufficient simply to orient one's self in it, not to get lost. "My odd feelings of the other week seem to me quite ridiculous today: I can no longer enter into them. I am quite at ease this evening, quite solidly *terre-à-terre* in the world. Here is my room facing north-east. Below the Rue des Mutilés and the construction-yard of the new station. From my window I see the red and white flame of the *Rendezvous des Cheminots* at the corner of the Boulevard Victor-Noir. The Paris train has just come in. People are coming out of the old station and spreading into the streets."

This is the world as map, the world as total Other, over which

49. Jean-Paul Sartre, *Nausea*, trans. Lloyd Alexander (New York, 1964).

one glances; it is a world one can always feel good about, simply by contemplating the fixity of all locations and therefore of all things. The structure of Roquentin's consciousness, his point of view, is the classically real one. He sits in his window, confined in his body, observing the world from above. He watches another body move in the world, and sees the map of her actions spread out before her, beneath her. The street corner preexists for the woman Roquentin sees from his vantage point, as the concluding goal exists for a realistic novelist; it is the space into which her temporality collapses: "Old wood louse! I suppose she's going to turn right, into the Boulevard Victor-Noir. That gives her a hundred yards to go: it will take her ten minutes at the rate she's going, ten minutes during which time I shall stay like this, watching her, my forehead glued against the window." Thus time like everything else is "tarnished," "deflowered," dissolved by the administrative, maplike forms of the real world. "I *see* the future. It is there, poised over the street, hardly more dim than the present."

This timelessness has its strongest grip in the structure of objects in Roquentin's world. The world is real because it is objective, because objects exist outside the confines of our subjectivity. Thus objects necessitate a map consciousness, and objects spatialize time: they are there, and we walk among them, between them; they orient us:

> The books were still there, arranged in alphabetical order on the shelves with their brown and black backs and their labels UP lf. 7.996 (For Public Use—French Literature—) or UP sn (For Public Use—Natural Science) . . . powerful and squat, along with the stove, the green lamps, the wide windows, the ladders, they dam up the future. As long as you stay between these walls, whatever happens must happen on the right or the left of the stove. Saint Denis himself could come in carrying his head in his hands and he would still have to enter on the right, walk between the shelves devoted to French Literature and the table reserved for woman readers.

This is the quality of the ordinary world Roquentin lives in: objects are indifferent and have nothing to do with human events, except as those human events are objective, that is, except as they take place in the map of objective space. Objects have been pushed to the furthest corner of their objectivity; they have receded as far as possible from human significance. This is why Roquentin is fascinated, like schizophrenics, by waste, by objects emptied of even their utilitarian meaning: "I very much like to pick up chestnuts, old rags and especially papers. It is pleasant to me to pick them up, to close my hand on them; with a little encouragement I would carry them to my mouth the way children do. Anny went into a white rage when I picked up the corners of heavy, sumptuous papers, probably soiled by excrement."

The psychological overtones of this passage were intended by Sartre. Roquentin's fascination with waste, his play with waste objects, is a symbolic manipulation of his own feces. The implications of the passage foreshadow one of the central themes in Burroughs, the theme from which the title *Naked Lunch* is taken: when objects have been pushed into the radical extreme of their definition, when they have been made to regress, to fold into themselves, then only the radical extreme of human gestures can deal with them, i.e., incorporation, devouring: "with a little encouragement I would carry them to my mouth the way children do." The irony is that this way of dealing with objects is simply a way of dealing with oneself, with oneself as a product, as waste, as feces; it is eating oneself. This is reality as regression, the final atomistic state of objectivity, in which everything disappears into itself. It is the central theme of Beckett's work. Molloy nourishes himself on sucking stones, and Malone surrounds himself with junk, a needle stuck into two corks, a pipe bowl, a boot, a hat without a brim, a photograph, a stone, a scrap of newspaper, buttons, the cap of a bicycle bell, all functional objects deprived of their function and thus possessed only of their objectivity.

Both Malone and Roquentin exist as parodies of the traditional hero of realistic fiction. It is no mistake that Roquentin reads Balzac and Stendhal, two novelists who defined human beings economically, by what they possess. If he were English, he would have read Defoe or Galsworthy, and if he were American, Dreiser, Lewis, or John O'Hara. Malone and Roquentin are human because they possess, and for no other reason. They are human beings at the extremity of humanity, and their possession is pure, stripped of all justification—use, pleasure, success—since the objects they possess have been stripped of all but their objectivity. Malone's desire is, finally, the same as Roquentin's; he wants to incorporate his objects, his waste, his products, since they have objectified him and consequently have made him their father: "Yes, a little creature, I shall try and make a little creature, to hold in my arms, a little creature in my image, no matter what I say. And seeing what a poor thing I have made, or how like myself, I shall eat it."

Thus the subject-object dichotomy seems to present no alternatives: the subject is transformed into an object by his possessions, and devours himself—this is the case of Malone and the only path that seems open to Roquentin. But there is another possibility, the one that Roquentin suddenly finds himself in the midst of and that he calls the Nausea: rather than the subject being transformed into an object, objects are transformed into subjectivities and suddenly become alive: "objects should not *touch* because they are not alive. You use them, put them back in place, you live among them: they are useful, nothing more. But they touch me, it is unbearable. I am afraid of being in contact with them as though they were living beasts." The alternative to the self-devouring tendency of realism is psychosis, but it is a polar alternative, an alternative born out of the schizophrenic nature of reality itself.

Reality demands that we hoard objects, since objects are merely objective; and hoarding, Arieti shows, is a common element of schizophrenia.[50] But schizophrenic patients also hallucinate, and objects also become alive to them. This is what *La Nausée* shows: the way reality becomes fantastic, the way reality and fantasy are two inseparable sides of the same coin, and not despite but because of the attempt to separate them. "A schizophrenic," says Merleau-Ponty, "feels that a brush

50. Arieti, *Schizophrenia*, pp. 352ff.

placed near his window is coming nearer to him and entering his head, and yet he never ceases to be aware that the brush is over there."[51] The paradox of *La Nausée* lies in Roquentin's realization of the dead weight of objects around him, of their inertia, their absolute neutrality and Otherness, to the radical extent that objects pose a threat to the subject, their deadness becomes alive to the subject, their neutrality is a taking sides, an attitude, and to touch things is to be touched. When the Nausea strikes, objects leave the shell of their inertness behind and present themselves, but they do it by the very fact of inertness. This is clear in what is perhaps the novel's most striking passage: "For instance, there is something new about my hands, a certain way of picking up my pipe or fork. Or else it's the fork which now has a certain way of having itself picked up, I don't know. A little while ago, just as I was coming into my room, I stopped short because I felt in my hand a cold object which held my attention through a sort of personality. I opened by hand, looked: I was simply holding the door-knob."

Roquentin's experience with the doorknob unfolds to penetrate his whole world. The Self-Taught Man's hand becomes a fat worm, the world holds its breath and makes itself small, and the quality of Roquentin's very gestures changes. Realism's structure of absolute necessity, by which objects are limited to their eternal immutable natures, bounded by other objects in a map organization, becomes its own extreme and its own opposite: the structure of absolute contingency, by which an object has no nature, since it is everything: "In vain I tried to *count* the chestnut trees, to *locate* them by their relationship to the Velleda, to compare their height with the height of the plane trees: each of them escaped the relationship in which I tried to enclose it, isolated itself, and overflowed." This "overflowing" is the structure of the *en-soi*, the in-itself, according to Sartre's philosophy. And since the *pour-soi*, the for-itself, incorporates the *en-soi* precisely by being an *en-soi* that reflects, that is at a distance from itself, subject and object are the same. Hence Roquentin's famous chestnut root becomes a black nail, boiled

51. Merleau-Ponty, *Phenomenology*, p. 290.

leather, mildew, a dead serpent, a vulture's claw, a sealskin, and thus "All the objects that surrounded me were made of the same substance as myself, of a kind of shoddy suffering," and finally, "I *was* the root of the chestnut tree."

All this takes place in a garden, a park, and the height of Roquentin's vision occurs when he sees "soft, monstrous masses, all in disorder—naked, in a frightful, obscene nakedness." If the ordinary world is a disguise for Roquentin's subjectivity, it is a disguise that has transformed that subjectivity into something grotesque and obscene. Indeed the ordinary world can be sane and chaste only by creating a pure space of fantasy and obscenity. Reality needs fantasy, but it needs it there, as Other; for the real world to become fantastic is a nightmare, since it means that the Other is no longer other, but here, where it has been all the time. This is true also of the garden that map consciousness has repressed and made Other. It is here, and because it is here, when we thought it was there, it is obscene and monstrous. *La Nausée* shows the revenge the garden takes for being made to retreat, the diabolical alliance it makes with man's hidden subjectivity, with the fantastic world repressed by all ordinary map structures:

> Once the city is dead, the vegetation will cover it, will climb over the stones, grip them, search them, make them burst with its long black pincers; it will blind the holes and let its green paws hang over everything. You must stay in cities as long as they are alive, you must never penetrate alone this great mass of hair waiting at the gates; you must let it undulate and crack all by itself. In the cities, if you know how to take care of yourself, and choose the times when all the beasts are sleeping in their holes and digesting, behind the heaps of organic debris, you rarely come across anything more than minerals, the least frightening of all existents.

Roquentin has found the reason Robbe-Grillet's soldier will never leave the city he wanders around in. The final condition of realism is this: dead objects on one hand and live objects on the other; the mathematical and mechanical fantasies of a labyrinth on one hand and the grotesque life of organic forms on the other. One is incomplete without the other; taken together, they represent a fundamental schizophrenia, implicit in all the forms of realism and naturalism, from the feud of mechanism and vitalism in biology to the chutes and elevators that channel the wheat of life in Frank Norris' *The Octopus*. And each, as a dead end of realistic structures, represents the way those structures turn around and become fantastic, the way objectivity gives way to the frightening depths of subjectivity and sanity gives way to madness.

At the end of *La Nausée*, Roquentin climbs a hill and looks out over Bouville—the traditional closing stance of many realistic and most naturalistic novels. He sees the map of Bouville unfold beneath him, but penetrating it he also sees the fantastic, subjective world that map consciousness has taken such pains to repress and has transformed into something grotesque by its very act of repression:

> I watch the grey shimmerings of Bouville at my feet. In the sun they look like heaps of shells, scales, splinters of bone, and gravel. Lost in the midst of this debris, tiny glimmers of glass or mica intermittently throw off light flames. In an hour the ripples, trenches, and thin furrows which run between these shells will be streets, I shall walk in these streets, between these walls. These little black men I can just make out in the Rue Boulibet—in an hour I shall be one of them.
>
> I feel so far away from them, on the top of this hill. It seems as though I belong to another species. They come out of their offices after their day of work, they look at the houses and the squares with satisfaction, they think it is *their* city, a good, solid, bourgeois city. They aren't afraid, they feel at home. All they have ever seen is trained water running from taps, light which fills bulbs when you turn on the switch, half-breed bastard trees held up with crutches. They have proof, a hundred times a day, that everything happens mechanically, that the world obeys fixed, unchangeable laws.... They are peaceful, a little morose, they think about Tomorrow, that is to say, simply, a new today; cities have only one day at their disposal and every morning it comes back exactly the same.... And all this time, great, vague nature has slipped into their city, it has infiltrated everywhere,

in their house, in their office, in themselves. It doesn't move, it stays quietly and they are full of it inside, they breathe it, and they don't see it, they imagine it to be outside, twenty miles from the city. I *see* it, I *see* this nature . . . I know that its obedience is idleness, I know it has no laws: what they take for constancy is only habit and it can change tomorrow.

What if something were to happen? What if something suddenly started throbbing? Then they would notice it was there and they'd think their hearts were going to burst. Then what good would their dykes, bulwarks, power houses, furnaces and pile drivers be to them? It can happen any time, perhaps right now: the omens are present. For example, the father of a family might go out for a walk, and, across the street, he'll see something like a rag, blown towards him by the wind. And when the rag has gotten close to him he'll see that it is a side of rotten meat, grimy with dust, dragging itself along by crawling, skipping, a piece of writhing flesh rolling in the gutter, spasmodically shooting out spurts of blood. Or a mother might look at her child's cheek and ask him: "What's that—a pimple?" and see the flesh puff out a little, split, open, and at the bottom of the split an eye, a laughing eye might appear. . . . And someone else might feel something scratching in his mouth. He goes to the mirror, opens his mouth: and his tongue is an enormous, live centipede, rubbing its legs together and scraping his palate.

This is schizophrenia, and it is the terrible significance of *La Nausée*; Roquentin was an ordinary man in an ordinary world, but holes have opened up in the most substantial, firm aspect of that world, in its objectivity. Overlooking Bouville, Roquentin sees the same "soft, monstrous masses" he saw in the garden, and now in more detail, born out of the very map, the very objective space of realism. The side of meat on the street, the laughing eye in the child's pimple, the centipede in the man's mouth, all are the revenge of the sexuality that is displaced by realism and the Life that is capitalized by naturalism. Sexuality is displaced and Life is capitalized because the person has been broken up into the mutually exclusive components of mind and body, and both of these exclude the organic life that synthesizes mind and body. Organic life, the life of the garden and of the whole person, has a space of its own in a world organized by maps, a pure space of exclusion, and thus becomes, by virtue of its exclusion, displaced sexuality in realism, Life in naturalism, and the grotesque images of *La Nausée*.

This is the final condition of realism's schizophrenic subject-object separation. Since this separation is implicit in all realistic forms, in the objective space of the novel, in the image of the body in the novel, in the multiplicity of roles assumed by the novel's characters, it works relentlessly toward uncovering itself, toward becoming what it is. But it can uncover itself only on its own terms; it can show the subject-object dichotomy as false only by showing it as mad, and it can reveal fantasy, the subjectivity that impregnates the world, only as a nightmare.

The worlds of Robbe-Grillet and Sartre complement and complete each other. Sartre reveals the minotaur hidden in Robbe-Grillet's labyrinth; if the city is a labyrinth, and a labyrinth is structure externalized, that is, objective, mechanical structure, then the grotesque forms Roquentin sees inside the city are subjective and organic life shaped by that objective, mechanical structure, and thereby made grotesque. The world William S. Burroughs was to write about twenty years after *La Nausée* is essentially this one, a world in which the organic and the mechanical, as well as the subjective and the objective, have each been made grotesque and frightening by virtue of their schizophrenic separation.

3 / William S. Burroughs

The romantic image of the artist as madman becomes with William S. Burroughs the reality of the madman as artist. What Barth, Pynchon, Robbe-Grillet, and others attempt to show, that if the properties of the real world are taken seriously enough there is something essentially insane about that world, is taken for granted by Burroughs in his novels *Naked Lunch, The Soft Machine, Nova Express,* and *The Ticket That Exploded.* Burroughs' world is reality; there can be no doubt about that. It is Martin's reality film, Luce's *Time-Life-Fortune* monopoly, the machinery of visual and auditory control—"encephalographic and calculating machines film and TV studios, batteries of tape recorders." But it is also an assault upon reality, an attempt to storm the reality studio and blow it up, to splice all the tape recorders into each other. ("Communication must be made total. Only way to stop it.") What is real about Burroughs is precisely the image of the world as machinery that Zola and the nineteenth century saw. But this reality is so total as to be fantastic, insane, grotesque; it is a reality in the process of exploding—"Only way to stop it." Thus it is a reality whose machinery has come to life, like the kitchen gadgets that assault the housewife in *Naked Lunch.* It is a world whose objects (as in Sartre's *La Nausée*) "stir with a writhing furtive life," and whose living beings are either programmed machines or Vegetable People who "tend gardens of pink flesh."

Burroughs' vision, as at the end of *La Nausée,* is one in which the world has flown into two opposing principles, a labyrinthine, external, mechanical structure and a reified organic content. I use the word "content" in the same sense as it is used by Mc-Luhan, who rightly sees Burroughs' origins in the Industrial Age, when Nature became a vessel of aesthetic and spiritual values, that is, a content.[1] The underlying roots of this condition lie in the schizophrenic structures of thought in the West, which can comprehend Nature only by siphoning it off into a pure, separate space. The romantic movement, by emphasizing the inner, the creative, the vital, the natural, against the outer, the mechanical, the static, and so on (see Carlyle's *Characteristics*, for example), reinforced rather than challenged those structures of thought. Its result can be seen in Burroughs, for whom the natural and organic are always shaped by the repressive nature of the mechanical, so that their manifestations are always stained by violence and evil.

The most common image of the mechanical and external in Burroughs is the City, "a labyrinth of lockers, tier on tier of wire mesh and steel cubicles joined by catwalks and ladders and moving cable cars." Maps, bureaucracies, IBM punch cards, and machines are also common images of this principle, as is the recurring notion of the real world as a movie film. The most common image of the other polarity, of organic content, is protoplasm, the blob, jelly: "Some way he make himself all soft like a blob of jelly and surround me so nasty. Then he gets wet all over like with green slime. So I guess he come to some kinda awful climax." At times this organic content is given the traditional name of "garden," for example, the Garden of Delights (G.O.D.) or the Amusement Gardens, both pure areas into which Nature as a reified entity has been channeled by the structures of the real world:

> The Amusement Gardens cover a continent—There are areas of canals and lagoons where giant gold fish and salamanders with purple gills stir in clear black water and gondolas piloted by translucent green fish boys—Under vast revolving flicker lamps

1. Marshall McLuhan, "Notes on Burroughs," *Nation* (28 December 1964), p. 517.

along the canals spill The Biologic Merging Tanks sense with-drawal capsules light and soundproof water at blood tempera-ture pulsing in and out where two life forms slip in and merge to a composite being often with deplorable results slated for Biologic Skid Row on the outskirts: (Sewage delta and rubbish heaps—terminal addicts of SOS muttering down to water worms and floating vegetables—Paralyzed Orgasm Addicts eaten alive by crab men with white hot eyes or languidly tortured in cha-rades by The Green Boys of young crystal cruelty). . . .

Structurally, the mechanical and the organic in Burroughs are exact opposites. A machine is comprised of discrete movable parts, each confined to its location, in no other location, and each related along its border areas to other parts. All these parts are brought together one by one to perform an action, the coordina-tion of which is not a synthesis but rather a reified object itself, with its own space: a circuit, a map, or in an extended sense, a program or punch card. The organic, on the other hand, reverses the tendency of the machine to unfold and separate into isolated, discrete spaces. As in the Amusement Gardens, objects struc-tured as organic content merge with each other; they become a diabolical parody of the romantic "All" and of the fluid life of the original garden. Mergence in this sense approaches the same condition as the mechanical, that of isolation and con-finement. This is seen most clearly in the plan of the Liquefac-tionists in *Naked Lunch*. They propose that everyone merge by protoplasmic absorption into one person, who would then be totally alone, as confined in his space as any discrete mechanical part in its space. Thus although the mechanical and organic in Burroughs are exact opposites, there is an underlying sameness to them, a kind of inert, imprisoned objectivity; this is why the mechanical and organic are often merged, as in the recurring image of "metal excrement."

All of this is schizophrenia. It is a making explicit of the schizophrenic nature of reality in our culture by a man diag-nosed as schizophrenic (Burroughs mentions this fact in the preface to *Junkie*, an early realistic novel), in ways that are ap-propriately schizophrenic, i.e., hallucinatory. Burroughs' world is structured upon either-or polarities—the organic and the mechanical, consciousness and the body, the self and the Other. This is most apparent in the image of the body in his novels. The body is variously seen as a machine (a tape recorder, a camera, a programmed computer, a robot), and as a soft, amorphous mass, transparent, wet, penetrable, and finally as a combination of the two, a "soft machine." As a "soft machine," the body's shape, skin, or surface is the external, mechanical principle that contains its soft, amorphous content (a view that derives ultimately from the reification of shape and form as properties of objects in Aristotelian thought). Thus bodies are "boneless mummies," and people wear uniforms of human skin, their own skin, which they can discard for the purpose of merging their soft, skinless content with someone else's.

This combination of a kind of dismemberment and merging is seen most explicitly in an incident that occurs repeatedly in the two later novels, *Nova Express* and *The Ticket That Exploded:* the merging of two homosexuals by means of the dismemberment and flaying of their external bodies in a film.

> The screen shifted into a movie—Bradley was lying naked with the attendant on the cot—The divide line of his body burned with silver flash fire shifting in and out of the other body—rectal and pubic hairs slipping through composite flesh—penis and rectums merged on screen and bed as Bradley ejaculated—He woke up with other thoughts and memories in Cockney accent of that attendant standing there with a plate of food—saw himself eating on screen composite picture tasting food in the other mouth intestines moving and excrement squirming down to the divide line of another body. . . .

Many significant features of the schizophrenic experience are expressed in this passage. There is a subject-object split, a polarization between one's self and one's image on a movie screen (the modern equivalent of objective mirror space); this split, coupled with the experience of being controlled or persecuted by an external power and with the experiences of dismemberment and merging, is a common element of schizophrenia.

Compare the passage by Burroughs with the following letter

of a hospitalized schizophrenic patient to a television station, in which she accuses television personalities and fellow patients of stealing parts of her body:

Dear Sir,

This is not my shape or face Mary —— has given me her glass eye and she has my noise. Bob Hope. Crooked mouth Peter Lin Hayes, has given me his lop sided shoulder. & terrible mans figure. He sold his shape to Mr. Albright, I want my own things

Frances ——, Pinky tongue. She has my noise.

Cathy Crosby has most of my things I want them. I have little Reds Kork leg, from the —— Hotel he lives most of the time & a few other bad features I cant mention he gave me. I guess knowing him you must know what it is.

Dolores —— club finger & two other fingers she had smashed in a defense plant Ruth —— one finger she had off in a defense plant.

Peggy —— or Hildegard has my hands & has gave me her large lump in the back of the neck & her large head:

Ida ——

Jeanette —— has my eyes & hair & other things so make her give them back. I don't want these things any more the Contest is over.

I want my own things back & also my daughter.

Dr —— has patricia & I want her back immediately Im going to the police. I know all her markings & I have all hers & my pictures with my attorney. Patricia took 3 screen test I have proof for these I took one also.[2]

The schizophrenic delusions expressed by both Burroughs' passage and this letter are expressions of the schizophrenia that is the realistic and objective world. In both, the reality that consciousness relates to exists as an image on a screen, either a movie screen or a television set. Reality has taken on the condition of machinery; it is a movable representation of what we are familiar with, only more focused; it exists in a frame that delineates it from its surroundings and gives it an authenticity and potency that the world it copies lacks. This is the classical image of the real carried to its full technological embodiment;

2. Quoted in Rosen and Gregory, *Abnormal Psychology*, p. 310.

it is the structure of mirror objectivity and map space in the realistic novel become what it always implicitly was, mechanical. The camera metaphor of human perception, subscribed to by Kepler, Galileo, Newton, Leibnitz, and others,[3] becomes literal in Burroughs, and the object-world exists as an image, as something we face, something we see or have, not something we are. Thus the dismemberment that is virtual, as in Fielding's mechanical descriptions of the actions of the body in objective space, becomes actual in Burroughs, in a space that is itself an object, a movie screen.

This dismemberment in space in Burroughs is pushed to the extreme condition of a total atomization of all things. Burroughs' world is the Newtonian world of discrete objects and entities existing in objective space, confined to their own locations, and it is this world carried to such an extreme that space explodes, and each object wraps its own space around itself. Space is polarized into the totally frozen map space of administration (maps, punch cards, bureaucracies), and the atomistic space of objects overflowing their administration ("This book spill off the page in all directions"). This kind of polarization cuts across many of the features of Burroughs' novels. On one hand there is immobility and catatonia, a condition made possible (as in Beckett's *Unnamable*) by the diffusion of space into total objectivity, into a void, to the extent that one exists anywhere and cannot move: "I lived in one room in the Native Quarter of Tangier. I had not taken a bath in a year nor changed my clothes or removed them except to stick a needle every hour in the fibrous grey flesh of terminal addiction." On the other hand there is frenzied activity, frantic action, a salad of actions that increase to maximum intensity as their space shrinks: "Diamonds and fur pieces, evening dresses, orchids, suits and underwear litter the floor covered by a writhing, frenzied, heaving mass of naked bodies."

In any world, space always exists as the relationship between objects; in Newton's universe, objects are impenetrable, discrete, and this relationship of exclusive juxtaposition generates

3. Turbayne, *The Myth of Metaphor*, p. 205.

absolute, objective space, space as a container.[4] The space of Burroughs' world encompasses at one polarity this Newtonian space: objects clash and bounce off each other, and the world generally exists in a shattered, fragmented state. But the space of Burroughs' world also shrinks to the skin of objects and bodies themselves, and this is why things don't always stand outside each other—they can merge. In objective space, the shape or skin of an object represents its absolute boundary, since that shape is made possible by space as an absolute ground. This is why, carried to its logical conclusion, Newtonian science (and the structures of Western thought in general) posits shape as a thing-in-itself. And this is why the rigid split between the external shape or surface of the human body and its internal content exists also for any object in space.

Burroughs clearly sees that when shape is a thing-in-itself, it is of a different order of being from what it contains. If shape is hard, content is soft. If shape keeps things apart, content wants to run together and merge. And if shape is removed, or simply dissolves as each separate thing wraps its own space around itself, then things (and people) do, in fact, merge: "The Vigilante, The Rube, Lee the Agent, A.J., Clem and Jody the Ergot Twins, Hassan O'Leary the After Birth Tycoon, The Sailor, The Exterminator, Andrew Keif, 'Fats' Terminal, Doc Benway, 'Fingers' Schafer are subject to say the same thing in the same words, to occupy, at that intersection point, the same position in space-time."

Thus there are two spaces in Burroughs; as well as being contained by external, objective space, objects and bodies are able to contain each other, to merge, to be each other's space. The rhythm of isolation and merging seen in Conrad, which according to R. D. Laing is the final stage of schizophrenia, is in Burroughs a rhythm of the expansion and contraction of space. As space expands into objectivity, objects and bodies exist in a state of fragmentation and isolation. Each thing is frozen, timeless, and immobile, since it exists in a void and hence is trapped in itself. But as space contracts, those things

4. Capek, *Contemporary Physics*, pp. 54ff.

(and people) are brought together, first in frantic activity ("a writhing, frenzied, heaving mass of naked bodies") and finally in complete mergence, so that people step out of their shapes and merge or people and things lose their shapes entirely in "Biologic Merging Tanks." The space of Burroughs' world is the space of objectivity and subjectivity at odds with each other, the juxtaposed experience of an external map space with its absolute boundaries and of a mythic space by which bodies are not subject to the limitations of a map and can merge; the mutually exclusive presence of both, of external and of mythic space, Merleau-Ponty calls the basis of schizophrenia.[5]

One of the underlying structural characteristics of this dual space is the concept of "image," which Burroughs refers to repeatedly. The image refers primarily to the camera metaphor of perception and hence to the space of reality as a movie, but it also refers to the discrete, atomistic entities that wrap space around themselves. "The human body is an image on screen talking." "Word begets image and image *is* virus." "Junk is concentrated image." Image, as in the last statement, is always a concentration, a focus, a fixation. It is completely objectified reality, reality broken into bits and served up for consumption, or addiction. But it is also a datum of consciousness. Image is the discrete entity that spatializes consciousness itself, that gives consciousness the same structure as external space. "Images" in Burroughs are like James's "states of consciousness," which are things, or like Locke's "ideas," which exist as atomistic objects in the mind. Burroughs frequently refers to conditioning processes that depend upon the theory of association of ideas, and he even asserts, not entirely ironically, that a movie and sound track of sexual activity are as good as the real thing. In this respect, Burroughs' world is firmly anchored in the structures of classical Western thought, in such figures as Locke and Pavlov, whom he refers to now and then.

His world is anchored in structures of control. "The scanning pattern we accept as 'reality' has been imposed by the controlling power on this planet, a power oriented toward total control."

5. Merleau-Ponty, *Phenomenology*, pp. 287ff.

Image is a discrete entity, and the only organization discrete entities can have, since internal synthesis is impossible, is one of external control—a map, a circuit, or a punch card. Because image is both a datum of consciousness and an object of the public world, all organization is by necessity control; the condition of the world is one of total maplike administration: "The point at which the criminal controller intersects a three-dimensional human agent is known as 'a coordinate point'. . . . Now a single controller can operate through thousands of human agents, but he must have a line of coordinate points— Some move on junk lines through addicts of the earth, others move on lines of certain sexual practices and so forth." The counterpart of the map, which administers control of the society, is the IBM punch card, a virus that administers control of the body:

> Transparent sheets with virus perforations like punch cards passed through the host on the soft machine feeling for a point of intersection—The virus attack is primarily directed against affective animal life—Virus of rage hate fear ugliness swirling round you waiting for a point of intersection and once in immediately perpetrates in your name some ugly noxious or disgusting act sharply photographed and recorded becomes now part of the virus sheets constantly presented and represented before your mind screen to produce more virus word and image around and around it's all around you the invisible hail of bring down word and image.

The obsessive reproduction of images that Burroughs refers to is his own literature: an orbit of snapshots of "ugly noxious or disgusting" acts, a camera that can't be shut off.

Control imposes violence. In Burroughs the act of contact itself is violent, for it is always a seizing, a taking over, and the body, since it is a mere object, is easily seized. In *Naked Lunch* the Latah attaches himself to a person and "imitates all his expressions and simply sucks all the persona right out of him like a sinister ventriloquist's dummy." Burroughs' apprehension of the world is one of frightening relevance: a society organized and administered by the map structures of control is necessarily sadistic, since everything exists by virtue of the fact that it is organized, by virtue of being an object, something to be used. The use of human beings as objects accounts for the most obsessively recurring action in Burroughs' novels, what he calls the "orgasm death": homosexual rape coupled with murder by hanging or strangling of the passive partner at the moment of climax. For Burroughs, violence is an absolute space into which one enters—it is like madness or sex; it is the "Other Half" that our culture has repressed, has siphoned off into a pure, separate area.

The recurring association of sex and death is due to their mutual occupation of this separate area, and that area is specifically flesh, the body, "the 'Other Half,' a separate organism attached to your nervous system." In one respect, the concept of "Other Half" is an expression of the internal-external split of the body; the "Other Half" is the body as an outer mechanical structure attached to an organism. But the "Other Half" is the bottom half of the body as well, the seat of sexual energies and anal violence, which has become anal and violent, regressive, because it has been made Other. On top, the body exists as a consciousness and a mental structure, but beneath it is a private space that the schizophrenic forms of realism and objectivity have repressed. "Sex words evoke a dangerous that is to say *other* half of the body. . . . You see the caustic layers of organic material? That is what they need from earth: Three other boys to make more marble flesh, ass and genitals vibrated by the iridescent attendant—Orgasm death is to other half of the body. . . ." The phenomenon of violence in our culture is to a large degree due to this schizophrenia, to the repression of the "Other Half" of the body, its objectification, and its consequent association with evil. Burroughs says, "Sex and pain *form* flesh identity," that is, the body is the siphoned-off object of sex, the object of pain. Or at least the form of the body, its surface, is the object of sex and pain, which implies that inside there is a content, an organism, which experiences sex and pain.

Both dual structures of the body, its external-internal and its top-bottom schizophrenia, are perfectly suited to the sadist. The pleasure of sadism lies in the simultaneous knowledge that one treats the body as an object (the "Other Half" of the body, its bottom half and its external half), yet that that object contains an organism and a consciousness that feel and experience pain. The knowledge that the body one gives pain to contains an organism is titillating to the highest degree, for it enables all organic aspects of experience to ally themselves with the obscene and ugly, with pain and evil. This is the world Burroughs writes about: one in which sex has achieved the space of evil, by virtue of the objectification of both sex and evil, their mutual predisposition as Other: "Another instrument of these pain tourists is the *signal switch* sir . . . what they call the 'yes no' sir . . . 'I love you I hate you' at supersonic alternating speed. . . . Take orgasm noises and cut them in with torture and accident groans and screams sir and operating-room jokes sir and flicker sex and torture film right with it sir." Sex and torture are allied because they are subject to the same manipulative control that objectifies the world as image and that creates a pure separate image of violence. This is why Burroughs' roots are in the underground literature of the eighteenth and nineteenth centuries, the literature of the Marquis de Sade and of all the anonymous nineteenth-century pornographers, the "Other Half" of the civilized Victorian era.

If control is the result of map structures (patterns, coded punch cards) applied to the content of reality, then one important means of control in a civilized society is the circulation of goods, the map that guarantees the distribution of movable objects. In Burroughs, movable objects control the body literally because they are junk. "Junk" means both waste objects and heroin, and the two are collapsed into one symbol in Burroughs' world. Civilized society is the consumer culture; it produces objects for instant consumption, objects with their waste function built in, objects to be emptied of their use and thrown away. The object most repeatedly emptied of its use in Burroughs is the needle, and it is emptied into the body. The complements of sadism and its fantasy of control are masochism and passive homosexuality and their fantasies of being controlled. The drug experience is the perfect image of these, for its act is totally receptive, an act that is not an act but the object of one. Thus the junkie is the perfect consumer; his body awaits the distribution of goods and is totally controlled by the map of that distribution.

"The world network of junkies, tuned on a cord of rancid jissom . . . tying up in furnished rooms . . . shivering in the sick morning." And junk, Burroughs is careful to point out, is "the ideal product . . . the ultimate merchandise. No sales talk necessary. The client will crawl through a sewer and beg to buy. . . . The junk merchant does not sell his product to the consumer, he sells the consumer to his product. He does not improve and simplify his merchandise. His degrades and simplifies the client." Junk seals the objectification of the body, for the junkie's life consists of a series of actions performed on himself for the purpose of fulfilling a need; the body becomes the medium of that need, the passive vessel of junk. "Passive" is the important word. The heroin experience is an offering oneself up to be penetrated, either by another or by one's own self as other. Junk satisfies the need to be passive, to be controlled, to be relieved of the burden of initiating any actions, to be fed, to incorporate, to consume. As Burroughs said in an interview, "if drugs weren't forbidden in America, they would be the perfect middle-class vice. Addicts would do their work and come home to consume the huge dose of images awaiting them in the mass media."[6] The extent to which drugs, especially pills, have in fact become a middle-class institution testifies to the truth of Burroughs' words.

To be controlled by a world of movable objects, of consumer goods, is a schizophrenic experience of the world—and again a kind of schizophrenia that reflects upon the nature of reality itself. Addiction in Burroughs is the natural outgrowth of the addiction to material goods found in, for example, *Moll Flanders*. The difference is that in Burroughs, material goods threaten the addict at the same time they fulfill his need. "Every object raw

6. Conrad Knickerbocker, "William Burroughs," an interview in *Writers at Work: The Paris Review Interviews*, third series (New York, 1967), p. 149.

and hideous sharp edges that tear the uncovered flesh." The significance Burroughs invests in the material world is paranoid; objects spring to life and penetrate the body, and the world exists as a threat. "In the beginning his flesh was simply soft, so soft that he was cut to the bone by dust particles, air currents and brushing overcoats."

This is the same apprehension of the world by Sartre or Beckett carried one step further. Roquentin and Malone are fascinated by a world of movable objects, objects to pick up and touch, to count, to handle. Burroughs' characters are persecuted by that same world. They are like a schizophrenic patient of Minkowski who feared imminent punishment by a system called the "residue politics": "Every leftover, all residue, would be put aside to be one day stuffed into his abdomen—and this, from all over the world. Everything would be included without exception. When one smoked, there would be the burnt match, the ashes, and the cigarette butt. At meals, he was preoccupied with the crumbs, the fruit pits, the chicken bones, the wine or water at the bottom of the glasses."[7] The subject-object split that produces the external-internal structure of the body also produces a split between the hard-edged objects of the world and the vulnerable, soft body, a split that gives the world the continual character of attack, of bombardment.

This bombardment of objects in Burroughs' novels is the visible manifestation of a world fragmenting itself, refining itself through the map of administration to the degree that it becomes total administration, hence total clutter. In Burroughs' world everything is on the verge of achieving complete separation and complete autonomy; it is a world in the state of explosion. "Explosion" is finally (and paradoxically) the most uniform quality of Burroughs' novels, the polarity toward which his world most consistently gravitates. Even administrative control and map space cannot finally help objects to cohere, since administration and maps have their own separate space.

This is why context and landscape in Burroughs always exist in pure states; they are the ground out of which objects fly and

7. *Existence*, p. 128.

explode, but they are motionless and ideal, sealed off from those objects. There is the landscape of the City, a mechanical labyrinth, and the landscape of Nature, the Garden of Delights, a swamp, or a mud flat; these are not so much environments in which actions occur as they are pure spaces for themselves. Actions and incidents that have any continuity usually occur in ill-defined rooms or on an ill-defined plain. Between these, which become less frequent with each novel, the wanderings of consciousness describe objects in a constant state of permutation and explosion, objects deprived of their context, each one in the context of itself, in its own exclusive space: "Lord Jim has turned bright yellow in the woe withered moon of morning like white smoke against the blue stuff, and shirts whip in a cold spring wind on limestone cliffs across the river, Mary, and the dawn is broken in two pieces like Dillinger on the lamster way to the Biograph. Smell of neon and atrophied gangsters, and the criminal manqué nerves himself to crack a pay toilet sniffing ammonia in a bucket. . . . 'A caper,' he says. 'I'll pull this capon I mean caper.'"

Burroughs' solution to the repressive control that the image of reality imposes is to fragment it and mix it together, to erase all lines between things. If reality is a film, one loosens its grip by submitting it to a state of explosion, by cutting it up and splicing all spaces and times randomly together:

> "The Subliminal Kid" moved in seas of disembodied sound—He then spaced here and there and install opposite mirrors and took movies each bar so that the music and talk is at arbitrary intervals and shifted bars—And he also had recorder in tracks and moving film mixing arbitrary intervals and agents moving with the word and image of tape recorders—So he set up waves and his agents with movie swirled through all the streets of image and brought back street in music from the city and poured Aztec Empire and Ancient Rome—Commuter or Chariot Driver could not control their word dust drifted from outer space—Air hammers word and image explosive bio-advance—A million drifting screens on the walls of his city projected mixing sound

of any bar could be heard in all Westerns and film of all times played and recorded at the people back and forth with portable cameras and telescope lenses. . . .

Burroughs' explosion of the reality image, as this passage illustrates, is an explosion of language too, the very language he uses to describe that explosion. The flat space of the objective world exists as a page as well as a film. To break its regimental control over consciousness, one must "Shift linguals—Cut word lines," two phrases that occur over and over in the later novels, *Nova Express* and *The Ticket That Exploded.*

This is the feature of Burroughs' novels that has won him a great deal of attention, the cut-up method of writing, by which a text is cut into short phrases of six or seven words, shuffled around and pasted together. Burroughs claims that he used this method unconsciously in *Naked Lunch,* and later had it brought to his attention by Brion Gysin. Together with Gregory Corso and Sinclair Beiles, Burroughs and Gysin published *Minutes to Go,* a collection of cut-up poems and articles, in 1960. Burroughs' novels subsequent to *Minutes to Go* have all displayed a rhythm of cohesion and fragmentation made possible by cutting up passages and printing the cut-up text after the original. With each novel the lines between cohesive writing and cut-ups have been increasingly blurred, and Burroughs has shuffled in cut-up newspaper articles and cut-up literature as well (*Lord Jim, The Waste Land,* passages from Shakespeare and Rimbaud).

As Burroughs himself has indicated, the cut-up method is not entirely new. "When you think of it, 'The Waste Land' was the first great cutup collage, and Tristan Tzara had done a bit along the same lines. Dos Passos used the same idea in 'The Camera Eye' sequences in *U.S.A.*"[8] Of these three figures, the mention of Tristan Tzara is perhaps most important. Tzara founded the dada movement, out of which surrealism grew, and Burroughs' literary roots are deeply imbedded in dada and surrealism. The

8. Knickerbocker, "William Burroughs," p. 153.

rationale for Burroughs' cut-up method has been best expressed by Brion Gysin—"the poets are supposed to liberate the words . . . who told the poets they were supposed to think?"[9]—and this rationale stems ultimately from that of dada. As the catalog of a recent retrospective dada show put it, "Man Ray untiringly transformed his surroundings from the useful to the useless . . . setting them free, and us at the same time."[10] Thus the typical dada work of art wrenches an object out of the context of its use and juxtaposes it with other such objects, a bicycle wheel upside down on top of a stool, for example, or a fur-lined teacup. Burroughs accomplishes with words what the dadaists did with objects; he cuts them out of the context that defines their use and that consequently binds us to the real world.

At the bottom of dada's use of objects and Burroughs' use of words is a sense of contradiction. In dada, objects become at once static and dynamic—static, purely objective, by virtue of their lack of function, and dynamic by virtue of the contradiction that strangles their function (as in a fur-lined teacup). Dada objects impose their inertness (as objects do in *La Nausée*), and they do so by the energy released through contradiction. Dada and surrealism also apply this sense of contradiction to language. In poems by Tristan Tzara or André Breton, not only is there a general atmosphere founded upon what in realistic terms is contradictory, that is, an atmosphere that merges fantasy and reality, dream life and waking life, but there is also a focused contradiction in every image. As one critic has put it, "in order for the surrealistic image to provoke us out of our passivity, it must have a strength greater than the mere comparison of two similar things. It gathers its peculiar intensity from an inner contradiction powerful enough to free the imaginer from banal ways of judging a familiar phenomenon."[11] Or as Reverdy has said, the profundity of an image is in an exact ratio to the distance between its elements.[12] This is why, accord-

9. Brion Gysin, "Cut-Ups," *Evergreen Review*, VIII (April-May 1964), 60.
10. Quoted in the *San Francisco Chronicle* (18 October 1968), p. 50.
11. Mary Ann Caws, *Surrealism and the Literary Imagination* (The Hague, 1966), p. 56.
12. Quoted in ibid., p. 59.

ing to Kenneth Burke, surrealist images are always violent; by bringing together objects of reality that don't belong together, surrealism rapes the order of reality.[13]

More precisely, surrealism rapes the order of language, which is analogous to the order of reality. This is what Burroughs does also. As Steven Koch puts it, "in literature, meaning and structure are virtually coextensive"; hence Burroughs gives words "their affect priority over their roles as signs quite simply: by de-structuring, by destruction."[14] The extent to which this destruction is a natural extension of surrealism can be seen in Reverdy's formula for reenergizing language, which is precisely one of destructuring. He proposes to eliminate conventional syntax and punctuation, to have no linking words, no adjectives, and no adverbs, so that only the force of nouns clashing together would be left.[15] The next step, as Swift showed in Book III of *Gulliver's Travels*, would be to eliminate nouns and communicate simply by holding up actual objects (or not so simply, as Swift saw, since one's vocabulary would have to be carried around on one's back). Swift's joke is the reality of an important aspect of twentieth-century consciousness. When the structure of language is invisible, when language itself is transparent, as it necessarily is for the realist, then it exists only as a glue to hold objects together. Surrealism carried over, perhaps as an unconscious expression of its parody of realism, this invisible function of language; as Aragon said, "the content of a surrealist text is decisively important."[16]

The space of language is invisible in surrealism, just as the space of surrealistic paintings is the invisibly "real" space of academic perspective, space as a container. This is why surrealism, to reverse Frost's definition of poetry, is what is *not* lost in translation. The content of surrealism consists of the objects it juxtaposes, and thus consists of words themselves as objects. When language is only a glue, its grip on objects can be loos-

13. "Surrealism," in *New Directions 1940* (Norfolk, Conn., 1940), p. 576.
14. "Images of Loathing," *Nation* (4 July 1966), p. 26.
15. Caws, *Surrealism*, p. 59.
16. Quoted in Maurice Nadeau, *The History of Surrealism*, trans. Richard Howard (New York, 1965), p. 81.

ened; as Roquentin in *La Nausée* says, "things are divorced from their names." Consequently names themselves are things, are objects to be cut up and shuffled around, "all the words of the world stirring around in a cement mixer," Burroughs says. Surrealism makes the invisible structure of language visible; it carries the objectification of words in realism necessitated by that invisible structure to its inevitable conclusion. In this sense Burroughs is the supreme realist: in the cut-up passages of his novels, his world is there, consisting of the words on the page. For example, "And love slop is a Bristol—Bring together state of news—Inquire on hospital—At the Ovens Great Gold Cup—Revived peat victory hopes of Fortia—Premature Golden sands in Sheila's cottage?—You want the name of Hassan i Sabbah so own the unborn?—Cool and casual through the hole in thin air closed at hotel room in London. . . ." Burroughs' world is one in which objects have become so objective, so one-dimensional, so thin, that they have dropped out of the words they are dressed in, leaving only those words—as objects—behind.

This is why there is no silence in Burroughs' world (although he strongly desires it, as he states several times), and no shadows. Silence is built into the expressive nature of language, into what R. P. Blackmur calls "language as gesture,"[17] not into language as an invisible structure. Just as there is no expressive synthesis to the body in Burroughs, so there is no expressive synthesis to language, and words are consequently objectified and fragmented. This is how and why they can be exploded, cut up. Words are an image of separate existence, existence in a body, in flesh, which is torment for Burroughs. One of the most striking passages in Burroughs' works occurs at the end of *The Soft Machine*, when tentative humans are born into separate existence excrementally, and take on the condition of words through their birth: "We waded into the warm mudwater. hair and ape flesh off in screaming strips. stood naked human bodies covered with phosphorescent green jelly. soft tentative flesh cut with ape wounds. peeling other genitals.

17. See his collection of essays published under that title, *Language as Gesture* (New York, 1952).

fingers and tongues rubbing off the jelly-cover. body melting pleasure-sounds in the warm mud. till the sun went and a blue wind of silence touched human faces and hair. When we came out of the mud we had names."

This is Burroughs' version of the Garden of Eden—it is one of the few actually serene passages in all his novels, even though that serenity is laced with matter-of-fact violence. Eden is the childhood mud of excrement and anal pleasure, and childhood is the only peace possible for bodily existence, since it is poly-morphously perverse—"body melting pleasure-sounds in the warm mud"—and the body hasn't channeled into its separate existence yet. For this reason the body hasn't channeled into the separate existences of its individual senses either, and there is "a blue wind of silence." The fall consists of emerging from childhood and receiving a name. Anality then becomes simply repulsive and can be enjoyed only in regressive fantasy and violence, since a name indicates a bodily existence, a separate existence in flesh: "What scared you all into time? Into body? Into shit? I will tell you: 'the word.' Alien Word 'the.' 'The' word of Alien Enemy imprisons 'thee' in Time. In Body. In Shit."

The solution to separate existence is to atomize it, to make it totally separate, to cut it up, to explode it. In this sense Bur-roughs, for all the fantastic nature of his novels, participates in the structures of realism. Realism's function is a separating one, and the primary separations it makes are between the self and the body, and the self and the world. Language is always in-visible in realism because the body has disappeared and is no longer the intersection of self and world. Burroughs fastens upon the necessary fragmentation entailed by draining the co-hesive force of the self out of the world of things, out of the body, and out of language. He aggravates that fragmentation, cuts it up, and completes the transformation from the invisible structure of language to the objectification of words, to the making of all words into names, a transformation that enables words to become an image of totally separate existence.

The cut-up, or more exactly, being cut up, accounts in part

for the experience of time in the world of Burroughs' novels. Time, like other aspects of that world, exists at two polar extremes, the first of which is explosion, being cut out of a context, the experience of total transportation out of oneself, out of a location, out of materiality. This is the temporality of flying and of release; it is ejaculation, the experience of being emptied, the experience of weightlessness. One is emptied of the body and its corporeality: "the soft bones spurted out in orgasm leaving a deflated skin collected by the guards." This is why ejaculation is so often associated with flying. Boys masturbate in roller coasters, on high wires, in planes, or simply while flying through the air—"boys swing from rings and bars jissom falling through dusty air of gymnasiums." The drug experience also is a "high," and being hit is flying, exploding, often an actual experience of leaving the body: "I project myself out through the glasses and across the street, a ghost in the morning sunlight, torn with disembodied lust."

When this experience exists in the body, it is temporality as frenzied activity, the body flinging itself in all directions, each organ at the pitch of its activity and pushing at its walls, eyes popping, throat screaming, arms and legs thrashing. This is temporality as overflow and overreach, the temporality of fire or of water as a fountain: "This book spill off the page in all directions, kaleidoscope of vistas, medley of tunes and street noises, farts and riot yipes and the slamming steel shutters of commerce, screams of pain and pathos and screams plain pathic, copulating cats and outraged squawk of the displaced bull head, prophetic mutterings of brujo in nutmeg trances, snapping necks and screaming mandrakes." At one polarity, temporality is the experience of boundlessness, specifically a release from the boundaries, the gravity, of the past.

At the other polarity, time is a being completely bounded, a being trapped, specifically by the body and by the decay of the body. If at one extreme, temporality can be seen orally as screaming, at the other it is orally a being devoured: "This Sex Skin is a critter found in the rivers here wraps all around you like a second skin eats you slow and good." Decay consists of this devouring as an action the body performs on itself, as the growth of the body over itself. The most explicit instance of this occurs at the end of the story of the talking asshole in *Naked Lunch*, when the anal function seizes control over the body and literally devours it:

> After that he began waking up in the morning with a transparent jelly like a tadpole's tail all over his mouth. The jelly was what the scientists call un-D.T., Undifferentiated Tissue, which can grow into any kind of flesh on the human body. He would tear it off his mouth and the pieces would stick to his hands like burning gasoline jelly and grow there, grow anywhere on him a glob of it fell. So finally his mouth sealed over, and the whole head would have amputated spontaneous . . . except for the *eyes* you dig. That's one thing the asshole *couldn't* do was see. It needed the eyes. But nerve connections were blocked and infiltrated and atrophied so the brain couldn't give orders any more. It was trapped in the skull, sealed off.

The result is "one all-purpose blob," the body sunk into its own weight.

If time at one polarity is a being emptied, at the other it is a being filled, a filling itself and spreading into itself of the body. Thus weightlessness at one polarity becomes a total surrender to weight at the other, flying becomes falling, and being high on drugs becomes coming down. Temporality as fire and a fountain becomes temporality as a stagnant pool and inorganic matter; the last is Burroughs' definition of a virus—"the renunciation of life itself, a *falling* towards inorganic, inflexible machine, towards dead matter." Temporality as exploding becomes temporality as the settling of debris after explosion. This settling can be seen in one of the frequent devices Burroughs uses to modulate his prose. After describing a frenzied activity, he elongates the description, flattens it out and allows it to echo through the narrator's unconscious. The effect produced is rhythmically like the aftermath of an explosion:

> The scream shot out of his flesh through empty locker rooms and barracks, musty resort hotels, and spectral, coughing corridors

of T.B. sanitariums, the muttering, hawking, grey dishwater smell of flophouses and Old Men's Homes, great, dusty custom sheds and warehouses, through broken porticoes and smeared arabesques, iron urinals worn paper thin by the urine of a million fairies, deserted weed-grown privies with a musty smell of shit turning back to the soil, erect wooden phallus on the grave of dying peoples plaintive as leaves in the wind, across the great brown river where whole trees float with green snakes in the branches and sad-eyed lemurs watch the shore out over a vast plain (vulture wings husk in the dry air).

This kind of rhythmic settling represents the settling of Burroughs' world as a whole, as it descends into the flat, shadowless, and timeless consciousness of cut-ups in the later novels. If the first polarity of time in Burroughs represents the release of time from the boundaries of the past, that is, explosion, then settling as the second polarity represents a return to those boundaries and a total release from the possibilities of the future.

The moment in Burroughs at which these two polarities intersect is the moment of his most recurring image, the "orgasm death." The most common manifestation of this is hanging; the hanged man in Burroughs always ejaculates at the moment of death, an act that combines the weightlessness and transportation of the body at the pitch of its activity with the sudden grip of the body's own weight, and its falling into the death of that weight. When time has been separated into schizophrenic polarities, as it has in Burroughs' world, only a totally violent act can hold time together, and that act is the orgasm death, "the whole birth death cycle of action." Burroughs' obsession with this image is a desperate attempt to overcome the frightening schizophrenia of his world, an attempt that is self-defeating the more it is returned to, not only because its violence feeds that schizophrenia but also because it fragments time into islands of repetition, into purely exclusive moments, repeated orgasm deaths, which are exclusive in that they are related to neither the continuity of the past nor the becoming of the future. This is the result of Burroughs' polarization of time; temporality now lacks a past and is total explosion, it now lacks a future and is settling, and it now lacks a past and a future and is orgasm death. Temporality thus falls apart into discrete components; it doesn't ripen or become.

Time in Burroughs takes one step beyond the spatialization of time in realism, but a step that realism makes inevitable. Time as a line, or a series of converging and diverging lines— time as the plot and reified continuity of realistic fiction— hardens and becomes brittle for Burroughs, so that it shatters and exists as a series of discrete, atomistic points or moments (as it exists for Descartes). If reality is addicting, as Burroughs claims, the proper time of realism is the time of the addict, which is atomistic, discontinuous. As one psychologist, Von Gebstattel, puts it, "the addict, having lost the contextual continuity of his inner life-history, exists therefore only in punctate fragmentation, at the moment of illusionary fulfillment, that is, discontinuously."[18] Burroughs' warnings against junk (as well as his warnings against the orgasm death) are thus warnings against reality and the control over temporality that reality imposes by repetition. Junk is image, and "the image past molds your future imposing repetition as the past accumulates and all actions are prerecorded and doped out and there is no life left in the present."

But despite his own warnings, Burroughs' world is most completely his world when it exists as pure repetition, when it is cut up. The cut-up world is the final condition of time, as it is of space, in Burroughs: it is atomistic time, time as a series of separate instantaneous flashes, time objectified and shattered into pieces, thus no time at all. This is why the completely bizarre becomes the completely monotonous in Burroughs (I refer to his later novels, especially *Nova Express*). Realism that has been amputated into pure fantasy, and therefore into an ultimate realism, simply repeats itself if it exists only by virtue of being amputated. Time in the cut-up world of Burroughs is the same as what Von Gebstattel calls manic time: "The

18. Quoted by Binswanger in *Existence*, p. 347.

manic always does the same, experiences the same, and in the medium of experientially immanent time moves nowhere."[19] Burroughs' world is precisely this: a movement toward immobility, toward frozen space. He arrives at this immobility from a different route than, say, Beckett's characters. He imposes explosion, and Beckett imposes catatonia. But the result is finally the same: a "real" world that consists of words as physical entities on the immobile space of a book's pages.

In many ways, Burroughs' world represents a direct attack upon the world of realism. "I have said the 'basic pre-clear identities' are now ended," he asserts in *Nova Express*, and indeed the concept of the world as "identity," and of characters as "identities," is destroyed by Burroughs. But Burroughs' destruction of reality is accomplished with the very tools of reality, not only with junk but with scissors. The result is an object-world whose preconfusion, whose nonidentity, *is* its identity, and whose schizophrenia is precisely the accelerated schizophrenia of the real world. There is no plot in Burroughs' world, but its frozen space is similar, for example, to the frozen space of Fielding's world, to the extent that the permission Fielding grants the reader in *Joseph Andrews* to skip chapters becomes in Burroughs the permission to "cut into *Naked Lunch* at any intersection point."

Burroughs' novels thus become diabolical maps, maps whose surfaces have been so intersected with conflicting directions, so cut up, that they are unreadable; they are maps of hell. Even the "conflicting directions," the sense of surrealistic contradiction in Burroughs, are finally neutralized by a cut-up world, a world existing in pieces that can't relate to each other enough to contradict. This is more true of the two later novels, *Nova Express* and *The Ticket That Exploded*, than it is of *Naked Lunch* and *The Soft Machine*. In *The Soft Machine* Burroughs makes his best use of cut-ups by establishing with them a dynamic rhythm of cohesion and fragmentation that becomes the experience of the novel. In the later novels, however, cut-ups come to seize their own space, to have less to do with other sec-

19. Ibid.

tions of the novels, except as waste bins to catch those sections when they drop. They become stagnant pools of amputated language and space through which the reader has to wade.

The amputation of language and space becomes also, at its extreme, an amputation of the body. Although the body in Burroughs is reified into two principles, an organic and a mechanical one, the mechanical is the final condition of the body, since even purely organic life, the body as blob, eventually swallows itself and falls into mineral existence, into death. Thus the objectification of the body in realism becomes in Burroughs a total dismemberment of the body, an explosion of it into separate existence, into pieces whose parts are all equal to each other and equal to any other object in the vicinity. This is the final condition of realism: schizophrenic atomism, living in pieces, in a world of pieces. Burroughs' world is the "real" world broken down into the components that Democritus began "reality" with, into atoms. Cut-ups finally strip away all the illusions Democritus talked about; they tear objects out of any context they may have created in combination and give their pure context back to them, so that "in *reality*," as Democritus said, "there are only Atoms and the Void."

4 / The Symbolic World: The Garden

The works of Burroughs, Robbe-Grillet, and Sartre all demonstrate that the structure of reality, pushed far enough, becomes the structure of fantasy. Reality is schizophrenic, displaying the most apparent quality of schizophrenia: hallucination, the impregnation of the world with fantasy. But reality accomplishes this precisely by separating fantasy and reality and thereby making the real all the more incomplete and unreal, or fantastic. Separation, the principle of the map, the principle of either-or, is thus the underlying structure of reality. This principle is manifest in the absolute separation of here and there that produces the fantastic labyrinth in Robbe-Grillet; in the separation of subject and object that produces the fantastic contingency of the objective world in Sartre; and in the separation of all things in Burroughs that produces the most fantastic, grotesque world of all, one whose shattered pieces are grafted together and then torn apart only to be grafted again, in a continuing series of random combinations.

All of this is schizophrenic, since its fantasy is the result of the separation of reality and fantasy, of waking and dream life. This separation constitutes Jung's definition of schizophrenia. There is not so much a regression inward, he says, as there is a separation of that inwardness, the pool of fantasy and childhood, from the outer world of objects.[1] The point is that separation

1. Carl Jung, *Symbols of Transformation* (vol. 5 of *Collected Works*), trans. R. F. C. Hull (Princeton, N.J., 1956), pp. 173–74.

itself makes "inwardness" a pool, a pure space to which the schizophrenic can regress.

But this question naturally arises: What can that condition previous to schizophrenia, previous to the separation of inner and outer, fantasy and reality, be called, and what are its structural contours? A preliminary sketch of this condition was given in Chapter One, in order to make clear what map structures are not. In that chapter it was called "garden." It is important to keep in mind that this term does not refer to the garden as a pure space, whose condition is mergence, as in *Heart of Darkness* and in Burroughs. The garden is the principle of unity, or integration, rather than mergence. Mergence is brought about when integration is separated from separation, when integration is thought of in terms of map structures and made one of a pair of mutually exclusive polar opposites, mergence and separation. But the true sense of integration unites itself and its opposite, integrates mergence and separation, which is the same as saying that the true sense of the garden unites the garden and the map, in a condition previous to the separation of these two. We saw with regard to Burroughs and Conrad that mergence and separation are so opposite as to be reduced to the same thing—in fact the irony of those principles is that they are so separate as to merge—and that the chief feature of their mutual reduction, or mergence, is a kind of inert objectivity, a confinement or imprisonment. When mergence and separation are united, however, the opposite is true: they are so much themselves as to be each other, are totally open to each other while being themselves; hence their chief feature is freedom, liberation.

This unity of mergence and separation is the major structural contour of the garden. The question posed above can now be changed to a more particular series of questions. If time is spatialized by map structures, how is time experienced in the garden? If space itself is given the structure of a map or of a container by map structures, how is space experienced in the garden? If the body is an object in the map, what is the body in the garden? And if objects themselves are experienced as inert and objective in the map, how are they experienced in the garden?

Perhaps the major paradox of the garden is that the answers to these questions can initially be found in the experience of schizophrenia. If reality is mad, or schizophrenic, then schizophrenia, from the point of view of its own world, can be said to be sane, or real—not the narrow real that excludes fantasy but the full reality that is infused with the fantastic, the marvelous, the dream. There is a schizophrenia whose structure is integration rather than separation, a schizophrenia that unites such opposites as subject and object, fantasy and reality, space and time, self and body, rather than polarizes them into either-or, a schizophrenia that unites either-or and both, and thus unites the garden and the map.

We saw in Chapters One and Two that when fantasy and reality are separated, the real becomes fantastic; similarly, when time and space are separated, time becomes spatialized, and when madness and sanity are separated, sanity becomes insane. But in the garden the opposite is true: the fantastic becomes real, space becomes temporalized, and madness becomes sane. The world seen in Sartre and Robbe-Grillet lays the foundation of this new kind of schizophrenia on the soil of the old, for it reveals the dream, the madness, that exists at the very heart of reality. The world in Kafka, and even more so in Theodore Roethke, completes the shift from the old schizophrenia to the new, from the schizophrenia of an insane reality to that of a real insanity, a sane insanity.

I say new schizophrenia, but it has always existed, no matter how invisibly. But there is a new view of schizophrenia that several psychologists have recently taken, notably Norman O. Brown and R. D. Laing, a view that is essentially the one I am taking in this chapter. Their point is that the schizophrenic experience can be healthy rather than pathological, and that schizophrenia has thus come to mean the opposite of what it traditionally has meant. As Brown says in *Love's Body*, "It is not schizophrenia but normality that is split-minded; in schizophrenia the false boundaries are disintegrating."[2] Thus, as Laing says in *The Politics of Experience*, "madness need not be all breakdown. It may also be breakthrough. It is potentially liberation and renewal as well as enslavement and existential death."[3] Laing knows there is a great deal of fear and suffering involved in the schizophrenic experience, and he knows that few schizophrenics (particularly given our treatment of the insane in mental institutions) achieve this "liberation and renewal." He is trying to point out, however, that there is a certain quality in the schizophrenic experience, a quality that used to be called "visionary," which represents an alternative to normalcy and the world of either-or. This quality is a certain structure of thought or perception, precisely that structure which unites such opposites as subject and object, fantasy and reality, mind and body. This is the meaning of Blake's schizophrenia. The structure of Blake's world at every point is the exact antithesis of the old schizophrenic world, the world of either-or.[4]

In this respect, the experience of schizophrenia becomes a bridge between two very different notions of reality, a bridge that spans the traditional structures of Western thought and the changes those structures have undergone in the twentieth century. We have seen how the world is experienced in the old schizophrenic world, the world of the map. In this chapter and the next, I want to look closely at the experience of objects, time, and the body in the new schizophrenic world, the world of the garden. I hope to show that this world is the most fundamentally real one, in that it is the world of our primary experience—which, Merleau-Ponty says, is "not indeed abolished, but repressed by everyday perception or by objective thought."[5] As we shall see, this world is also a symbolic world, a world whose beings are incarnate with significance rather than fragmented and inert. Finally, I examine some works of Theodore Roethke, a poet who, like William S. Burroughs, has been diag-

2. (New York, 1966), p. 159.
3. P. 110.
4. See Northrop Frye, *Fearful Symmetry* (Boston, 1962).
5. *Phenomenology*, p. 291.

nosed as schizophrenic and whose images are often similar to those of Burroughs, but whose world is the opposite of Burroughs', whose schizophrenia represents liberation and renewal rather than confinement and death, and thus in every respect represents a return to the garden and its structures.

1. Schizophrenia and Symbolism

The fact that the schizophrenic experience has often been equated with the experience of children or of primitives should be evidence enough that schizophrenia contains a dimension directly opposed to classical Western civilization. Levin, Boisen, Werner, Von Domarus, Kasanin, Roheim, Storch, and Brown are psychologists who have explored this connection.[6] The major point underlying what they say is that schizophrenics, like children and like primitives, are capable of thinking in ways that are somehow prelogical, that is, their thinking can embrace what from a logical point of view would be called contradiction. Werner says this explicitly: "It is one of the most important tasks of the developmental psychology to show that the advanced form of thinking characteristic of Western civilization is only one form among many, and that more primitive forms are not so much lacking in logic as based on logic of a different kind. The premise of Aristotelian logic that, when a thing is A it cannot at the same time be B, will not hold true for the primitive."[7]

Von Domarus has called this prelogic "paleologic," and has explicitly identified it with schizophrenia. The principle of

6. Max Levin, "Misunderstanding of the Pathogenesis of Schizophrenia, Arising from the Concept of 'Splitting,'" *American Journal of Psychiatry*, XCIV (1938); A. T. Boisen, "The Form and Content of Schizophrenic Thinking," *Psychiatry*, V (1922); Heinz Werner, *Comparative Psychology of Mental Development* (Chicago, 1948); E. Von Domarus, "The Specific Laws of Logic in Schizophrenia," in J. S. Kasanin, ed., *Language and Thought in Schizophrenia: Collected Papers* (Berkeley, 1944); J. S. Kasanin, "The Disturbance of Conceptual Thinking in Schizophrenia," in *Language and Thought in Schizophrenia*; Geza Roheim, *Magic and Schizophrenia* (New York, 1955); A. Storch, *The Primitive Archaic Forms of Inner Experience and Thought in Schizophrenia*, trans. C. Willard (New York, 1924); and Norman O. Brown, *Love's Body*.
7. Quoted in Arieti, *Schizophrenia*, pp. 196–97.

paleological thought, he says, is that identity can be inferred on the basis of identical predicates rather than identical subjects.[8] Arieti gives an example that explains what Von Domarus means: "A patient thought she was the Virgin Mary. Her thought process was the following: 'The Virgin Mary was a virgin; I am a virgin; therefore, I am the Virgin Mary.' The delusional conclusion was reached because the identity of the predicate of the two premises (the state of being virgin) made the patient accept the identity of the two subjects (the Virgin Mary and the patient)."[9]

What is similar between this kind of thinking and primitive thinking is the ability to see two supposedly separate entities as both separate and identical. An African native says to a European: "During the day you drank palm wine with a man, unaware that in him there was an evil spirit. In the evening you heard a crocodile devouring some poor fellow. A wildcat, during the night, ate up all your chickens. Now, the man with whom you drank, the crocodile who ate a man and the wildcat are all one and the same person."[10] As Lévi-Strauss points out, this combination of separation and identity (expressed as a unity of opposition and integration) is the underlying structural principle of totemism in primitive society.[11] And as Eliade tells us, a ritual for a primitive unites two separate times, two separate places, and two separate beings, the actor in the ritual and a totemic animal, an ancestor, a god, or a hero.[12] Schizophrenics and primitives can thus in a sense step out of their skin and be in it at the same time; they can be transported to a different time and a different place, and they can become a different being, while remaining themselves and remaining in their own time and place.

I say that schizophrenics and primitives can "in a sense" experience the world in this way, but that "sense" has to be

8. Ibid., p. 194.
9. Ibid., p. 195.
10. Levi-Bruhl, quoted in ibid., p. 197.
11. *Totemism*, trans. Rodney Needham (Boston, 1962), p. 99.
12. *Cosmos and History: The Myth of the Eternal Return*, trans. Willard Trask (New York, 1959), p. 28.

made more clear. Von Domarus' and Arieti's categories falsify such an experience. They assert that a schizophrenic infers identity according to predicates, and Arieti even talks about this inference as a kind of process: I am a virgin, the Virgin Mary is a virgin, I am the Virgin Mary. But this is the most fanciful possible representation of schizophrenic thought; it has no resemblance whatsoever to the experience of schizophrenia. Not only have Von Domarus and Arieti failed in their major task, to characterize schizophrenic and primitive thought, but also they have positively distorted that thought by imposing upon it categories that are antithetical to it in all respects, those of classical Western thought. Hence they have also imposed a very explicit negative judgment upon it. The patient's assertion that she is the Virgin Mary is a "delusional conclusion," and the reason is clear: she has committed a logical fallacy. The fact that the idea of a logical fallacy is understandable only from Arieti's "normative" point of view makes no difference. Arieti is consistent only when he asserts at the end of his treatment of schizophrenic thought that "paleologic thought per se must be considered inferior to the Aristotelian."[13]

Arieti is closer to a description of the experience of schizophrenia and primitivism when he mentions the symbolic dimension of schizophrenic thought. Yet his definition of a symbol also depends upon Von Domarus' principle: "A symbol of X is something which stands for X, but also something which retains some similarity with X—a common predicate or characteristic."[14] Arieti's description contains two basic points, both insufficient to define "symbol." A symbol "stands for" something else, which implies that the identity of the symbol and its referent is not, in fact, an identity, but an external connection that preserves the discreteness of the two terms in question. But even if this relationship were an identity, it would be implicitly fallacious, since it is inferred by "a common predicate."

Arieti's definition is a perfect example of the impossibility of defining the concept "symbol" with the structures of Western

13. Arieti, *Schizophrenia*, p. 269.
14. Ibid., p. 199.

thought. His concept of symbol is in fact the Freudian concept, by which "symbol" indicates the meaning disguised by an object; this is the only view of the symbol that Western thought is capable of. At bottom it depends upon a structure whereby all meaning relationships are mappings. This is why it was necessary for Freud to interpret dreams with a structure that is essentially spatial, that of the "conscious" and the "unconscious." Symbols in dreams are the conscious manifestation of meanings imbedded in an entirely separate space, the unconscious.[15] Freud's mechanism is essentially that of allegory, a literary mode more prominent in the West, at least until the last century, than symbolism. In allegory, a figure represents a quality that exists in a different space from that of the figure itself (usually heaven or hell). This itself is schizophrenic, in the sense of the word used in the first three chapters.

The true sense of symbol is the opposite of the mapping function by which a symbol stands for something else. This is so radically true in schizophrenia that one patient has described the feeling of words in his mouth as the very objects those words stand for: "When I said 'street,' the whole street would be in my mouth, and it would be difficult for me to pronounce it."[16] Such an experience dramatizes a world in which words are made flesh, a world incarnate, thus a world in which, as Goethe put it simply, "everything is a symbol."[17] "For the schizophrenic," says Roheim, "word and object, symbol and content, are the same thing," just as for the primitive, Eliade asserts, all objects "live" and "speak."[18] The symbol, in other words, represents "the coexistence of contradictory essences,"[19] the unity of subject and object, of thing and meaning, of flesh and spirit.

This unity is the central dynamic at the heart of the notion "symbol" that such thinkers as Jung, Cassirer, Eliade, and Lang-

15. See in particular "Distortion in Dreams," chap. 4 of Freud, *The Interpretation of Dreams*, trans. James Strachey (New York, 1965).
16. Quoted in Roheim, *Magic and Schizophrenia*, p. 160.
17. Quoted in Brown, *Love's Body*, p. 239.
18. Roheim, *Magic and Schizophrenia*, p. 108; Eliade, *The Sacred and the Profane*, p. 165.
19. Eliade, *Patterns*, p. 29.

er have emphasized. It is a dynamic that destroys the spatial bias of formal logic whereby things in the world are confined in their locations and items of consciousness themselves are things confined in their locations, and the two, internal and external things, are related as a map and terrain. This is why Eliade is able to say, "whatever its context, a symbol always reveals the basic oneness of several *zones* of the real."[20] Symbols destroy map space: a stone, as the symbol for the center of the world, *is* that center, a tree *is* the axis of the world, the earth *is* a woman, and so on. Or, returning to Arieti, a young girl *is* the Virgin Mary, not because she "accepts identity based upon identical predicates" but because, as Eliade puts it, "magico-religious experience makes it possible for man himself to be transformed into a symbol," and thus "only insofar as man himself becomes a symbol, are all systems and all anthropo-cosmic experiences possible.... Man no longer feels himself to be an 'airtight' fragment, but a living cosmos open to all the other living cosmoses by which he is surrounded."[21]

The symbolic world is the antithesis of the classical structure whereby the self is separated from the body and the body separated from the world. In the symbolic world, the body and the world are saturated with the self. The body is open to objects, and objects themselves live for the body; they point themselves out *with* man's body. This is the implication of Baudelaire's famous lines in his sonnet "Correspondences": "Man passes through forests of symbols / Which watch him with familiar eyes." The experience of the schizophrenic, of the child, and of the primitive is precisely this, that of a significant world intimately related to the body. When Minkowski's patient asserts that the smallest piece of thread has been purposely laid in his way or that the cigarette smoke of a passerby is a signal,[22] it is in fact true, since the world is alive and watching and arranges itself around one's body.

As Heidegger, Merleau-Ponty, Cassirer, and others attempt

20. Ibid., p. 452. Italics mine.
21. Ibid., p. 455.
22. *Existence*, p. 135.

to show, this is also in a basic sense the experience of everyone. Cassirer specifically opposes the theory of symbols to empirical and rationalist theories of knowledge, on the basis that it doesn't, as they do, "modify the pure content of consciousness, the experienced phenomenon."[23] The world of symbols is the world of primary experience, previous to objective thought and map consciousness. Cassirer demonstrates this strikingly by examining the phenomenon of aphasia. One of the principle features of aphasia is the inability to orient oneself in space, or to co-ordinate the movements of the body with the dimensions of objective space. An aphasic patient can, if left alone, unconsciously draw a match from a box and light his cigarette, but if he is asked to perform this action, hence must put the action in front of him, so to speak, he cannot.[24] Aphasic patients can somehow feel up and down, left and right, but cannot carry this feeling into space.[25] Thus some can't tell if they are lying or standing, and others know that above is over their head but can't identify above correctly when they are lying down.[26] For the aphasic, each coordinate of space has the same inert meaning, which is no meaning at all; thus the various coordinates are indistinguishable. This includes near and far as well as up, down, left, and right. A patient asked to place an object on a certain side of a ruler between him and the doctor cannot.[27]

For the aphasic both sides of the ruler are objectively equal, and only objectively equal, since neither has a reference to him, to his body. Each item in space is an entity, sealed off from all others, and each dimension in space is discrete; everything "out there" lacks the synthetic and integrative infusion of the body to animate it and make it a space-for-him, a living place. It is the primary world of significant objects and significant space, the world of symbols, that is absent in aphasia. The important point is that this world is the world itself, in the sense that Hegel used that word—"individuality is what its world, in

23. *Symbolic Forms*, III, 235.
24. Ibid., p. 243.
25. Ibid., p. 246.
26. Ibid., p. 242.
27. Ibid., p. 247.

the sense of its own world, is."[28] This is Cassirer's point—that what we call the world exists always in perfect sympathy with the body, and is in this sense a world of symbols. Otherwise we couldn't—as many aphasics can't—walk across the room. Our world is always incarnate with meaning, even when we perform the most simple actions, and its meaning is neither subjective nor objective nor referential, but is one of "symbolic pregnance." "This pregnance," says Cassirer, "can be reduced neither to merely reproductive processes nor to mediated intellectual processes—it must ultimately be recognized as an independent and autonomous determination, without which neither an object nor a subject, neither a unity of the thing nor a unity of the self would be given to us."[29]

The key concept of Heidegger's philosophy, being-in-the-world, makes exactly the same point; he uses the phenomenon of left and right, up and down, to demonstrate that the body is always already in, and in sympathy with, a world: "By the mere *feeling* of a difference between my two sides I could never find my way about in a world. The subject with a 'mere feeling' of this difference is a construct posited in disregard of the state that is truly constitutive for any subject—namely, that whenever Dasein has such a 'mere feeling,' it is in a world already *and must be* in it to be able to orient itself at all."[30] Or as Merleau-Ponty puts it: "The parts of space seen as breadth, height or depth, are not juxtaposed, but . . . coexist because they are drawn into the hold that our body takes upon the world."[31]

This is the significance of the lines by Baudelaire quoted above: objects, as symbols, watch us, because our body takes hold of them through its own expressive space. "As in schizophrenia," Brown points out, quoting Storch, "what happens to the person's own body . . . is identical with what happens in the

28. G. W. F. Hegel, *The Phenomenology of Mind*, trans. J. B. Baillie (New York, 1931), p. 335.
29. Cassirer, *Symbolic Forms*, III, 235.
30. Martin Heidegger, *Being and Time*, trans. John Macquarrie and Edward Robinson (New York, 1962), p. 143.
31. Merleau-Ponty, *Phenomenology*, p. 275 .

universe."[32] This is why the primitive mentality shows a profound mistrust of maps. A map extracts the world out of its unity with the body. McLuhan quotes an educated Nigerian who tried to bring back the secret of maps to his people and was surprised to find himself rebuked by his father: "Maps are liars, he told me briefly. From his tone of voice I could tell that I had offended him in some way not known to me at the time. The things that hurt one do not show on a map. The truth of a place is in the joy and the hurt that come from it. I had best not put my trust in anything as inadequate as a map, he counseled."[33] In the most basic sense this is true for all of us. Space as it is experienced in the symbolic world, the world of primary experience, is never abstract, but always endowed with an "accent," as Cassirer says.[34] Significant objects in our environment to which our attention is directed, such as a painting on the wall, are closer to us than our glasses or the floor on which we stand. My body, like that of the schizophrenic, qualifies space; it does not quantify it.

This unity of body and world, in literature, underlies both the symbolist movement in France and the emphasis upon point of view in American and English fiction. The two movements are inseparable; both occurred at the turn of the century, both were reactions to the map space of naturalism, and both posited a world in which the body and objects reciprocally secrete significant space for each other, a world that constitutes and is simultaneously constituted by the body. Symbolism, Feidelson points out, is the antithesis of discreteness (which is the basis of map space) since it unites part and whole,[35] and thus does not separate aspects of experience into mutually exclusive locations. Similarly, point of view posits a world whose horizon always circles the body. The structure of point of view makes the "in front of me" or "below me" of map space impossible, by establishing a world I am in, a world that surrounds me. Space in

32. *Love's Body*, p. 226.
33. *Understanding Media*, pp. 145–46.
34. Cassirer, *Symbolic Forms*, I, 85.
35. Charles Feidelson, *Symbolism in American Literature* (Chicago, 1953), pp. 57, 60.

such a world arranges itself around the body as that body moves, "the way Vermont throws itself together" for the narrator of one of Stevens' poems. Stevens fixed the connection between the concept of symbolism and that of point of view in one superbly cryptic sentence: "The absolute object slightly turned is a metaphor of the object."[36]

The point is that the object is never absolute, since it is always slightly turned, that is, seen from a point of view—which means that it is always a metaphor, a unity of itself and the observer, a symbol. This sense in which point of view, like symbolism, constitutes a unity of subject and object has been best explained by Ortega y Gasset. Two men looking at the same object see, in a sense, two different objects, since each sees the object "slightly turned," to use Stevens' phrase. But as Ortega asserts, this does not mean that one version of the object is false; nor does it mean that both versions are false and the object has an absolute true reality behind its various perspectives. Rather it means that the reality of the object completes itself in each point of view.[37] Because of this, it is misleading to even use the word "object," which is the reason Baudelaire has man pass through a "forest of symbols," not a forest of objects. The object doesn't exist—that is, the object as objective, as something purely out there. This is certainly the lesson of Sartre's *La Nausée*.

The object is an abstraction created by philosophical discourse. Someone says, "There, there's a chair—it is there, a *thing*; it isn't *you* by any stretch of the imagination, so it is an object." But to call the chair to attention in such a way is to localize it with the very act of calling it to attention. It is to throw it against itself outside of me ("object" literally means "something thrown against") by the act of holding my point of view back from it. The act of isolating the object in such a way creates, naturally, an isolated object, something objective. In reality, however, the objects in our environment are never experienced in this man-

---

36. *Opus Posthumous*, ed. Samuel French Morse (New York, 1966), p. 179.
37. José Ortega y Gasset, *The Modern Theme*, trans. James Cleugh (New York, 1961), pp. 89ff.

ner. That chair is not simply that chair, but an aspect of my whole world, part of that world's history and future, since it entered that world at one time and in a certain way and since it will leave that world similarly, carrying its own beauty or ugliness. It is not isolated from my world, but something at hand, literally arranged in and with my world. I walk around it, and it has different ways of facing me. It is thus a potentiality in my world, a quality, a way my world bends and allows me to sit in it. It is a metaphor, a metamorphosis of my world; it is a symbol in a symbolic world, incarnate with my own body, saturated with my subjectivity.

The writer with whom the doctrine of point of view originated, Henry James, best displays this symbolic world, the dense world of human intersubjectivity, whose atmosphere—the very space between things—is permeated with consciousness. All of James's novels concern what could be called the problem of the novel form itself, the problem of map space. His characters are initially presented with a world foreign to themselves, a world in which they don't participate—a world whose condition for them is the flat, two-dimensional space of a map. The most familiar manifestation of this situation is the theme of the American in Europe. But the point of that theme is that the map of Europe breaks down when a character begins to participate in its world—the world of Paris for Strether in *The Ambassadors*, for example—as he begins to feel its contours and know its objects, and as those objects begin to arrange themselves around him. A map eliminates shadows, and Strether sees Europe and its society initially as shadowless—he has no sense of the other sides of things that make their surfaces possible. This is true in several senses. First Liverpool and then Paris represent "fronts" to Strether, as the wall surrounding Liverpool and the imposing flat wall of Chad's apartment in Paris make literally clear. (These constitute the only detailed descriptions of Strether's environment in Books I and II.) Chad and his social world are also initially flat for Strether: he has no conception of its forces, its composition, its dimensions, no conception of its relation to him.

But as the novel progresses, objects and people emerge from

the homogeneous background that is Paris, and the complicated shape of the society around Strether begins to form. This is dramatized in the incident that precipitates the novel's turning point—Strether's excursion in the eleventh book to a small village outside Paris. He approaches the village as if it were a painting, a flat two-dimensional surface—indeed it reminds him of a painting he had seen in a Tremont Street store in Boston. But rather than simply observing the scene and keeping it in front of him, Strether steps into it and becomes a part of it, to the extent that he enables it to fall into place and fully become itself around him: "The oblong gilt frame disposed its enclosing lines; the poplars and willows, the reeds and river—a river of which he didn't know, and didn't want to know, the name—fell into a composition, full of felicity, within them; the sky was silver and turquoise and varnish; the village on the left was white and the church on the right was grey; it was all there, in short—it was what he wanted: it was Tremont Street, it was France, it was Lambinet. Moreover he was freely walking about in it." A few pages later, James remarks that Strether "has never yet so struck himself as engaged with others and in midstream of his drama," a fact about to be confirmed with a shock when he discovers Chad and Madame de Vionnet in the same village. From then on Strether is part of the fabric of his world, part of the density of it, and his space, rather than existing in front of him, surrounds him and comes to be filled with his actions and decisions, almost as if it were a continuum of his own consciousness, carrying the ripples that consciousness makes to other characters.

This density and richness of the world, and the need such a world has for a point of view, a subjectivity, to animate it and give it form, are also the major theme of *Wings of the Dove.* Milly Theale is the dove of the title because she moves in a rarified atmosphere, the thin upper air of peace, beauty, and frailty. Yet her "wings"—her money and social grace—provide the density in which the other characters exist. But the story of the novel is not so much Milly's as it is Densher's—the character who moves from the upper atmosphere of his polite European education into the dense world of will, choice, and consequence (hence the pun on his name). Milly's importance consists in providing a point of view with which Densher can impregnate his world to give it structure and form. The novel thus comes to be about the integration of a rarified upper atmosphere on one hand and the cluttered world of things and of moral responsibility on the other.

In this respect, like many of James's novels, *Wings of the Dove* is about how all unlike things penetrate each other and make each other possible—about how the ideal informs the real, the foreign informs the familiar, death informs life, or silence informs speech. The interplay of silence and speech is one of the most evident qualities of all of James's fiction. His world is such an intersubjective one that characters in it often communicate through a kind of telepathy, through the subtlest gestures, the slightest innuendos in conversation, through silence as much as through words. Brown says, quoting Carlyle, "To let the silence in is symbolism. 'In symbol there is concealment and yet revelation: here therefore, by Silence and by Speech acting together, comes a double significance.'"[38]

James shows that underlying the unity of body and world, subject and object, silence and speech, all of which constitutes the symbolic world, is a more general unity of Being and Nonbeing. This is why the unity of subject and object, body and world, etc., is never a mergence of them, a reduction of one to the other. Mergence is made possible when either-or separates isolation and mergence into two mutually exclusive polarities. The symbolic world, on the other hand, embraces and transforms the structure of either-or, since it unites either-or and both; thus it establishes the autonomy of the body and the world, subject and object, etc., on the very grounds of their unity, by virtue of their unity.

In other words, the symbolic world preserves what it unites. The world is the body, yet it is also the world; objects are subjective, yet they are also objects; similarly, sanity and reality are mad and fantastic, yet they are also sane and real. By sepa-

38. *Love's Body*, p. 190.

rating sanity and madness, map consciousness reduces the sane to the insane, and only to the insane; but by uniting sanity and madness, the symbolic world reveals the most true kind of madness (Blake's, for example) as sane by virtue of being mad. Schizophrenia, Binswanger says, is the condition whereby a person is and is not himself,[39] but is and is not himself in the unity of himself, that is, in the symbolic world.

A writer whose world is one of the most schizophrenic in modern literature, Kafka, uncovers in all respects this unity of unity and separation, of Being and Nonbeing. Kafka simultaneously unites and preserves those opposites that structure the world—subject and object, body and world, inner and outer, and above all, fantasy and reality. Before Kafka, the fantastic existed in literature for the most part as a diversion, as the sporadic intrusion of the unknown upon a civilization that had created that unknown by draining fantasy out of the world and sealing it off as Other. This is schizophrenic in the sense of the word used in the first three chapters. Kafka's world in one respect presents just this kind of schizophrenia: it is a real world upon which the fantastic intrudes, with surprising and sometimes terrifying results. But once this intrusion has been accomplished, Kafka fuses fantasy and reality, and his world becomes schizophrenic in the sense of the word used in this chapter: his world becomes incarnate with significance, and fantasy impregnates every object, animating it and arranging it around the protagonist.

If Robbe-Grillet and Sartre reveal to us the fantastic nature of reality, Kafka reveals both that and, more important, the real nature of fantasy. Reality in the most narrow sense, as something Other and objective, is always present in Kafka, just as its opposite, a unity of the real and fantastic, the objective and subjective, is present. The "dark penumbra," which Jung asserts surrounds our world when we restrict the real to objective, material reality,[40] exists in Kafka as the great shadow that is cast by in-

39. *Existence*, p. 297.
40. "The Real and the Surreal," in *The Structure and Dynamics of the Psyche* (vol. 8 of *Collected Works*), trans. R. F. C. Hull (New York, 1960), p. 383.

stitutions like the "remote, inaccessible Courts" in *The Trial* and the castle itself in *The Castle*. But Kafka simultaneously re-integrates shadows and the world; he carries into the world and places behind every object the absolute shadow, the Other, that the objective world casts. Thus the Other is always both there and here in Kafka; it is the Law that is inaccessible and that is in every attic. Fantasy in Kafka's world also is both there and here, both strange and familiar, both enigmatic, like the am-biguous gesture from the window of a nearby house at the end of *The Trial*, and apparent, like Gregor Samsa's metamorphosis into a cockroach. Kafka's world is dreamlike, but it is a dream in which one is awake; it is real, but irrational and illogical; it is arbitrary and fortuitous, but infused with necessity.

We read Kafka and perceive his world with the mental struc-tures of realism, particularly when the text seems to invite it, when the dream that impregnates the world is least visible. But inevitably the dream appears, and the structures of objectivity and realism, of schizophrenia in the initial sense, are forced to shift, as the dream turns out to have been filling space all the time, like air, and schizophrenia turns out to be real, that is, fantastic. This is one of the most common experiences in reading Kafka. K.'s shock at being arrested in *The Trial*, for example, is a natural and real reaction, but the caution that follows indig-nation is strangely inappropriate, as when K. leaves the door to his room open to demonstrate to his wardens that he is not taking his life. Gradually, as this inappropriateness is manifest more and more, K. and the reader with him are shown to have been implicated in a fantastic world all along. A brilliant passage deleted from *The Trial* demonstrates how subtly and yet how totally this implication takes hold:

> As someone said to me—I can't remember now who it was—it is really remarkable that when you wake up in the morning you nearly always find everything in exactly the same place as the evening before. For when asleep and dreaming you are, ap-parently at least, in an essentially different state from that of wakefulness; and therefore, as that man truly said, it requires enormous presence of mind or rather quickness of wit, when

opening your eyes to seize hold as it were of everything in the room at exactly the same place where you had let it go on the previous evening.[41]

The boundary between reality and dream, which the narrator of this passage presumes is actual, is totally shattered by that very presumption. This is the feeling of all of Kafka's work: the perfect reasonableness of the most fantastic things, to the extent that those fantastic things are born out of the very heart of that reasonableness.

This dual mode, this new kind of schizophrenia that unites the real and the fantastic, is established by two conflicting, or apparently conflicting, assumptions about space, assumptions that can be seen in the passage just quoted and in all of Kafka's work: first, that space is objective and that the things in it retain their absolute positions when they do not fall under our gaze (when we are asleep); second, that space is given by the body and that things have a position only by virtue of our perception of them (when we wake up). The point is that in Kafka's world, which is the world itself, both of these kinds of space are present and are held in a unity. This is the meaning of the statement that schizophrenia unites (integrates) separation and integration, or discreteness and mergence: it unites a space that is objective and alienating with one that is subjective and whole. K.'s environment in *The Trial* is both impersonal, foreign to him, and constituted by him, familiar to him; he is both separated from it and one with it. Its impersonality and Otherness are established from the beginning with K.'s arrest and subsequent persecution by the enigmatic Court. But this persecution is shown to be a structure that K. himself constitutes as well; he implicates himself in it, not only through his growing caution but simply by living in a world whose objects always face him, whose environment always directs its gaze at him.

Thus, although K. is alienated, his world is strangely small—as when he finds the room and building that his first interrogation is in without having the address, or when he is traveling

41. Appendix II, "The Passages Deleted by the Author," in *The Trial*, trans. Willa and Edwin Muir (New York, 1968).

across town for that interrogation and notices his three clerks, two of them in a streetcar crossing his path, one sitting on the terrace of a café. "All three were probably staring after him and wondering where their chief was rushing off to." In fact they probably were. K. is always imagining people eavesdropping behind doors, and they usually are. His world is one in which persecutions are both fantastic and real, one which simultaneously reaches out *for* him and is made possible *by* him.

The Court persecutes K. and follows him, but as the priest tells him, "the Court wants nothing from you. It receives you when you come and it dismisses you when you go." This is the significance of the whipping scene, in which K. discovers his two warders being whipped behind a remote door in his bank. K. intrudes upon the space of this scene, as characters in realistic fiction intrude upon a space in disclosure scenes (the example of Mrs. Tow-wouse in *Joseph Andrews* was given in Chapter Two); yet as Kafka makes clear, the scene is made possible only by K. himself. There is total silence when he closes the door, although the screams of the men had filled the bank when the door was open; and when K. returns the next day and opens the door again, the warders and the whipper are there in the same position as the previous day, and the warders are still imploring K. for mercy, as they were then. The clear implication is that K.'s very intrusion upon the scene is a creation of it; K. constitutes the world his body opens upon, while through that very action he is simultaneously constituted *by* the world. His world, like the world we all live in, is both subjective and objective, both real and fantastic, and is not a reduction of either of these to the other but a perfect unity of them.

This is the symbolic world at its extreme, but an extreme in which it can only exist, an extreme that is necessary due to the radical severance of subject and object, and of symbol and reality, in the classical "real" world. Kafka unites symbol and reality, and he restores to metaphor the reality of metamorphosis, as his story of that title makes clear: Gregor Samsa is not *like* a cockroach, but *is* a cockroach. There is a striking passage in *The Trial* that also makes this apparent. Caught in a conversation between the Assistant Manager and a manufacturer, K. feels as though he has shrunk to the size of a midget: "Slowly, lifting his eyes as far as he dared, he peered up to see what they were about, then picked one of the documents from the desk at random, laid it flat on his open palm, and gradually raised it, himself rising with it, to their level."

This lifting, which is both imaginative and real, both internal and external, contains the full meaning of the symbolic world: there is a perfect unity of the literal and the figurative, of the metaphoric and the metamorphic. And this is why the "delusion" of Arieti's schizophrenic patient is real: she *is* the Virgin Mary. Some psychologists, although they are in the minority, have attempted to carry this sense of symbolic reality—which is really a sense of primary experience, of phenomena only as they manifest themselves—into their descriptions of psychic events. Wittels asserts that it would be more suggestive of the actual state of things if rather than speaking of an Oedipus complex or introjecting father images, one spoke about *being* Oedipus or *being* father.[42] And Boss makes a similar assertion with regard to dreams: "In our dreams we experience real physical facts: a thing is a real thing, an animal is a real animal, a man is a real man and a ghost is a real ghost."[43]

One more dimension of *The Trial* needs to be discussed, a dimension for which the idea of symbol presents a problem. If the symbol unites subject and object, inner and outer, then what does a symbolic world mean for our experience of time? In the world of classical Western thought, time is purely objective, spatialized. How is a time that is neither objective nor subjective—or to say the same thing, both objective and subjective—experienced? In *The Trial*, K.'s doom hangs over him; his future is closed, since it is in the hands of the Court. Time is spatialized by the plot of *The Trial* as it is in realistic and naturalistic fiction, and K. moves along the inevitable line of his future. Yet there is an element of improvisation to K.'s life, just as there is to *The*

42. Cited in Herbert Fingarette, *The Self in Transformation: Psychoanalysis, Philosophy, and the Life of the Spirit* (New York, 1963), p. 185.
43. Medard Boss, *The Analysis of Dreams*, trans. Arnold J. Pomerans (London, 1957), p. 106.

Trial's plot. K. dismisses his lawyer, something unheard of in the annals of the Court. At times he is defiant in the face of the Court, as at the close of his first interrogation, and he always holds out hope for his future, even to the end. There is, then, a sense in which K.'s future is also open, a fact made more apparent in *The Castle*, which is unfinished precisely because K.'s life is unfinished, because he leans to a possible future, even if, paradoxically, the act of leaning exists in stasis. The question is how can time be experienced as both static and dynamic, and how can a future be both open and closed. A close examination of the phenomenon of time in terms of a symbolic world is necessary for the answer.

2. Time

Temporality, Heidegger said, is a "falling"[44]—but it is not a falling through any medium. If temporality fell through a medium, say through space, then space would be somehow outside of time, and time would thus be defined at its border areas, that is, in terms of space. And to spatialize time is to preserve that separation of subject and object that our primary experience in a symbolic world tells us is false.

Yet, sitting in my room, I wonder how "time" can possibly be in it, in the space of the room, except in the form of the gradual decay of its objects. The actual space of my room is apparently no different from what it was yesterday, last week, or last year. Space, in a certain sense, must be timeless, and time must be encapsulated in a subjectivity. I could say, as Bergson says about consciousness,[45] that my room is in time in that it interpenetrates itself in time, but on the face of it, that is a meaningless, tautological statement. A great deal of the difficulty entailed in talking about time is due to the dead ends that the tautologies and paradoxes of language throw in front of one's assertions. "My room interpenetrates itself"; "time falls, but not through anything." The problem stems from the fact that language is a fixed

44. Heidegger, *Being and Time*, p. 421.
45. Bergson, *Time and Free Will*, p. 101.

entity, while time is a moving one; as a cultural entity, language is fixed, just as my room and the furniture in it, as cultural entities, are fixed.

But is language only a cultural entity? Is it a timeless package of meanings one animates by picking up and using them? No, because meanings only exist in predefined boundaries (as timeless) when the words that comprise language exist in isolation. And words in isolation, as in a dictionary, are not language. In language, words are always in context, and they delimit or expand each other, play upon each other; they gesture toward and away from each other.[46] Since we use language, not words, we do not pick up words one by one and then combine them to form meanings. "Speech," Merleau-Ponty says, "does not translate ready-made thought, but accomplishes it," and it does this in the act of speaking.[47] Then what about the space around me—my room and its furniture? Do I "pick up" objects and then animate them in time? Clearly not, as the previous section of this chapter implied. My room does not exist in isolation outside of me but exists in the context *of* me and gestures toward me, plays upon me, disposes of me, delimits me, as and with my gestures toward it, my playing upon it, disposing of it, delimiting it.

I couldn't possibly exist in an encapsulated time, for there would be no connection between myself and the world outside if I did. If I tried to walk around in a timeless room, the floor would not slide concurrently beneath my feet, and either I would never arrive at the other side of the room or I would already simply be there. My act of moving implies that my feet can extend and meet and dispose of an area of floor, and this implies that that area already exists in a certain relationship to me. As we have seen, many aphasics, for whom this relationship doesn't exist, cannot walk across their rooms. And, as we have also seen, this relationship is the basis of the symbolic world. This symbolic world, which is neither subjective nor objective, always exists in and of time. If the world were objective and timeless, I could not even walk around things, because to walk

46. See Blackmur, *Language as Gesture*.
47. Merleau-Ponty, *Phenomenology*, p. 178.

around something implies that there is a gap between me and the other side of things; and this gap cannot simply be broken up into units, since the concept "unit" contains an instantaneousness that it preserves no matter how many units are added together, an instantaneousness that is manifest for any number of units when only one of them is manifest. The gap must be a lapse, and that very intersection of myself and the symbolic world must be temporal.

It is important that the sense in which that intersection is temporal be made clear. The connection that exists between me and the chair when I touch it, or even when I see it, is a connection in time, not a connection that exists as a pipeline pumping time into the chair; it is a connection that participates in the structure already uniting my chair and me. And this structure, in turn, is not like a hanger inside a shirt, but rather interpenetrates my chair and me; it is inseparable from things and me, since it is the symbolic world. Structure is nonspatial. The structure of a Bach fugue is not in the score (we can't hear the score), not in the piano or the fingers passing over the keys, not in my ear or eardrums or even exclusively in my consciousness. It is not in any of these to the exclusion of the others, and is not in all of them as a sum. Rather it unfolds through them and brings them together in the time that it constitutes. Time itself, in this sense, is a structure similar to a musical piece, as Bergson and others have noted.[48] And because time is such a structure, because it is not encapsulated, the space it penetrates is forced to bend across it, or as Whitehead puts it, to stretch with it.[49] This, Capek shows, is the implication of Einstein's theory.[50] And it is why both Hegel and Whitehead define space as a relationship between events, not between objects.[51] Time in this sense unites juxtaposition and succession, the two relationships that define space and time, respectively, in the classical world.

48. Bergson, *Time and Free Will,* p. 105. See also Straus, *Primary World,* p. 56.

49. Cited in Capek, *Contemporary Physics,* p. 170.

50. Ibid., pp. 175ff.

51. Hegel, quoted in Heidegger, *Being and Time,* pp. 481–82; Alfred North Whitehead, *The Concept of Nature* (Cambridge, 1920), p. 142.

The symbolic world is above all dynamic; it is time that stuns this world into life and gives to it its very power to unite contradictory things. Thus the problem of defining time as "falling" has begun to be solved. Since time is united with space, falling is of the medium itself as well as through that medium. Time is what falls through itself. Or, as Merleau-Ponty puts it, time is both "a general flight out of itself"[52] and "a flow which never leaves itself."[53] Time falls and accumulates its falling and accumulates the world of its falling, all in a motion which is itself, which is time.

All of this is illustrated in an extraordinary poem by James Dickey titled "Falling." Dickey's poem tells of an airline stewardess on a plane who is swept through an emergency door when it suddenly springs open. The poem, about two hundred and fifty lines long, accompanies her on her fall to the earth and recounts the horrible thrill of this experience "that no one has ever lived through." But the point of the poem is that everyone, in a sense, "lives" through this experience; everyone falls toward his death. Falling in the poem becomes the primordial experience of time that we all undergo. It is as if we were released from all the bulky interference that objectivity crowds us with, and the repressed experience that lies beneath that bulk were allowed to stand forth, or to "fall," naked. The last act of the stewardess, before the earth finally swells up to meet her, is to strip off her clothes and fall naked, an act that expresses the helpless freedom the bare experience of falling is.

"Helpless freedom" is only one of the many paradoxes that describe the feeling of the poem and that also describe the experience of time. Heidegger calls time an "anticipatory resoluteness,"[54] and this enables the stewardess to begin experimenting with her falling, to accept it and play with it. "She develops interest she turns in her maneuverable body," and in that turning feels for the first time the excitement of her body in its world, in its falling.

52. Merleau-Ponty, *Phenomenology*, p. 419.
53. Ibid., p. 425.
54. Heidegger, *Being and Time*, p. 372.

she clasps it all
To her and can hang her hands and feet in it in peculiar
    ways and
Her eyes opened wide by wind, can open her mouth as
    wide wider and suck
All the heat from the cornfields can go down on her back with
    a feeling
Of stupendous pillows stacked under her and can turn turn
    as to someone
In bed smile, understood in darkness can go away slant
    slide
Off tumbling into the emblem of a bird with its wings half-
    spread
Or whirl madly on herself in endless gymnastics in the growing
    warmth

The stewardess's helpless freedom is fully helpless, but as she is realizing, fully free; she snatches at her existence, she makes it up, and she glides with it. The image of freedom is the bird, and she opens her jacket like a bird's wings, begins to fly, and "turns gravity / Into a new condition showing its other side like a moon." The other side of gravity is weightlessness, and the synthesis of weight and weightlessness is the stewardess's experience of falling, therefore of time.

This should be distinguished from the experience of time in Burroughs, where weightlessness and weight—flying, floating, being released, and sinking, settling, being trapped—are two separate polarities of time. Their combination occurs only in a kind of atomistic instant that is obsessively repeated, the instant when death takes place at the climax of sexual activity. Burroughs' world and the structures of Western thought have in common this obsession with the concept of "atom"; in general, the only way Western thought can conceive of time is to break it up into such atomistic instants (as in Hume or Descartes) as those that combine weight and weightlessness in Burroughs. But in Dickey's "Falling," weight and weightlessness stretch across time—they *are* time in their unity; not time broken up into a series of "nows," but time as it flows out of itself; not time as a system of objective, discrete positions, but time that unites and synthesizes total mobility and total immobility. In other words, the falling of the stewardess is also a floating; there is a stasis, a timelessness, at the heart of its movement.

This stasis, timelessness, or weightlessness, and its relation to the flow of time need to be more fully explained. Within the structures of Western thought, there have been attempts to overcome the atomistic bias of descriptions of time by comparing the flow of time to that of a river (as Bergson does). But this description doesn't address itself to that enigma by which the present slides by and yet is always here; it fails to account for the stasis at the heart of the movement of time. It polarizes these two aspects of time, stasis and movement; it extracts the presence of the present out of its unity with the flow of time and places it outside that flow as a kind of observer on the bank of a river, as an entity past which the stream of events travels. This is the implication of those descriptions of time that assert that a new present is always coming at us and the old one is going away, no matter how fluid this movement from new to old is conceived to be. Such descriptions always isolate us as an entity to which time happens; consequently we are returned to the problem this section began with: time falling through an external medium and defined at its border areas—and spatialized.

Needed is a description of time that can dynamically unite both the sliding away and the presence of the present, both its weight and weightlessness, without allowing them to fall apart into polarities and without uniting them only in atomistic instants. The existentialists have perhaps best accomplished this description; for them, time is what unites the presence and absence of the present, unites weight and weightlessness, movement and stasis, and, in general, Being and Nonbeing. Sartre puts it this way: "The present is precisely this negation of being, this escape from being, inasmuch as being is *there* as that from which one escapes. . . . Thus we have precisely defined the fundamental meaning of the Present: the Present *is not*. . . . It is impossible to grasp the Present in the form of an instant, for the instant would be the moment when the present *is*. But the present is not; it makes itself present in the form of flight."[55] This is exactly the experience of Dickey's poem. There are no "nows" in the poem except the one that kills time, the moment of impact with the earth that throws time totally into the past. The only "instant" in the poem is that which was. And there is no polarity of stasis and flow, of the person who falls and the act of falling. There is rather a perfect unity of passing and presence, a perfect timelessness of time that allows the stewardess to glide, roll, and swoop, to "take up her body / And fly," to become into a totally open future.

The stewardess can become into an open future only by being propelled forward out of the great weight of a closed past. I should say a closing past, since the past, rather than being a static bulk, is always simultaneously catching up with the present and falling behind it. If the present is not, then the past unites the presence and passing of time. This argument applies also to the future: if the present is not, then the future combines the presence and arriving of time, since it is always falling back into the present and leaping ahead of it. The point is that the present is not because it is a unity of the two most contradictory things, the past and the future. It is a unity of these, not simply an intersection of them. This constitutes the central enigma of time, an extension of its weight and weightlessness, which Heidegger has expressed in the concept of the "ecstases" of time.

"Ecstasis" means "standing outside" (for example, Donne's use of the word in "The Extasie"), and the ecstases of time are the past, present, and future, the three relationships of time that stand outside each other.[56] These are ecstases of a being that in turn stands outside of itself, a being that is present wholly in each of its parts. So time stands both in and out of itself; as Heidegger puts it, "temporality is the primordial 'outside-of-itself' in and for itself."[57] And Merleau-Ponty says, "my present outruns itself in the direction of an immediate future and an immediate past and impinges upon them where they actually are,

55. *Being and Nothingness*, trans. Hazel E. Barnes (New York, 1956), p. 123.
56. Heidegger, *Being and Time*, p. 377.
57. Ibid.

namely in the past and in the future themselves."[58] The past and the future are fully past and future—and fully present. With regard to the past, this amounts to saying that falling is always a falling *out* of itself; it simultaneously retains the past and throws it away. As Sartre puts it, "everything happens as if the Present were a perpetual hole in being—immediately filled up and perpetually reborn."[59] Or as Whitehead puts it, time is "the perpetual transition of nature into novelty."[60] In this sense the future for the stewardess is always opening, and the past always closing.

But the concept of the ecstases of time also means that the opposite is true, that falling is a falling *into* itself, that the future is virtually present in the present, and that the future is always closing and the past always opening. This amounts to saying that the future impact of the stewardess with the earth intersects the perpetual present of her falling, and seals that present—the impact by which she buries herself in the world and dies is a condition by which she is always *in* the world. This radical sense of being-in-the-world is expressed by Dickey at both ends of the poem: at the beginning when he says, "She is hung high up in the overwhelming middle of things in her / Self," and at the finish when he describes her as literally buried in herself, or in the world.

Neither of these senses of the ecstases of time is true without the other: the future and the past are both always opening and always closing; each shifts and transforms with the movement of time, and falling is both a falling into and out of itself. Falling is always a momentum, and it gathers itself; but because it also loses itself, the expression of that momentum is in the future as well as in the past: in the earth below, as the poem makes clear, as well as in the sky above. Falling is growth: it is that action which both gathers and loses itself, that action in which the future pours into the past and swells it—and that action in which the past pours into the future and swells it:

58. Merleau-Ponty, *Phenomenology*, p. 418.
59. *Being and Nothingness*, p. 147.
60. *The Concept of Nature*, p. 178.

nine farms hover close   widen   eight of them separate,
leaving
One in the middle   then the fields of that farm do the same
there is no
Way to back off

The momentum of the poem tells us that falling is the present, but, Sartre says, the present is not. So falling is the past and the future united in a single act, not despite but because of the fact that the past and the future are where they are, in the past and in the future. Falling is an act that is not only a falling but also a rising. This is to say that if the stewardess is the world of her falling, then she is that world, as Heidegger says, which comes "towards itself futurally in such a way that it comes back."[61] She is her world and she is not her world, since her world, the world itself, is rising up to meet her.

This is why the point of view toward the end of the poem shifts often to the world below the stewardess, and why the action of rising occurs with reference to that world:

She goes toward   the blazing-bare lake
Her skirts neat   her hands and face warmed more and more
by the air
Rising from pastures of beans   and under her   under chenille
bedspreads
The farm girls are feeling the goddess in them struggle and rise
brooding . . .
and will wake
To see the woman they should be   struggling on the rooftree to
become
Stars: for her the ground is closer   water is nearer

The stewardess is not her world, because her world is below; yet she is her world because her falling is also a rising. Thus she begins to feel the same rising sexuality that the farm girls feel as she runs her hands "deeply between / Her thighs"—also "for her the ground is closer." This dynamic unity of opposites, of is and is not, will cease only when the simultaneous rising and fall-

61. Heidegger, *Being and Time*, p. 373.

ing of time ceases, when the past and the future totally close by
being passed and arrived (not passing and arriving), and when
the stewardess is reduced to herself in the instant—"This is
it THIS"—that paralyzes time and funnels the process of growth
into death.

Time is and is not itself; it is falling. The way in which time
unites opposites in Dickey's poem—weight and weightlessness,
helplessness and freedom, immobility and mobility, passing and
presence, falling and rising—and unites them not by reducing
one to the other, but by preserving the full meaning of each, is
an indication of the sense in which time is at the core of the symbolic world, as the very membrane which holds that world together. And as a unity of Being and Nonbeing, that membrane
holds the symbolic world apart also, unites unity and multiplicity in such a way that they are and are not each other. The
stewardess in "Falling" is her world by not being her world: she
is, as Sartre puts it, "the being which is its own nothingness of
being."[62]

This is to say that time is that phenomenon which unites both
aspects of schizophrenia, separation and mergence, the map and
the garden, either-or and both. Laing describes the experience
of schizophrenia as that of a voyage, but a voyage for which
there are no navigational charts.[63] As with Marlow in *Heart of
Darkness*, the voyage taken without a map is that motion in
which the person becomes his movement; it is the experience of
time, of falling into and out of oneself. Laing quotes one patient
who perfectly describes this feeling: "But I had this feeling all
the time of—er—moving back—even backwards and forwards
in time, that I was not just living in the present moment."[64] In
this sense, schizophrenia, as a temporal and dynamic experience,
unites the garden and the map: it propels us forward by reach-
ing back into the garden, and thus unfolds the map only as it is
experienced, only as it bends across time, bringing Being and
Nonbeing together. Or to return to a theme discussed in Chap-

62. *Being and Nothingness*, p. 117.
63. *Politics of Experience*, p. 117.
64. Ibid., p. 128.

ter One, there is no fall out of the garden into the map, but a falling, an act that embraces the condition of Adam and Eve both before and after the Fall, an act that unites the Fall and the Redemption in that it is both a falling and a rising, and an act that is virtual in every moment of our lives.

Before considering some of the specific ways in which time lies at the core of the symbolic world, particularly with regard to the experience of the body and of objects, there is another aspect of Dickey's poem that needs to be discussed. That is the poem as a poem, as a form which itself can be considered according to the structure of falling. There is a kind of improvised inevitability to Dickey's poem, as there is to so much modern literature, a temporal form that is the antithesis of the already constituted space of realistic and naturalistic fiction. As Feidelson asserts, the elements of a poem interpenetrate each other, in that any relation of part to part is also a relation of part to whole.[65] This is equivalent to saying that the space of a poem unfolds in time, that the elements of a poem are not simply juxtaposed but play upon each other in the act that constitutes the poem. This is certainly true of Dickey's poem: just as the act of falling is not a series of discrete positions but a unity of presence and passing, and just as falling continually relates to its wholeness by falling into and out of itself, so the elements of the poem "Falling" are transformed as our eyes fall from line to line, and the past of the poem never remains as a static bulk but changes qualitatively with each new presence in it.

Formally, a poem is similar to Straus's description of music. We do not, he says, add the sounds of a musical piece together mathematically in order to arrive at a whole. The piece is rather a living transformation of its elements, and "we apprehend the unity already while listening; it is not constructed in retrospect. . . . In other words, we organize our experience as becoming beings."[66] We always perceive the whole of a poem in each element of it, and we do this while falling through the poem. In Dickey's "Falling," the act the poem describes, the act of the

65. *Symbolism in American Literature*, p. 60.
66. *Primary World*, p. 56.

poem itself, and our act of reading the poem are all held in a unity, the unity of falling. The sense of a poem as act, says Burke, unites form and content,[67] and the particular temporal act of falling accomplishes that unity, and accomplishes it in the unity of the poet and reader as well. The experience of poetry is that of time, a fact Stevens has expressed in his poem "A Primitive Like an Orb":

> It is and it
> Is not and, therefore, is. In the instant of speech,
> The breadth of an accelerando moves,
> Captives the being, widens—and was there.

Realism and naturalism neutralize this experience by rendering language transparent, by hollowing out the act of reading. This is why the world of realistic fiction is spatial, in the Newtonian sense, and why time in that world is spatialized. And it is why that world is exactly the opposite of the symbolic world described in this chapter.

Form, in literature that is specifically a reaction to realism and naturalism, is temporal. This view is directly opposed to a theory of modern literature that has received a great deal of attention, Joseph Frank's theory of spatial form. According to Frank, writers like Eliot, Pound, Proust, and Joyce "ideally intend the reader to apprehend their work spatially, in a moment of time, rather than as a sequence."[68] Thus, while the "word-groups" of *The Waste Land,* for example, "follow one another in time, their meaning does not depend on this temporal relationship," and "to be properly understood, these word-groups must be juxtaposed with one another and perceived simultaneously."[69] This means that modern works of literature like *Ulysses* are not read but reread, since only through reflection, not through the temporal act of reading, can such works be apprehended.[70] "The reader is forced to read *Ulysses* in exactly the same manner as

---

67. *The Philosophy of Literary Form,* p. 75.
68. Joseph Frank, "Spatial Form in Modern Literature," *The Widening Gyre* (New Brunswick, N.J., 1963), p. 9.
69. Ibid., p. 12.
70. Ibid., p. 19.

he reads modern poetry, that is, by continually fitting fragments together and keeping allusions in mind until, by reflexive reference, he can link them to their complements."[71]

Frank's theory depends upon a certain definition of space and time, and it is significant that his definition is precisely what constitutes space and time for classical Western thought. Space, he says, following Lessing, consists of a relationship of juxtaposition, and time of a relationship of consecutiveness.[72] Time is unable to handle the cross-references necessary to apprehend modern poetry, since it is pure succession, since its parts are mutually exclusive and succeed each other as a series of "nows." Thus, form is spatial. But space and time defined in this way are so opposite that they are the same; both are inertly spatial, and both are atomized; and Frank has made his point before he gets to it. Frank simply carries into the twentieth century the false split between space and time implicit in Greek thought and explicitly incorporated into seventeenth-century thought (it is significant that he refers to Locke as a precursor of Lessing), the split that reduces time to spatiality. His view of modern literature is the same as my view of realism and naturalism, that of a literature structured to enable a consciousness distant from it to apprehend it as one apprehends a map frozen in space.

The alternative is the structure of time as falling, time whose elements are not mutually exclusive but time which embraces and transforms the relationship of juxtaposition, time whose ecstatic structure asserts that all of time is present in each of its parts, as time falls in and out of itself. The refutation of Frank is in all that I have said about time and temporal form. There is a spatial aspect to temporal form, but it is a space united with time, not split from it, a space that bends across time. For it to be necessary, as Frank asserts, to finish a poem before I get a sense of the whole implies that the poem builds mathematically, piece by piece, up to that whole. But for the space of a poem to bend across the temporal act of reading means that the whole of the poem is given in each of its parts, and further means that

71. Ibid., p. 18.
72. Ibid., p. 6.

that whole cannot be conceived of as a bulk, but is something dynamic that changes and becomes as we constitute it in the act of reading, in the act of falling into, through, and out of it.

This is so much the case in *The Waste Land* and *Ulysses* (Frank's two major examples of "spatial form") that it is thematically as well as formally a major element in each. Both works concern themselves with a kind of map space; in Eliot, the map of London, and in Joyce, the map of Dublin. In both works this map space is established by overviews: the morning traffic over London Bridge in *The Waste Land*, or in an extended sense, the juxtaposed overviews of several different classes of society in section two of that poem; and the similar juxtaposition, specifically set in the map of Dublin, in *Ulysses*. But in each work the structure of the map is countered by structures of interpenetration. The shifting consciousness of *The Waste Land* metamorphoses into a number of different figures who are and are not themselves, who can't be nailed down by the relationship of discreteness that a map and "spatial form" necessitate. Eliot's authority for this is the best and is well known: "Just as the one-eyed merchant, seller of currants, melts into the Phoenician Sailor, and the latter is not wholly distinct from Ferdinand Prince of Naples, so all the women are one woman, and the two sexes meet in Tiresias."[73] The relationship of interpenetration is impossible in a space defined purely by juxtaposition; it is time that interpenetrates itself in the act of falling in and out of itself. The metamorphoses of the narrator of *The Waste Land* necessitate a temporal form, a form that is its own motion, not one that moves through an already existing space but one that creates that space as it moves. The map terrain of *The Waste Land* exists for the purpose of being ripped up and carried along by the temporal flood that falls through it, a flood that spills into the actual content of the poem at the end.

Similarly, in *Ulysses* acts of consciousness are given as interpenetrations of each other in time. To search for clues by which we can piece the puzzle of the novel together and attain "a uni-

73. *The Complete Poems and Plays: 1909–1950* (New York, 1952), p. 52.

fied spatial apprehension"[74] of it in retrospect is to leave behind the most important dimension of it, the novel as an act or series of acts of consciousness. *Ulysses* is such an elaborately structured novel that there are, of course, juxtapositions in it; but as Frank Kermode says, "there is a polarity of static and dynamic; there is a mimesis of change, potential, as well as a structure of the kind we call spatial."[75] Indeed this is a unity rather than a polarity, and the static is swallowed up in the temporal, in the acts of consciousness and language that are not only a "mimesis of change" in the novel but are change itself.

Molly's soliloquy is the emotional and structural summary of these acts, and it is totally impossible to think of the soliloquy spatially: it unfolds in time and becomes, as the novel as a whole does. Frank's theory presumes that the novel is broken up into chunks or pieces, which we rearrange reflexively. But Molly's soliloquy does not descend from piece to piece, from "now" to "now," as on a stairway; rather it descends with the passing presence of falling; it accumulates itself and comes toward and away from itself, as Molly is literally "falling" asleep. And we know from the nature of Joyce's next work, *Finnegans Wake*, that all of *Ulysses* falls into Molly's act of falling asleep, that the novel as itself and as a summary of the novel form gathers momentum into sleep in preparation for the act of dreaming that is *Finnegans Wake*. Even those sections of *Ulysses* that are naturalistic and spatial are carried in the temporal form of the novel and dynamized by it.

It is insufficient to talk about simply spatial cross-references in either *The Waste Land* or *Ulysses*. The point of repeated images, of cross-references, is that the image accumulates new meaning with each new appearance, since it is arrived at in the act of reading, in time; it therefore possesses not only its first appearance but a whole intermediary part of the poem or novel, as the past that constitutes its presence. Each time we arrive at the line "Those are pearls that were his eyes" in *The Waste Land*, it has gathered a momentum and no longer means what it

74. Frank, *Widening Gyre*, p. 19.
75. *Sense of an Ending*, p. 177.

previously meant. The case is somewhat like Bergson's description of listening to a clock: we do not put the successive ticks of the clock on a line and apprehend them spatially beside each other; rather we perceive one beat in the other, "each permeating the other and organizing themselves like the notes of a tune."[76] This is no doubt why F. R. Leavis compares the form of *The Waste Land* to a musical piece, and asserts that its themes, like those in music, move in and out of each other.[77]

It remains only to examine the nature of the dynamization of objects and of the body that the temporal dimension accomplishes, and that is the experience of schizophrenia, of the symbolic world. This is a prelude to looking closely at a unique example of temporal form in literature, the sequence of poems in Theodore Roethke's *Praise to the End!*

3. Time, Objects, and the Body

To summarize what has been said: as Straus puts it, "we experience ourselves together with and facing things,"[78] and this is to say that we experience things as they face us and therefore experience ourselves *in* things, in the organization they have from our point of view. This organization is specifically a temporal one: we know things are "slightly turned" because we can walk around them, because distances exist in the world that are not merely geometrical distances. A distance is always my distance, a lapse for my body, as I fall and rise toward and from things and therefore toward and from myself, in the ecstases of time. This is why things "rise" up before me and "fall" behind me when I move through the world.

I have said that in such a world it is inappropriate to use the word "object" if that word is taken to indicate an objective thing lying outside of me, isolated from me and from the world. As seen in Chapters One and Two, this view of objects supposes

---

76. Bergson, *Time and Free Will*, p. 105.
77. "*The Waste Land*," in Hugh Kenner, ed., *T. S. Eliot: A Collection of Critical Essays* (Englewood Cliffs, N.J., 1963), pp. 95–96.
78. *Primary World*, p. 180.

that a changeless substance underlies or is inherent in each object and that all attributes of an object—color, taste, shape, even its movement through space—are secondary qualities. This division of things into primary and secondary qualities is necessitated by the absolute space of the classical world; since objects exist as isolated, discrete entities in absolute space, their attributes also exist as isolated, discrete entities in space. Whitehead has pointed this out: "What we find in space are the red of the rose and the smell of the jasmine and the noise of cannon."[79] Objects are thus shattered, atomized; not only is there an inner core, a substance, which is divided from its external qualities, but also those qualities themselves are divided from each other, like broken armor. Thus objects are a perfect image of schizophrenia as originally defined, as a principle of separation.

The alternative to this view of objects lies in the definition of schizophrenia as a principle of integration, as a voyage in which the voyager unites with his motion—as time itself. The distinction between the full and the void upon which the classical conception of matter and objects depends is not valid in a space that has been dynamized by time and is therefore no longer absolute. As Capek points out, in the relativity theory, which explicitly unites time and space, matter is no longer a substance, a thing in itself, but is a displacement of the time-space continuum.[80] Ultimately the distinction between space and matter is a false one, which means that the distinction between time and matter is also false.

For this reason my analysis of time as falling also applies to the movement of objects: when an object moves, it does not change its location with respect to a medium, but in a sense becomes both its motion and the medium it is moving through. Such is the clear implication of modern physics: the relativity theory tells us that the mass of an object increases with its velocity,[81] and Heisenberg's Indeterminacy Principle shows that the velocity of a subatomic particle is inseparable from the par-

---

79. *The Concept of Nature*, p. 21.
80. Capek, *Contemporary Physics*, p. 270.
81. Max Jammer, *Concepts of Mass* (Cambridge, Mass., 1961), p. 170.

ticle itself, that is, it *is* the particle, and vice versa.[82] This is why the antinomy between corpuscular and wave theories of matter is a false one, as Capek shows.[83] My analysis of time does not apply simply to moving objects; it also reveals the sense in which every object is, in fact, a movement, an act, an event. Objects are not airtight packages that exist in or move through time and space. The opposite would be more accurate: time-space moves through objects, composes them, animates them. This is Whitehead's point when he says that objects are always situated in events and thus cannot be considered isolated "things."[84] The unity of time, space, and objects is given in the "passage of events" that is nature,[85] and "each object is in some sense ingredient throughout nature."[86] "In a certain sense, everything is everywhere at all times,"[87] and it is also itself in one place and one time.

The sense in which time falls in and out of itself, and therefore is and is not itself, is the fundamental condition of all objects in the world. It also enables those objects to be called symbols. Objects are both themselves and not themselves; they are both themselves and their medium, their world. This doesn't mean that objects are one fluid mergence into each other; such a mergence is simply the world as a solid block, the world as Other, and exists as the necessary opposite pole of objects as discrete, atomistic entities. The true sense of an object is neither of these, but both, in a condition that unites them.

As the physicist Schrodinger says, all things have both the discrete structure of particles and the continuous structure of a wave or field.[88] All things exist both in and out of themselves, not only subatomic particles but all things we see and touch, all objects carved out of our own visual dimension, all symbols in the symbolic world. An object's shape is not a coat it wears, a

82. Capek, *Contemporary Physics*, pp. 292–94.
83. Ibid., p. 376.
84. *The Concept of Nature*, p. 169.
85. Ibid., p. 142.
86. Ibid., p. 145.
87. Quoted in Capek, *Contemporary Physics*, p. 271.
88. "Our Image of Matter," in Rapport and Wright, *Physics*, p. 235.

thing in itself, as the shapes of bodies and objects are in Burroughs; nor does that shape belong to the world around the object as the limit of that world. Rather, "shape" is the membrane that unites the object and its world, and unites the object, world, and my point of view. It is the intersection of these three and manifests itself as both the negation and assertion of the object, as the act that both encloses and liberates it, as the object itself and as everything else. This is true not only of shape but of all an object's attributes—color, weight, taste. The reason an object is extended through all other objects is because it is extended through itself, through its attributes, just as each of those attributes, as Sartre points out, is extended through the others: "It is the sourness of the lemon which is yellow, it is the yellow of the lemon which is sour."[89] This is why, Straus points out, when we see with our eyes, we do not see pictorial representations of objects but objects themselves;[90] the object itself, as well as its texture, its weight, and its taste, is fully present in its visual appearance.

There is a persistent strain in modern poetry that has a great deal to do with this sense of objects. The conclusion to Yeats's "Among School Children" is one example:

> O chestnut-tree, great-rooted blossomer,
> Are you the leaf, the blossom or the bole?
> O body swayed to music, O brightening glance,
> How can we know the dancer from the dance?

The answer to both questions is each possible answer. The chestnut tree manifests itself in each of its parts, as with the Tree of Life; and the tree can be a unity of these parts only because it is totally proliferated in each of them. Similarly, the dancer is and is not herself in the perfect unity of the dance. The dance is not a shape imposed upon her body; it is shape as act, as the unity of the dancer with her motion and her medium, her space, just as in modern physics a particle is perfectly united with its trajectory, its act.

89. *Being and Nothingness*, p. 186.
90. *Phenomenological Psychology*, p. 258.

Many of Wallace Stevens' poems are also about this sense of objects. His persistent theme is the relationship of seer, world, and object. In "Someone Puts a Pineapple Together" he asserts that each person sees in the pineapple a "tangent of himself," and that "the fruit so seen" is also "a part of the nature that he contemplates." In "Connoisseur of Chaos" he says that "the pensive man . . . sees that eagle float / For which the intricate Alps are a single nest." The point of both poems is that the wholeness of the world is composed by a single object that opens upon it, the pineapple or eagle, and this unity of object and world in turn passes through the perspective that opens upon *it*, the someone who puts the pineapple together or "the pensive man" who sees the eagle.

This is why the jar in "Anecdote of the Jar" can "make the slovenly wilderness / Surround that hill." And it is why such an object as the jar couldn't possibly be an inert thing enclosed in its shape; it reaches out for the eyes of whoever is watching and with those eyes arranges the world around it—it infuses the world with itself and itself with the world by means of the point of view, the body, it is anchored in. Objects are like the glass of water in the poem of that title; they are both defined and released by their boundaries:

> That the glass would melt in heat,
> That the water would freeze in cold,
> Shows that this object is merely a state,
> One of many, between two poles.

The two poles are not only heat and cold but also the seer and the world. If objects are events as Whitehead says, they are events that mediate between the body of the seer and the world, events that carry that body into the world and the world into that body.

The sense of an object as an event rather than a thing goes hand in hand with the sense of form as act, as temporal form, which characterizes a great deal of modern poetry. Because an object is an event, its form or shape is not a reified suit of armor but an organic act, a wave, a process—which is true for those objects called poems also. Coleridge made this point in a well-known statement that indicates the changes occurring in the structure of Western thought even in the nineteenth century:

> The form is mechanic, when on any given material we impress a pre-determined form, not necessarily arising out of the properties of the material;—as when to a mass of wet clay we give whatever shape we wish it to retain when hardened. The organic form, on the other hand, is innate; it shapes, as it develops, itself from within, and the fulness of its development is one and the same with the perfection of its outward forms . . . each exterior is the physiognomy of the being within,—its true image reflected and thrown out from the concave mirror. . . .[91]

This idea of form as act is another expression of the basic structural principle of schizophrenia, as the term has been used in this chapter; it is what unites a poem and its parts, matter and its attributes, inner and outer, body and world; it is what animates the symbolic world and makes possible its quality of being symbolic; it is the temporal dimension as it can only exist, in objects, not an object itself; and it is nature itself, the world of events that falls in and out of itself in the ecstases of time.

Perhaps the best way to summarize and conclude this chapter is to look closely at that aspect of ourselves which is woven into the world by objects themselves—the body—and to look at it in terms of temporal form. In a sense, the implication of all I have said about objects is that objects are bodies, possessing for us the same kind of animation and structural organization that our bodies do. This enables objects to be symbols, to be incarnate. And it is possible only because the converse is not true, because my body is not primarily an object, since it does not exist, for me, in objective space. Merleau-Ponty says, "I am not in front of my body, I am in it, or rather I am it."[92] My body is not a collection of parts juxtaposed in space, as in the woodcuts of

---

91. S. T. Coleridge, "Lectures and Notes of 1818," *Lectures and Notes on Shakespeare and Other English Poets*, ed. T. Ashe (London, 1893), p. 229.
92. Merleau-Ponty, *Phenomenology*, p. 150.

COLLEGE OF THE SEQUOIAS
LIBRARY

Vesalius. Rather it describes space, generates space, through the affective power of its actions. Merleau-Ponty says in a beautiful passage:

> My body appears to me as an attitude directed toward a certain existing or possible task. And indeed its spatiality is not, like that of external objects or like that of "spatial sensation," a *spatiality of position*, but a *spatiality of situation*. If I stand in front of my desk and lean on it with both hands, only my hands are stressed and the whole of my body trails behind them like the tail of a comet. It is not that I am unaware of the whereabouts of my shoulders or back, but these are simply swallowed up in the position of my hands, and my whole posture can be read so to speak in the pressure they exert on the table.[93]

The spatiality of my body is temporal; it literally bends, in this example, across the body's posture, its direction, its gesture. As in the temporal structure of objects, the whole of the body is present in each of its parts. When I lean with my hands on the desk, "my whole posture can be read so to speak in the pressure they exert on the table."

In any action I perform, the parts of my body are always variously absorbed in each other. When I dive into a pool, my body rushes ahead of me into my fingers and even beyond them. The movements of the body are always accumulations, and they accumulate the entire body itself. The movement of my hand down to my shoe is present in its arrival, and that movement is a complicated momentum that passes from my fingers through my arm, shoulders, and trunk, even to my foot itself. It is a momentum in that it gathers more of itself, more of the body; it gathers it in a gradual accumulation similar to the gradations of movement when I walk through the world, from the rapidly approaching objects in front of me to the sluggish ones in the distance. The structure of the body is a temporal form in the fullest sense: the body falls through itself in the performance of its actions and can do this because the whole of it is present in each of its parts, just as the whole of time is present in each of

93. Ibid., p. 100.

its ecstases. The whole of the body is accessible to each of its parts in the same way the past and future are accessible to the present—where it is, in the body. The body, like time and like objects, is and is not itself in the unity of itself.

This should clarify the sense in which the body and the world are united. It is not only in the parts of my body that my whole body can be present; it is also in the objects of the world. To take a simple example: when a baseball player swings and strikes the ball, his whole body is gathered into the bat he holds, and that body doesn't flow back into itself until his follow-through subsides and he drops the bat. In an extended way, this is true of every action we perform in the world. I always cast out of myself when I walk, and come toward myself in the temporality of the body, just as the stewardess in Dickey's poem falls toward herself, toward the world, precisely by falling out of herself in the ecstases of time. This falling, since it is also a rising, is that very act of growth that constitutes my life span and fills out the world, uniting my growth and that of the world. The world and the body dovetail perfectly and couldn't do otherwise; they interpenetrate each other, which is why the body is also an object and why objects are also bodies. This was implied in all I said about time in the previous section; I couldn't walk about in a timeless space, because the floor would not slide beneath my feet concurrently with their movement. Time is the connection between my body and the world, but time is not a thing. It exists only *in* things, and the connection is always already given as a perfect unity of body and world, a temporal form.

Once again it is necessary to emphasize that this unity of body and world is not a mergence, since it preserves their autonomy in that very unity. Their unity is given where they are, in the body and in the world, just as the whole body is given where it is to each of its parts, and just as the past and the future are accessible to the present where they are, in the past and in the future. Mergence is possible only when the body and the world are split off from each other; as in Burroughs, mergence is the polar opposite of that split and is made possible by it.

What I have said about shape with regard to objects also applies to the body, and serves as an effective contrast to Burroughs. The body's shape is its form, and since the body is a temporal form, that shape both holds the body together and releases it into its parts and into the world. This is the opposite of the situation in Burroughs, where the shape or skin of the body is a thing-in-itself and has to be removed in order for the body to enter the world; and of course that entry into the world can be only a mergence with it. Shape in its true sense is a transformation of body and world. This can be seen in those primitive rituals in which a dancer clothes himself in the skin of an animal or a human victim. That skin doesn't simply lie across the dancer's body as a thing-in-itself; the dancer becomes the animal or victim—he doesn't portray him or become like him but unites his body with the animal or victim through the transforming act of its shape. This is the point of two recent poems based on such primitive rituals, James Dickey's "Approaching Prayer" and Galway Kinnell's "The Bear." Shape is thus simply temporal form, the unity of one's body and the world in the being and not-being of each other. This temporal form makes the symbolic world possible, the world in which Arieti's patient can become the Virgin Mary.

The unity of body and world has been one of the most common themes of surrealist poetry. I said in connection with Burroughs that surrealism stripped objects of their context, their function, and left them completely objective; hence the contradiction upon which surrealism depended for its dynamic finally neutralized itself, for the simple reason that objects stripped of everything that defines them couldn't possibly contradict. But not all surrealism—in fact, little of it—has been this pure. Although surrealist poetry is born out of an aesthetic that shatters the world into pieces, the best surrealist poets have picked up those pieces and woven them together, and in doing so have rejected the classical organizing principle of the world—objective space—for a more basic and true one, the body. This is why surrealism is the most important literary movement of this century, and why its impact is still being felt strongly today. Surrealism is that form which destroys objective space by breaking it down into its elements, mutually exclusive juxtaposed objects; and it is that form which uncovers the fundamental unity of the body and objects by weaving the world back into the temporal form of the body.

Two poems by the best of the early surrealists, André Breton and Paul Eluard, should illustrate this point. The title of one of Breton's books, *L'Union Libre*, has been translated as "Freedom of Love,"[94] but a more accurate translation, though less evocative, would be "The Free Unity." The point of the best-known poem in that book is the open, free unity of all things in the temporal medium of the body. Here are the opening lines:

> My wife with her hair of wood fire
> With her thoughts of heat lightning
> With her shape of an hourglass
> My wife with her shape of an otter in a tiger's teeth
> My wife with her mouth of a cockade and of a bouquet of stars
> of final grandeur
> With her teeth of the footprints of white mice on the white
> earth
> With her tongue of polished amber and glass
> My wife with her tongue of a stabbed host
> With her tongue of a doll that opens and shuts its eyes
> With her tongue of incredible stone
> My wife with her eyelashes of strokes of a child's writing
> With her eyebrows of the edge of a swallow's nest

As Whitehead says, each object is extended throughout nature, and as Breton shows, the crossroad of this extension of things is the body. The body is the form that composes everything; it is the ground for all textures, for all visual and auditory experience, for all movement; it literally mediates and synthesizes these in the unity that substantiates itself and animates things, as well as vice versa.

Eluard's short poem "You Are Everywhere" makes the same point:

94. By Edouard Roditi, in *Young Cherry Trees Secured against Hares* (New York, 1945). The translation that follows and that of Eluard's poem are my own.

You get up the water unfolds
You lie down the water blossoms

You are the water diverted from its abysses
You are the earth which takes root
And upon which everything establishes itself

You blow bubbles of silence in the desert of noise
You chant nocturnal hymns on the strings of the rainbow
You are everywhere you abolish all roads

You sacrifice time
To the eternal youth of exact burning
Which conceals nature in reproducing it

Woman you place in the world a body always equal
Your own

You are its resemblance

The last line brings to mind the mirror space of realistic fiction that objectifies the body by reproducing it; Eluard's point is that the body is its own reproduction. The body thus unites subject and object in a new space that abolishes mirrors and therefore abolishes all maps ("you abolish all roads"). This is why "you are everywhere" and why, in the space of the body, the near is united with the far ("You get up the water unfolds"). In realism, the polarization of near and far, here and there, creates a map space; in Burroughs and in Conrad's *Heart of Darkness*, the other pole of this map space is mergence. But in Eluard's poem, the unity of body and world is one in which near and far can unite without merging, without obliterating themselves. This is simply the experience of our everyday world, an experience we all know once the film that objectivity lays over the world is peeled off. The tree I see out the window is both there and here; and it is not simply an image of the tree that is here, but the tree itself, since it is not a projection of me that is there, but me myself. In this sense, I *am* my resemblance. This is because I am "the earth which takes root / And upon which everything establishes itself," while I *am* my body as well.

Examples of this kind of perception in surrealist poetry are endless. Here are four lines from Pablo Neruda's poem "Gentle-man without Company":

> this immense forest, entangled and breathing,
> hedges me around firmly on all sides forever
> with huge flowers like mouths and rows of teeth
> and black roots that look like fingernails and shoes.[95]

Similarly, Lorca says, "Your belly is a battle of roots, / your lips are a blurred dawn,"[96] and Bert Meyers, a contemporary American poet, says, "the eyelid of a shadow shuts the hills." But it is not simply the fusion of organs of the body with objects of the world that expresses the unity of body and world. It is in general an apprehension of a symbolic world, a world of transformations, whose parts dovetail, absorb each other, liberate each other, whose forms, like the form of the body, fall in and out of themselves in their temporality—all this expresses that unity. Here, for example, is W. S. Merwin's poem "Provision":

> All morning with dry instruments
> The field repeats the sound
> Of rain
> From memory
> And in the wall
> The dead increase their invisible honey
> It is August
> The flocks are beginning to form
> I will take with me the emptiness of my hands
> What you do not have you find everywhere

The unity of body and world, of inner and outer, enables even the vacancy of the self to open simultaneously into the world and the body. And this unity, in the symbolic world, makes possible a poem that bends perfectly across the feelings of the poet, a poem whose speech is the speech of the world, since the world is interfused by the temporal form of the body.

95. Translated by Robert Bly, in *Twenty Poems of Pablo Neruda*, trans. Robert Bly and James Wright (Madison, Minn., 1967).

96. "Casida of the Reclining Woman," trans. W. S. Merwin, in *The Selected Poems of Frederico Garcia Lorca*, ed. Francisco Garcia Lorca and Donald M. Allen (New York, 1955).

To return to the theme that began this chapter: the body as a temporal form structures the world of primitive experience and of schizophrenia as well. In schizophrenia, what happens to one's body is identical with what happens in the world,[97] and this often means, Laing shows, that the schizophrenic voyage finds its goal "in the being of animals, vegetables, and minerals."[98] Such a unity of body and world is the foundation of primitive experience also, and accounts for the many creation myths in which the world is born out of the dismembered parts of a god's body: rivers from his veins, grass from his hair, wind from his breath, and so on.[99] The simple fact that the world has parts, or objects, is insufficient to enable us to apprehend it as a world. As in schizophrenia and primitive experience, and as in poetry and temporality, the parts of the world unite on the ground of the body's temporal unity of whole and parts. Those parts, the multiplicity of the world, absorb and release each other in the being and not-being of themselves, in the falling into and out of each other. This is the world of the garden in the most complete sense, the world that unites subject and object, space and time, fantasy and reality, madness and sanity, and also unites all of these pairs together. Yet it is far from being a chaotic world, a world of confusion. It is that world, as in Stevens' poem, in which

> A. A violent order is disorder; and
> B. A great disorder is an order. These
> Two things are one.

And it is Theodore Roethke's world, the world of a schizophrenic who returns us to where we have always been, to the garden. Roethke's world is one in which objects are bodies, and the world and the body are one. It is a world in which this unity is filled out by time, and particularly by that aspect of time that unites falling and rising—growth.

97. Brown, *Love's Body*, p. 226.
98. *The Politics of Experience*, p. 104.
99. Eliade, *Mephistopheles*, p. 115.

5 / Theodore Roethke

In Marvell's "The Garden" there is a well-known passage that recalls one of the points Eluard's poem "You Are Everywhere" makes:

> The Mind, that Ocean where each kind
> Does straight its own resemblance find;
> Yet it creates, transcending these,
> Far other World, and other Seas;
> Annihilating all that's made
> To a green Thought in a green Shade.

Marvell begins by citing the classical doctrine of perception, which says that sense images of external objects are accompanied by images in consciousness and that the latter resemble the former as mirror images resemble real things. But then, as Eluard did with the line "you are its resemblance," Marvell undercuts that doctrine by giving the mirror image a kind of integrative autonomy, by annihilating the absolute two-term map relationship and asserting a dynamic unity of external and internal, of subjective and objective: "a green Thought in a green Shade." This is the condition of the garden, as I have been describing it. And the world of Roethke's poetry is above all a garden.

As we have seen, the garden is not the polar opposite of the map; rather the garden embraces and transforms the map, temporalizes it, unfolds it in time. The garden is not total mergence and confusion, a scrambling of all things and all objects together, but unites mergence and separation, unity and multiplicity. This is why the garden in Roethke's world is often a greenhouse, the meeting place of the human and nonhuman, the organic and the rational, the natural—Kenneth Burke has said—and the artificial.[1] Or as Roethke himself put it in his notebooks: "What was this greenhouse? It was a jungle and it was paradise. It was order and disorder."[2] Even when the setting of Roethke's poems is not a greenhouse, his world has this feature of uniting the garden and the map. It is the perfect illustration of the symbolic world described in the previous chapter, of the world that unites space and time, body and world, discreteness and mergence, Being and Nonbeing.

It is also the perfect illustration of the schizophrenia that unites madness and sanity. The first of Roethke's many bouts with "insanity" that landed him in the hospital, and earned him such titles as "manic-depressive neurotic," "manic-depressive psychotic," and "paranoid schizophrenic,"[3] occurred in 1935. One night he wandered into the woods near his apartment in University Park, Pennsylvania (he was teaching at Pennsylvania State). He got lost, cold, and wet, but eventually found a highway and thumbed home. He returned to the same woods the next morning, skipping his classes; later in the day he appeared at the dean's office in a disheveled condition, told off the dean, and was sent to the hospital. Roethke's own description of what happened to him in the woods is also a description of the world of his poetry, the "insane" world of the child, the primitive, and the schizophrenic: "For no reason I started to feel very good. Suddenly I knew how to enter into the life of everything around me. I knew how it felt to be a tree, a blade of grass, even a rabbit. I didn't sleep much. I just walked around with this wonderful feeling."[4]

1. "The Vegetal Radicalism of Theodore Roethke," *Sewanee Review*, LVIII (Winter 1950), 82.
2. Quoted in Allan Seager, *The Glass House: The Life of Theodore Roethke* (New York, 1968), p. 196.
3. Ibid., p. 101.
4. Ibid.

This is "madness." But as Roethke showed in the poems he wrote ten years later (those published in *The Lost Son* and *Praise to the End!*), this is the world of everyone, stripped of repression; it is the world of the child, not as we leave the perceptions of childhood behind, but as those perceptions underlie our continuing experience; it is the world of the garden, and it is the garden itself as the world. The irony of the attempts of others to treat Roethke's schizophrenia, to analyze him, to "help" him, is that they are the very ones who needed help, for their inability to see and feel as Roethke was able to, for their inability to enter into the life of everything around them. Roethke's perception is normal; theirs, and by implication ours, is abnormal, since it neutralizes the primary experience of the symbolic world, of the garden, with the forms of the map and of objectivity, by which here and there, inside and outside, are absolutely separated.

In Roethke, the garden is not only a place; it is also a mode of experiencing, an organization of experience, or better, a process, a way experience happens. And it is a process exactly the same as what Laing calls the healing voyage of schizophrenia. In the previous chapter we saw that the experience of time in this voyage is simultaneously a rising and a falling, a going forward and a going back. Roethke makes precisely this point about his *Lost Son* and *Praise to the End!* poems in a notebook entry: "To go back is to go forward."[5] In these poems, regression is also progression; time loops back to gather itself as it goes forward to meet itself. The "itself" that time loops back to gather lies in the prehistory of the world as well as in Roethke's childhood. The landscape of the poems is both the greenhouse operated by Roethke's father in Saginaw, Michigan, and the primordial garden previous to the rise of civilizations; and the inscape of the poems is both the emotional state of Roethke as an adult and the childhood experience of life as an undifferentiated whole previous to the emergence of adult consciousness. Children lose this undifferentiated whole as they grow into adult-

5. Quoted in ibid., p. 166.

hood. One must go back and recover it in order to become a full man. "To go back is to go forward."

The *Praise to the End!* poems are a developmental sequence of fourteen long, experimental poems about childhood and the growth out of childhood into adolescence, first published completely in *The Waking: Poems 1933–1953* (1953). Four of the poems were initially published in *The Lost Son* (1948), and the whole sequence except for the last poem, "O, Thou Opening, O," was published in *Praise to the End!* (1951). In Roethke's arrangement (which was not followed in the posthumous *Collected Poems*), the sequence is divided into two major sections, the first consisting of "Where Knock Is Open Wide," "I Need, I Need," "Bring the Day!" "Give Way, Ye Gates," "Sensibility! O La!" and "O Lull Me, Lull Me," and the second consisting of "The Lost Son," "The Long Alley," "A Field of Light," "The Shape of the Fire," "Praise to the End!" "Unfold! Unfold!" "I Cry, Love! Love!" and "O, Thou Opening, O."

Taken as a whole, the sequence represents one long poem, each part of which (that is, each poem) contains and reaffirms that whole. The movement of progression and regression, of expansion and deflation, occurs rhythmically in each poem and in the overall sequence in such a way that the sequence sways as a tree does, with a unified gradation of movements and countermovements, from the small and quick to the large and ponderous.

The sequence gains its vitality from its regressions that carry the poet and the reader—and the language of the poems—back into that timeless childhood experience of life as an undifferentiated whole, being a radical means of recovering that experience for everyday life. "Whole" is an abstract word; as an experience, however, it is real and tangible, and not always pleasant, as Roethke shows. In Roethke's sequence the human body often regresses to its polymorphous wholeness, its being as a blob, to the womb, just as the world often regresses into a confusion of all its objects together, into slime, and just as language often regresses into nonsense and playing with sounds. These three regressions are inseparable; they are one in structure and feeling in portions of the sequence. Roethke's most explicit description of them occurs in "The Shape of the Fire":

> Who, careless, slips
> In coiling ooze
> Is trapped to the lips,
> Leaves more than shoes;

> Must pull off clothes
> To jerk like a frog
> On belly and nose
> From the sucking bog.

> My meat eats me. Who waits at the gate?
> Mother of quartz, your words writhe into my ear.
> Renew the light, lewd whisper.

In this passage, the mergence of the world—mud—threatens to swallow and merge with the body, and both these images of mergence are followed by a regression of language into nonsense. One is reminded of Burroughs and of all the instances of mergence, especially those occurring in canals or swamps, in his novels. But unlike Burroughs, Roethke emerges from this primordial confusion and liquid mergence of all things, not by flying toward the opposite polarity, toward atomistic separateness, but by combining mergence and separateness in the unity of opposites that is the condition of the garden: by channeling into the world, into separateness, and carrying the wholeness from which that separateness is descended into every manifestation of it.

In terms of temporality, this means that the sequence is about the evolution out of timelessness into that world which unites Being and Nonbeing in time, which unites timelessness and time, the continual absence and presence of time, the sway and countersway that *is* time. The sequence, more specifically, is about the child's growth in time, and about how growth is that act which is always leaving and simultaneously falling back into itself. The best image of this is the child's literal growth into his limbs, hands, feet, eyes, mouth, penis—and the point of this growth is that the child always both retains himself and moves out of himself, always unites his "parts" with his original and continual wholeness, his body. This is impossible to picture in a map space; it is impossible to "picture," period. In the realistic novel, we saw that "plot" in its basic sense is characterized spatially by a sequence of convergences and divergences; and in *The Octopus*, we saw the mechanical image of this structure in the railroad and the chutes and elevators that channel wheat into bins. In a map space, the whole is always separated from its parts, or at most is the sum of them. But in Roethke, the whole —whether it be language, world, body, or time—overflows into each of its parts, into the variety of its forms, into each small thing, in the becoming act of growth. This is why Roethke's world is a world of small things—pebbles, petals, slugs, leaves, cinders, seeds, tongues, fingers—but it is also why that world is a whole world.

Since each poem reflects the whole in Roethke's sequence, I will examine the first poem in detail and then move more quickly through the succeeding ones. The first poem says all that needs to be said—but only because the rest follow.

Here is the first section of the first poem, "Where Knock Is Open Wide":

> A kitten can
> Bite with his feet;
> Papa and Mamma
> Have more teeth.
>
> Sit and play
> Under the rocker
> Until the cows
> All have puppies.
>
> His ears haven't time.
> Sing me a sleep-song, please.
> A real hurt is soft.
>
> Once upon a tree
> I came across a time,
> It wasn't even as
> A ghoulie in a dream.

> There was a mooly man
> Who had a rubber hat
> And funnier than that,—
> He kept it in a can.

> What's the time, papa-seed?
> Everything has been twice.
> My father is a fish.

The first thing to be noted about these lines is their quality of nonsense and play. Roethke has begun his sequence as close to the condition of primordial mergence as possible, and the casting around of the language, the ranging of it in play, and its decided lack of "meaning" in the usual sense are expressions of this mergence. This is language at its most silent because it is language with little reference outside of itself. It is language as almost pure gesture, as a mouth, where the condition of all the body is that of a mouth. Thus the oral images in the first four lines are most appropriate; the child is truly at an oral stage of development, where everything, including language, partakes of that total narcissistic union for which a baby at his mother's breast is the most apt image. This is why, spatially, most of the images in these lines have to do with being enclosed and with the feeling of softness: play *under* the rocker, a hat *in* a can, "A real hurt is soft."

But the language in this section, for all its narcissistic play and its self-enclosedness, is not without a referential function. Indeed the hard edge of reality is beginning to impinge upon the soft primordial wholeness of the child's world; thus the mention of teeth or a hurt or a can, and also the matter-of-fact, almost abstract statements such as "Everything has been twice." This is also the feeling of the section's rhythm and movement: the casting around, the play and flow of language, is twice brought to an abrupt halt by some rather prosaic, flat lines. The language play and nonsense verse occur in four-line units, each line of which has two or three stresses and is not end-stopped; these flow smoothly until they are halted by three-line units with three or four stresses in each line, all of which are end-stopped.

This is the beginning of the strophe-antistrophe movement, the sway and countersway, evident throughout the whole sequence. Out of narcissistic play, Roethke pulls up short at the plain fact of the world: "His ears haven't time."

The awakening sense of time is perhaps the most important aspect of this opening section. The word "time" is mentioned three times in this section, the point being that out of a timeless condition of play and self-enclosedness, the child is losing himself into time and is beginning to feel a past grow behind him and a future come toward him. One of the mentions of "time" is born out of that very playfulness, out of the child's casting around with words: "Once upon a tree / I came across a time." These lines should "normally" read, of course, "Once upon a time / I came across a tree." Roethke's shifting of the normal syntax of words, which occurs throughout the sequence, is indicative of the unsettled state of the child's consciousness; a tree is just as new and unfamiliar to him as a time, and both are part of the new world he is inadvertently creating by tossing his words around. It is only natural that the child should come across a time while playing with his words, since that play is simply the birth of the poem itself and since the poem thus born can exist only in the falling away of its words, in time.

The closing three lines of this section accumulate most of the above themes and discoveries, and introduce some new considerations that are to be important in the sequence. The narrator asks, "What's the time, papa-seed?" a question that is to be taken literally: what is time? The appropriateness of asking papa this question is in the fact that the very awareness of the father *as* father constitutes a time consciousness, a historical consciousness. The latter is made explicit by the ensuing two lines: "Everything has been twice. / My father is a fish." These lines open up the particular nature of that time consciousness, and its difference from the primordial mergence the child is leaving behind. Everything has been twice; there is a dual mode to the world-in-time, as opposed to the self-enclosed nature of play and timeless mergence. Most of the rest of the sequence will be an attempt to unite that dual mode with the previous wholeness of the child, a unity prefigured by the father's being and not-being of himself as a fish.

Throughout the sequence, the father is identified with the male generative principle, what penetrates the amorphous wholeness of preexistence and infuses it with form, gives it parts, limbs, separations. This is why papa is "papa-seed" and why he is also a fish. The fish image in Roethke represents the only formed thing in the undifferentiated mass, the "body without skin," or water: it is the root of that body, which means it is also the father of that body. The identification of the fish with the penis, and thus of the father with the penis, is a natural one. Images of the penis—the fish, the rat, the foot, the worm—are a central focus of many of the sequence's conflicts and resolutions, and can be arranged opposite images of the vagina—holes, nests, gates, caves, water. The unity of male and female becomes the perfect image of the unity of separation and wholeness, of discreteness and mergence, that is the final condition of Roethke's world. This unity is equally a unity of father and mother and a unity, an integration, of the self. This is why a common image of the unity of male and female, the act of fishing, is expressed in one of the last poems of the sequence as a self-directed act of integration: "Fishing, I caught myself behind the ears."

Section two of the poem continues much of the playing with words that constitutes section one, but also introduces several new considerations:

> I sing a small sing,
> My uncle's away,
> He's gone for always,
> I don't care either.
>
> I know who's got him,
> They'll jump on his belly,
> He won't be an angel,
> I don't care either.

> I know her noise.
> Her neck has kittens.
> I'll make a hole for her.
> In the fire.

> Winkie will yellow I sang.
> Her eyes went kissing away
> It was and it wasn't her there
> I sang I sang all day.

The sensual richness of the child's language play reveals a world that is itself sensually rich, a world that plays with and tosses around each of the various senses that open upon it. The world of the child is synesthetic, and all his sense perceptions are present in each separate one, just as the whole of the body is present in each of its parts; thus "I know her noise. / Her neck has kittens," and "Her eyes went kissing away."

Synesthesia has been called a sign of schizophrenia,[6] and as such it reveals the sense in which our most primary experience is schizophrenic. Merleau-Ponty says, "the senses intercommunicate by opening on to the structure of the thing. One *sees* the hardness and brittleness of glass, and when, with a tinkling sound, it breaks, the sound is conveyed by the visible glass."[7] In this respect, "synaesthetic perception is the rule, and we are unaware of it only because scientific knowledge shifts the centre of gravity of experience, so that we have unlearned how to see, hear, and generally speaking, feel. . . ."[8] The experience of the child in Roethke's sequence is the opposite. He is learning how to see, hear, and feel, and is thus able to retain the undifferentiated wholeness of experience that converges upon and fills out each separate perception of the world.

These lines also contain the first ambiguous references to "her" in the poem. "Her" is in a certain sense the child's mother, the living representation of his primordial wholeness, and the ultimate object of his regressions. But as the sequence proceeds, "her" obviously comes to indicate another woman, who becomes the focus of all the vaginal images in the poems and thus represents a separate being whom the child, growing out of childhood, must unite with.

6. Wolfgang Born, "The Art of Schizophrenics," *Ciba Symposia*, VII (January 1946), 220.
7. Merleau-Ponty, *Phenomenology*, p. 229. Italics mine.
8. Ibid.

Two more points about this section: first, death is experienced for the first time by the child and handily disposed of in play—something that will become increasingly difficult to do as the sequence proceeds. Second, the phrase "I know" is repeated twice, an indication of the child's rapid growth in time. "I know" constitutes in both cases a kind of recognition, and recognition implies that the child possesses a past that is not simply a primordial mergence but a history, an accumulation of experiences.

"I know" triggers the next section, which in feeling, rhythm, and theme is substantially different from the first two.

> I know it's an owl. He's making it darker.
> Eat where you're at. I'm not a mouse.
> Some stones are still warm.
> I like soft paws.
> Maybe I'm lost,
> Or asleep.
>
> A worm has a mouth.
> Who keeps me last?
> Fish me out.
> Please.
>
> God, give me a near. I hear flowers.
> A ghost can't whistle.
> I know! I know!
> Hello happy hands.

If the sequence is structured on a kind of expansion-deflation rhythm, the meaning of "deflation" is made clear in the first two stanzas of this section. In the first section the expansive play of the child stopped at the hard edge of the real world; here that stoppage is given the explicit emotional character of fear and the temporal and spatial character of being lost. It is rhythmically expressed by the fact that all the lines are end-stopped, and some even have full stops in the middle. The lines have a kind of atomistic quality, a feeling of things broken apart and lying beside each other. In terms of time, this is to say that the growing time-awareness of the child has suddenly hit a nerve in consciousness that reveals time is slipping away as well as going forward. A kind of fear is produced in the child, a fear that makes him clutch at whatever is at hand in order to stop the passage of time.

This is "being lost," not the loss of orientation that can occur in a map space, but the loss of self in time that necessarily occurs in growing up. The loss of self in time is always accompanied by a coming toward one's self, but either may be experienced more intensely than the other, and in this case the former is. This is why the child grabs at things: in order not to slip away into the past. But the irony is that whatever he reaches for slips away itself—as if he were being blown backward, and reached out of desperation for doorknobs and handles that loosened and came off in his hand. Heidegger's description of fear is apt here: "When concern is afraid, it leaps from next to next, because it forgets itself and therefore does not *take hold of* any definite possibility."[9] Thus these lines:

> Eat where you're at. I'm not a mouse.
> Some stones are still warm.
> I like soft paws.

This feeling of jumping from one thing to the next is echoed throughout the sequence. In "The Lost Son," for example: "What a small song. What slow clouds. What dark water. / Hath the rain a father? All the caves are ice. Only the snow's here." Or in "Give Way, Ye Gates":

> Touch and arouse. Suck and sob. Curse and mourn.
> It's a cold scrape in a low place.
> The dead crow dries on a pole.

The further irony is that this jumping from thing to thing in order to stop time leads finally to regression. The child clutches at everything around him as time slips away, but nothing works, nothing is rooted, until he finally clutches at himself and his world once again becomes self-enclosed. Since the feeling of time slipping away is also a feeling of losing oneself, the

9. Heidegger, *Being and Time*, p. 392.

solution is to embrace oneself, to root oneself. This is the "near" the child asks God for. His world is not near, because he is being blown away from it, and all its handles come loose. But his hands are near, what he uses to clutch at the world: "I know! I know! / Hello happy hands." The hint of masturbation is unmistakable, especially given the accompanying references to "fish" and "worm." All that is necessary is for the child to direct the use of his hands toward himself, allowing himself to be blown totally back through time, to regress.

Masturbation is an ambiguous act throughout the sequence. On one hand, it is a dead end, a desperate attempt to stave off being lost. The penis itself is a perfect image of the separateness into which the primordial wholeness of the child's world has been channeling; to fasten upon it is to acknowledge the fragmentation of the world that being lost results in. It is to relinquish the world as such, to let it pass by, and to enclose oneself like a snake swallowing its tail. On the other hand, the act of enclosing oneself leads back to that pool of narcissistic and maternal wholeness out of which the child has been thrust, and therefore leads back to the original mergence with the world. The paradox is that the image of separation and isolation, the penis, leads to wholeness, and thrusts the child back into the world he has just relinquished. Masturbation becomes the act by which the child can connect with the erotic nature of his environment, with the life of nature itself. The child says, "I hear flowers," when masturbation is hinted at. This kind of fundamental erotic connection between the child and his world is made more explicit in passages where masturbation is made more explicit, in "Praise to the End!" for example:

> It's dark in this wood, soft mocker.
> For whom have I swelled like a seed?
> What a bone-ache I have.
> Father of tensions, I'm down to my skin at last.
> It's a great day for the mice.
> Prickle-me, tickle-me, close stems.
> Bumpkin, he can dance alone.
> Ooh, ooh, I'm a duke of eels.

> Arch my back, pretty-bones, I'm dead at both ends.
> Softly, softly, you'll wake the clams.
> I'll feed the ghost alone.
> Father, forgive my hands.

> The rings have gone from the pond.
> The river's alone with its water.
> All risings
> Fall.

The "near" the child asks for becomes the natural things of the world, as well as his own skin: "It's a great day for the mice. / Prickle-me, tickle-me, close stems." The being lost that had forced the child back on himself has become its own opposite, a being found. The deflation that is being lost has become, of its own movement, an inflation, both literally and figuratively, a mutual embrace of the child and his world.

But as the final lines of the above passage and the following section of "Where Knock Is Open Wide" make clear, that very inflation of the child's world, which is centered in the penis, becomes of its own movement a deflation; thus "All risings / Fall," and the emphasis at the end of that passage upon being alone: "I'll feed the ghost alone," and "The river's alone with its water." Similarly, in section four of "Where Knock Is Open Wide," the narrator says:

> That was before. I fell! I fell!
> The worm has moved away.
> My tears are tired.

The sway and countersway of time in the sequence, and the sense in which those two movements are born out of each other, is primarily felt in this recurring rhythm of being lost, regressing, and then out of that very regression, expanding and embracing the world erotically, and in turn out of that very expansion, finding oneself lost again. The emphasis at the beginning of the sequence is upon being lost, and at the end upon embracing the world and being found, but each is also present in the other.

The rest of "Where Knock Is Open Wide" reemphasizes, after the brief countermovement of embracing the world, the being lost and being alone of the child's fall into time. Here is section four:

We went by the river.
Water birds went ching. Went ching.
Stepped in wet. Over stones.
One, his nose had a frog,
But he slipped out.

I was sad for a fish.
Don't hit him on the boat, I said.
Look at him puff. He's trying to talk.
Papa threw him back.

Bullheads have whiskers.
And they bite.

He watered the roses.
His thumb had a rainbow.
The stems said, Thank you.
Dark came early.

That was before. I fell! I fell!
The worm has moved away.
My tears are tired.

Nowhere is out. I saw the cold.
Went to visit the wind. Where the birds die.
How high is have?
I'll be a bite. You be a wink.
Sing the snake to sleep.

The bulk of the section is given as a kind of reverie, a memory, perhaps the only one the child could fasten upon to prevent the recurrence of being lost. The feeling of the passage is a kind of uneasy stasis: there is no intensely felt fear and no radical regression, but neither is there any embracing of the world and progression.

And yet this section does contain the climax of this first poem: "That was before. I fell! I fell!" Out of the realization that the reverie is a reverie issues a temporal self-consciousness, a kind of being inside and outside of oneself that is the basis of time as falling. "I fell!" also refers to the child's sexual sin and to the correlation between the child's sin and that of the race, by calling to mind the fall of Adam. The traditional equation between the penis and the snake in the Garden is made in the next line: "The worm has moved away." The image of the penis also appears three stanzas earlier, and as in the first section of the poem, it appears in terms of a close connection between father and fish:

> I was sad for a fish.
> Don't hit him on the boat, I said.
> Look at him puff. He's trying to talk.
> Papa threw him back.

Not only is this passage another instance of the fact of death, but it is also an allegory which in general displays the authority over life that the father possesses, and in particular displays his displeasure with the son's attempt to express his sexuality, to "talk" with his penis. As in Eden, the child's sin is a sin of disobedience of the father; "Father, forgive my hands," he says in "Praise to the End!" His salvation, as the rest of the sequence shows, will be an attempt to reconcile himself with the father.

The end of the poem, section five, shows the final break with the father that is necessary before reconciliation is possible:

> Kisses come back,
> I said to Papa;
> He was all whitey bones
> And skin like paper.
>
> God's somewhere else,
> I said to Mamma.
> The evening came
> A long long time.
>
> I'm somebody else now.
> Don't tell my hands.
> Have I come to always? Not yet.
> One father is enough.
>
> Maybe God has a house.
> But not here.

The father's death dramatically heightens the son's sense of separation from himself, from his original mergence with the world. Time now is "a long long time" since it has fallen out of itself, and the son is "somebody else" since he has done the same. Nothing is in fact present, nothing is here. "Kisses come back," the son says; God is "somewhere else," and even God's house, the world itself, is "not here." The father's death shows that the narrator's reconciliation with the father will be in an important sense a reconciliation with everything, with God, with the world. Thus the line "One father is enough" will find an answer in the last poem of the sequence: "A son has many fathers."

The dominant theme of "Where Knock Is Open Wide" is being lost. There is a momentary interlude, an awakening and being found in section three—"I know! I know!"—but this quickly recedes, and the poem ends on a note of absence.

Being lost is the intense experience of time slipping away. There is an experience related to being lost that equally concentrates on only one aspect of time and therefore produces a similar sense of incompleteness, and that is desire. If being lost is the realization of time slipping away, desire is the realization of time slipping ahead, of time always eluding our grasp. The dominant theme of the next poem in the sequence, "I Need, I Need," is this experience of desire, as its title makes clear. Gramatically, most of the poem is concerned not with what has happened but with what may happen, or should happen. Thus many of the sentence forms are commands or wishes; in section one, for example:

> Whisper me over,
> Why don't you, begonia,
> There's no alas
> Where I live.

There's "no alas" because in this new orientation in time to the future there's no pausing to reconsider or catch one's breath. There is a kind of restlessness in this section, not exactly a searching but a quizzical wandering:

> Went down cellar,
> Talked to a faucet;
> The drippy water
> Had nothing to say.

This wandering breaks out into pure playful wish in the next section, followed in turn by a conscious realization that the leaping ahead of time means the world is always essentially incomplete:

> I wish I was a pifflebob
> I wish I was a funny
> I wish I had ten thousand hats,
> And made a lot of money.

> Open a hole and see the sky:
> A duck knows something
> You and I don't.
> Tomorrow is Friday.

The image of the hole in these lines and the realization that time is slipping ahead combine in the poem to form the essential structure of desire. Desire is a hole that is always being filled but never retains anything; it is a constant and pure progression, a continual outstripping of itself. It is pure mouth, which is why the predominant imagery of the poem is oral ("Sit in my mouth" at the beginning of the poem, and "My hoe eats like a goat" at the end). Desire is eating, and it is that particular eating, like fire, whose sustenance passes through it instead of being retained.

The images of eating—and of fire—congregate at the end of the poem and become explicitly sexual. At the poem's beginning, oral images appear in terms of the mother, but at the end they are presented in terms of the "her" introduced in "Where Knock Is Open Wide." It is almost as if in order to stop the ceaseless passing through and slipping ahead that constitute desire, the narrator had to invent an object of desire. This is the structure of all sexual awakenings: they are not precipitated by a "her," but the desire already existing casts around until it finds a "her" it can anchor in:

Who's ready for pink and frisk?
My hoe eats like a goat.

> Her feet said yes.
> It was all hay.
> I said to the gate,
> Who else knows
> What water does?
> Dew ate the fire.

I know another fire.
Has roots.

The anchoring of desire succeeds to such an extent that the final image of eating is of desire itself being eaten: "Dew ate the fire." The recurring use throughout the sequence of water and fire to represent the female and male principles indicates that this devouring of desire is simply the inevitable result of sexual fulfillment. It is anything but permanent; "another fire" already exists, its roots are already down, and it will inevitably burst forth to start the cycle over again.

But the last two lines—"I know another fire. / Has roots." —have a further possible meaning, a meaning more indicative of the direction the rest of the sequence will take. If fire, as an image of desire, represents a kind of pure becoming and pure progression, a temporality that always leaps ahead of itself, then a fire with roots represents, paradoxically, a becoming that has a permanence at its heart, a progression that retains itself. It represents the full structure of temporality, the structure for which being lost on the one hand and desire on the other are only partial manifestations. The fire with roots is the very act of growth that is temporality in its most complete sense.

The next poem, "Bring the Day!" is the shortest of the sequence, and represents a kind of peaceful interlude before the emphasis in the sequence shifts to growth and embracing the world. The dominant image of this poem is the kiss, again an oral action, but that particular oral action that is neither a devouring nor a being devoured but rather a kind of floating on the surface of both. The kiss is the image of gentle and mutual appropriation, of the cooperative alliance of things. Thus the poem opens with these lines:

> Bees and lilies there were,
> Bees and lilies there were,
> Either to other,—
> Which would you rather?
> Bees and lilies were there.

The feeling in the poem is one of compatibility. Except for a brief brush with being lost, there is no sense of incompleteness. Rather the images are of things that suit and complete each other:

> Leaves, do you like me any?
> A swan needs a pond.
> The worm and the rose
> Both love
> Rain.

The space of both being lost and desiring was a kind of atomistic space, a space broken up into the separate objects the narrator clutched at to steady and fix himself. Here the space is one that funnels through things and enables them to gently manifest themselves, to introduce themselves:

> The herrings are awake.
> What's all the singing between?—
> Is it with whispers and kissing?—
> I've listened into the least waves.

Things hold themselves out in this poem, as we hold objects out on our hands. Their space is a buoyant one that allows them to float before us, to stretch and feel themselves awakening:

> O small bird awakening,
> Light as a hand among blossoms,
> Hardly any old angels are around any more.
> The air's quiet under the small leaves.
> The dust, the long dust, stays.
> The spiders sail into summer.
> It's time to begin!
> To begin!

The peace of the poem is that quiet that exists before a storm, that stasis out of which beginnings proceed and which even the most violent kind of becoming and progression has to continually carry with it and have at its heart if it isn't to outstrip itself and swallow itself as pure desire.

This becoming with a stasis at its heart is the dominant theme of the next poem, and the continual resolution of the rest of the sequence. The title, "Give Way, Ye Gates," refers to floodgates but also has obvious sexual overtones. Throughout the sequence the gate is an image of the vagina, as in the line "My gates are all caves," in "The Long Alley." The gate is particularly a symbol of the forbidden nature of sexual union, since its function is to block entrance. But in this poem the gates literally give way, and the result is a reawakening and a rebirth of the narrator into the world, both sexually and existentially. Birth is an important theme in the poem, of equal importance to the theme of sexual union. The two themes are collapsed in the line describing the actual giving way of the gates: "Tufty, the water's loose." Tuft means a clump of hair, so refers to the female sexual organ; "the water's loose" calls to mind a release of stored sexual impulses on the one hand and a pregnant woman's breaking water on the other. Together these two meanings indicate the sense in which the giving way of the gates is a surge of energy that carries the child out of the womb into sexual union with another. The giving way of the gates is that surge of energy which is the child's act of growth.

Throughout the sequence, the two kinds of images that best reveal the structure of this act of growth are of openings—gates, holes, mouths, caves—and of water—streams, ponds, lakes, the amniotic fluid. With regard to the images of water, a flood is the most explicit image of growth, for that forward movement always accumulates itself; this is precisely what growth is, the movement forward in time that accumulates itself, the falling that is also a rising. Growth is that activity which never leaves itself behind and yet always goes forward. In this sense, not only a flood but any movement of water embodies the structure of growth, since water always carries its source—water—with it when it moves. The movement of water, precisely like growth, is that flow out of itself which retains itself. This is the point of the closing lines of "Give Way, Ye Gates":

> The deep stream remembers:
> Once I was a pond.
> What slides away
> Provides.

Just as water partitions itself out of an original wholeness into more and more refined parts—rivers and streams—but retains that original wholeness, carrying it into each of those parts, so growth is the activity of partitioning one's body into its parts, while always retaining that original mergence, that original wholeness, that "pool," out of which it came.

The imagery of holes reveals a similar structure. In the sequence, the concept of "hole" is used in two senses: as an enclosure, e.g., a pit, and as an opening out of an enclosure. The imagery of enclosures indicates regression and a return to the original condition of mergence. "Who stands in a hole / Never spills," says the narrator in "Give Way, Ye Gates," a sentiment echoed throughout the sequence in all the images of mergence and sinking, of pouring into one's self and filling one's self, that result in a kind of blob existence familiar from Burroughs' novels; thus, in lines already quoted:

> Who, careless, slips
> In coiling ooze
> Is trapped to the lips,
> Leaves more than shoes.

The "coiling ooze" is one's own body as well as the amorphous body of the earth; thus it is one's body as a hole or pit in which one is trapped. Similarly, the lines "Everything's closer. / Is this a cage?" in "Bring the Day!" or the phrase "I'm lost in what I have" in "O, Thou Opening, O" refer to the body as it funnels back into itself and fills the hole of itself, to a kind of regressive growth that never leaves itself. Opposed to these images in the sequence are all those of emerging from a hole, of flowing out of one's self. "I've crawled from the mire, alert as a saint or a dog," the narrator says in "Praise to the End!" a line echoed in "O, Thou Opening, O": "I've crept from a cry." This imagery of emergence is related to the experience of desire, of always leaping out of and ahead of one's self. And both are expressions of the becoming aspect of growth, of the structure of human existence as a continual progression; we are always "Looking toward what we are," Roethke says in "Give Way, Ye Gates."

The concept of growth embraces both these aspects of the imagery of holes. Growth is that activity in which we are always being filled and yet always emerging from ourselves; it is the grave and the nest united. Growth is time as falling, and particularly, in terms of the body, time as a falling into and a simultaneous rising out of ourselves. This is growth: we lose and gather ourselves, we slip by ourselves in the very act of falling into ourselves, and we always overflow ourselves without spilling. Roethke's most stunning image of a kind of overflowing that doesn't spill occurs at the end of "The Shape of the Fire":

> To know that light falls and fills, often without our knowing,
> As an opaque vase fills to the brim from a quick pouring,
> Fills and trembles at the edge yet does not flow over,
> Still holding and feeding the stem of the contained flower.

This is precisely the condition of the body in growth, a fact made clear by Roethke's description, several lines before this passage, of a rose "Rising slowly out of its bed, / Still as a child in its first loneliness." Growth is a perfect unity of stasis and silence with continual becoming, is sustained fullness that trembles at its own brim and simultaneously leaves itself in order to feed itself. That unity of the timelessness of the child's world with the successiveness of adulthood enables time to embrace both presence and absence, both passing and becoming. This is why Roethke's narcissism, evident throughout the sequence, is not idle self-indulgence but that perfect excess of being which is also perfectly trim, that complete absorption in one's self which is also completely impersonal. "Fishing, I caught myself behind the ears," he says in "Unfold! Unfold!" indicating that the reach into one's self, into the narcissistic pool, is also an emergence out of one's self.

In Burroughs, by contrast, the two aspects of growth in time—flying and sinking, emerging and submerging—exist beside each other, with no fundamental connection or unity between them. In Roethke's sequence they exist united, in that perfect unity of Being and Nonbeing which also preserves their separation. To submerge is to emerge in Roethke's poems, or as Roethke said about the entire sequence, to go back is to go forward. Growth is that activity in which one always falls back into the hole of the self, fills that hole, and is consequently impelled forward—all in one motion.

Growth is the activity that organizes all the countermovements of the poem, the sway and countersway of its rhythm, the progression-regression, expansion-deflation movement of the child's wanderings in the world. Growth unites being lost and desiring or needing—it is that fire with roots by which we are what we become, and it thus unites being lost and being found. The emphasis upon being found in the rest of the sequence is equally an emphasis on coming toward oneself in the world.

The emphasis is also upon uniting with the world, upon filling the world as one fills one's self, while always not being the world as well, while always flowing out of it. The ambiguity of masturbation in the sequence reflects this being and not-being of the self and the world, and indicates its connection with the concept of growth. Masturbation is a kind of ecstatic self-enclosedness, a being-filled that is also outside of itself and specifically is outside of itself by being in the world, by erotically plugging into nature. Growth is that very excess of being which overflows into the world, into the objects of the world, and enables the body both to define itself on the "ground" of the world and to unite with the world. This is the further significance of the image of catching oneself while fishing: to catch oneself is to generate oneself, to become the father of oneself, and this is possible only because one is united with "mother" earth, with the world. This is why all I have said about growth also applies to the world: the world overflows its objects while retaining itself among them, a phenomenon for which plant life offers the best illustration.

Growth, in other words, is the fundamental condition of the garden, that continual, becoming unity of mergence and discreteness, of unity and multiplicity, that is the full sense of the garden. This is the significance of the images of water and light in the final two poems in this first section of the sequence. Water and light are symbols of that wholeness which impregnates the world and fills it out, which holds things in their separateness while connecting them with everything else. Lines like "The lake washes its stones" in "Sensibility! O La!" and "Light fattens the rock" or "The sea has many streets" in "O Lull Me, Lull Me" all express the intimate reciprocal relationship between wholeness and separation in the natural world. The final poem, "O Lull Me, Lull Me," explicitly connects this organization of the natural world with the ongoing process of growth that the child is experiencing:

> The poke of the wind's close,
> But I can't go leaping alone.
> For you, my pond,
> Rocking with small fish,
> I'm an otter with only one nose:
> I'm all ready to whistle;
> I'm more than when I was born.

As a symbol of that wholeness and continuity which informs the process of growth, the pond in these lines is also a symbol of the world itself. The narrator "can't go leaping alone" because growth that isn't fed by the world and that doesn't simultaneously overflow back into the world is no growth at all. This is why, in the same poem, images of the connection between inside and outside and between body and world become prominent for the first time in the sequence:

> I see my heart in the seed;
> I breathe into a dream,
> And the ground cries.
> I'm crazed and graceless,
> A winter-leaping frog.

This is the kind of resolution that will occur often at peak moments in the second half of the sequence.

However, the resolution is still only partial at this particular point in the sequence; the process of growth has begun, but has not yet filled itself out completely. Thus in "O Lull Me, Lull Me," the narrator says: "Soothe me, great groans of underneath, / I'm still waiting for a foot." As in much of the rest of the sequence, the foot is an image of the penis. Roethke's fixation with the penis throughout the sequence is in many respects a fixation with growth, since as the body channels into its limbs, it channels most noticeably into the penis. (In another poem in the sequence, Roethke sings a song of encouragement to his penis to grow: "Be large as an owl, be slick as a frog, / Be good as a goose, be big as a dog, / Be sleek as a heifer, be long as a hog,— / What footie will do will be final.") In the line "I'm still waiting for a foot," however, the indication is that the process of growth is still in its beginning stages; the "foot" by which he is to grow forward and connect with the world, like his whole body, is "more than when I was born," but not quite enough yet.

The references to "her" in these last two poems make the same point. In "Sensibility! O La!" the opening lines are:

> I'm the serpent of somebody else
> See! She's sleeping like a lake:
> Glory to seize, I say.

Clearly "she" is no longer the mother, but is another, the very symbol of otherness that the poet must connect with in order to truly grow. But at the end of the poem there is a slipping back, not exactly a regression, but certainly a failure to achieve the other and a recognition that such achievement is difficult:

> My sweetheart's still in her cave.
> I've waked the wrong wind:
> I'm alone with my ribs.

And further on: "Mamma! Put on your dark hood; / It's a long way to somewhere else." The double function of growth, to retain itself and leave itself, is always in danger of slipping exclusively into one or the other. Particularly with regard to the world outside and to the most important manifestation of that world, another person, there is a temptation to draw back; thus "I'm alone with my ribs" and "It's a long way to somewhere else."

Despite these obvious setbacks, the emphasis of the rest of the sequence is upon union with the world in the act of growth. In Roethke's radical insistence upon the full meaning of this union, he abandons the references to "her" and "she" that occur in the first half of the sequence. It is as if before taking the step that most of us take—sexual union—he wanted to explore it fully in a more fundamental way, in terms of our relationship to the objects we encounter every day, at every moment. This is why the dominant emphasis in the rest of the sequence is upon the sexual nature of the world—upon the sexual nature of Being in general. Roethke's vision is of that gap in Being, that Nonbeing which passes through and fills Being out, and requires that the body and the world always mutually embrace and penetrate each other so both can truly grow. The peak moments of the rest of the sequence occur when the narrator and the world slip into each other's skin through the common hole they share, the hole in time that is growth. I will conclude by examining some of these peak moments.

The first occurs in "The Lost Son" and climaxes with a dizzy plunge into the hole of the world, into that pure Nonbeing at the heart of everything:

> These sweeps of light undo me.
> Look, look, the ditch is running white!
> I've more veins than a tree!
> Kiss me, ashes, I'm falling through a dark swirl.

This passage occurs several stanzas after a description of being lost in which the narrator says, "My veins are running nowhere." By contrast, the "running" of his veins in this passage, the new infusion of life, is the opposite of being lost; it is an intimate connection with the things of the world: "I've more veins than a tree!" The same dizziness that is found in the extreme state of being lost is there, but it moves in exactly the opposite direction;

it moves toward the world, penetrates the world: "I'm falling through a dark swirl." The next poem, "The Long Alley," contains lines that express a similar kind of dizzy union, except in this case the world penetrates the protagonist. Here is the entire passage, perhaps the most beautiful one in the sequence, or even in all of Roethke's poetry:

Shall I call the flowers?

> Come littlest, come tenderest,
> Come whispering over the small waters,
> Reach me rose, sweet one, still moist in the loam,
> Come, come out of the shade, the cool ways,
> The long alleys of string and stem;
> Bend down, small breathers, creepers and winders;
> Lean from the tiers and benches,
> Cyclamen dripping and lilies.
> What fish-ways you have, littlest flowers,
> Swaying over the walks, in the watery air,
> Drowsing in soft light, petals pulsing.

Light airs! Light airs! A pierce of angels!
The leaves, the leaves become me!
The tendrils have me!

As in "The Lost Son," this incident occurs after a period of being lost and regressing. Here the things of the world, their vegetal, sexual aspect, literally plunge through the body of the poet, and the result is a totally ecstatic experience of being-in-the-world: "The leaves, the leaves become me!" It is this kind of ideal metamorphic moment for which the whole sequence exists. One more example should suffice, from "Praise to the End!":

Arch of air, my heart's original knock,
I'm awake all over:
I've crawled from the mire, alert as a saint or a dog;
I know the back-stream's joy, and the stone's eternal pulseless
   longing.
Felicity I cannot hoard.
My friend, the rat in the wall, brings me the clearest messages;
I bask in the bower of change;
The plants wave me in, and the summer apples;

My palm-sweat flashes gold;
Many astounds before, I lost my identity to a pebble;
The minnows love me, and the humped and spitting creatures.

This is that complete openness which is also completely filled;
it is that total self-effacement in the presence of the world which
is equally a complete self-fulfillment, a complete realization of
the self. Roethke disperses himself, loses himself into even the
most inanimate objects, stones and pebbles, and by that very
dispersal finds himself fully and collects himself. And this losing
and finding oneself in intimate union with the world is the
"bower of change" that the poet basks in; it is growth itself.

The space of this union with the world is that perfect unity
of space and time which is the space of the garden. Each thing
presents itself as autonomous and independent, as something
with its own space, and yet all things participate in each other
and are drawn together in a common space; they are drawn
together by that particular hole in Being which is the body's
link with the world, by that mutual temporality of body and
world by which they fall into and out of each other, by growth.
The space of Roethke's world unites fullness and emptiness,
plenitude and nothingness, as growth itself does. All of this can
be seen in a passage in "A Field of Light":

I touched the ground, the ground warmed by killdeer,
The salt laughed and the stones;
The ferns had their ways, and the pulsing lizards,
And the new plants, still awkward in their soil,
The lovely diminutives.
I could watch! I could watch!
I saw the separateness of all things!
My heart lifted up with the great grasses;
The weeds believed me, and nesting birds.
There were clouds making a rout of shapes crossing a windbreak
    of cedars,
And a bee shaking drops from a rain-soaked honeysuckle.
The worms were delighted as wrens.
And I walked, I walked through the light air;
I moved with the morning.

The "separateness of all things" is preserved in Roethke's world, and so the space of that world is not one absolute objective block; but neither is it an atomistic space, as in Burroughs, in which each thing is confined totally to itself. Rather it is a space that gathers up objects in all their separateness, as a wave gathers up stones, and integrates them by virtue of that separateness —a space in which objects are always falling into place, a space that simultaneously contracts and expands, a becoming, temporal space.

This space both anchors things and releases them for the grasp of the body; it thus perfectly unites here and there, the subjective point of view and the absolute, objective world, fantasy and reality. It is a space that flows out of itself, as the body leaves itself in growth, and that simultaneously fills and impregnates itself. The image of things leaving themselves is common in Roethke, and the most general example of it, which reveals it as a basic structural principle of his world, occurs in "The Lost Son":

> From the mouths of jugs
> Perched on many shelves,
> I saw substance flowing
> That cold morning.

The space of all Roethke's poetry is a metamorphic space, dynamized by time, a space that leaves itself and becomes, changes, as the clouds in the previously quoted passage make "a rout of shapes crossing a windbreak of cedars."

We saw in Chapter One that the schizophrenic world of the map is one in which holes open up, holes such as absolute space or absolute consciousness, both of which are hermetically sealed and are of a different order of being from what they exclude. The space of Roethke's world also contains holes, but they are holes that are both continually being sealed and continually opening. It is space as a collection of mouths, not atoms. As he puts it in "Unfold! Unfold!":

> Easy the life of the mouth. What a lust for ripeness!
> All openings praise us, even oily holes.

The bulb unravels. Who's floating? Not me.
The eye perishes in the small vision.

Oral images opened the sequence and expressed the primordial wholeness of the child's world. Here they express that wholeness as it is carried into the growing world of everyday experience and united with each separate entity in that world. "The eye perishes in the small vision" because it is drawn into the bottomless hole of each separate thing, thus is drawn into the world itself. This is possible only because the space of Roethke's world —of the garden, and of schizophrenia as the most ideally sane state of consciousness—is one in which all things open upon each other and upon the body, in which subject and object, fantasy and reality, are perfectly united. Space is a hole and things are holes in Roethke's world, but space is also a medium and things are also things, and the pure potentiality of both is also pure actuality.

This metamorphic space, this space of mouths, is the reason Roethke's world, as in Baudelaire's sonnet, is a world of correspondences—correspondences between things and between the body and things. It is also the reason the objects of that world so often speak and sing, not only to the protagonist but also to each other. As Kenneth Burke points out, Roethke prefers verbs of communication to any others in describing the things of the world.[10] Weeds whine, a cracked pod calls, "Even thread has a speech." The world of Roethke's poetry is engaged in a constant energetic exchange with itself and with the body; it is the symbolic world in the fullest sense:

> Sing, sing, you symbols! All simple creatures,
> All small shapes, willow-shy,
> In the obscure haze, sing!
>
> A light song comes from the leaves.
> A slow sigh says yes. And the light sighs.

Each thing in Roethke's world manifests itself in every other thing, and even—or especially—all opposites exist in and of each

10. Burke, "Vegetal Radicalism," p. 97.

other. Roethke says in "Unfold! Unfold!": "Speak to the stones, and the stars answer." Or as he puts it more generally in "O, Thou Opening, O": "The Depth calls to the Height."

This unity of opposites indicates the way in which Roethke's world is a total alternative to the dualistic structures of classical Western thought, an alternative that is manifest in our most primary, everyday experience. Body and world, subject and object, time and space, fantasy and reality, child and man, all exist in a perfect unity, a unity given previous to any reflection, and a unity that couldn't conceivably be otherwise. But each exists also as perfectly autonomous; each is bounded and liberated by itself; each is a hole, a mouth. The garden, Roethke's world, is the condition of growth; it is open-ended, a mouth, since it leaves itself and fills itself in the becoming motion that is growth. This includes the world of inanimate as well as animate things, since the life of that world is the perfect unity of life and death, of Being and Nonbeing, that infuses every moment of our lives. The "other condition" that Roethke claims in the last poem of the sequence to be king of is the schizophrenia of the garden, the condition of the symbolic world, which embraces and unites the garden and the map, unity and multiplicity, life and death, fantasy and reality, while falling and rising in the single flow of growth:

> I sing the green, and things to come,
> I'm king of another condition,
> So alive I could die!

Epilogue

The difficulty of concluding with Roethke's vision—of a totally unrepressed world in which all things open upon each other and exist in a kind of intimate erotic community—becomes apparent as soon as I put my pen down and look up from the page. Such a world is an ideal one, and requires not only a totally different life-style but in general a totally different civilization from that in which we live. Few objects sing in our world as they do in Roethke's world, simply because the objects we encounter and use every day have been manufactured with a kind of built-in objectivity: they have been made to be used efficiently and thrown away when that use is drained out. From canned food and automobiles to doorknobs, shirts, and end tables, they are encrusted with an impenetrable objectivity that precludes all love, all sacred significance, in our relationships with them. A world filled with these kinds of objects is totally atomistic and can be arranged only with map structures, with shelves and floor plans, or on a larger scale, with timetables, file cabinets, bureaucracies, and maps themselves.

The particular nature of this objectivity of objects involves a structure seen repeatedly in dealing with forms of Western thought. Because objects are manufactured for mass consumption, they bear the imprint, stylistically and substantially, of the concept "mass." Such objects are always streamlined; their excess is trimmed off (and used to manufacture more of the same objects), and their measure is purely quantitative, having to do only with the amount of material used. Every object made from the same mold, whether it be a plastic comb or a tract house, is the same; the distribution of the "mass" into its parts is purely mathematical. The result is an object that is on one hand a kind of atom, in that it is mathematically discrete, and on the other a kind of massive block, in that its being is assimilated into the total conformal being of every object made from the same mold. These are two aspects of the structure of space in the classical world—atomistic and blocklike—and this is an alienating structure, a structure that drives the human body as well into the confines of its skin—or that molds all bodies into one blocklike existence, as Fascism does and as the Liquefactionists in Burroughs' world plan to do.

Natural objects are not much better off in such a world. They are channeled into their own pure space by maps, spaces such as parks in the cities or lawns in the suburbs. Our own involvement with natural objects is strictly limited to a maplike structure, and we consequently live in and move through spaces that are in all respects antitheses of the space of the garden. This mapping off of the objective and the organic into separate spaces occurs temporally as well as spatially: we parcel out our daily activities into certain mutually exclusive areas—work, play, home life—and only in the limited mapped-off leisure time of our day or week can we be surrounded by natural objects in an erotic environment. Marcuse has written a great deal about how our civilization has drained the erotic and organic out of their state of integration with the world and mapped them off into certain bounded places and times, and even into certain limited locations on the body.[1] As we have seen, civilization does this to all aspects of experience, especially to fantasy and madness, as well as to the organic and erotic.

The frightening truth is that Burroughs' novels are a more accurate description of our own world than is Roethke's poetry. Burroughs' vision is of a society whose institutions are structured upon total maplike administration, hence total repression. For all the sexual activity in his novels, their landscape is the most

1. Marcuse, *Eros and Civilization*, pp. 184–85.

unerotic in literature, for it polarizes our relationships with the world into alienation and mergence. In Burroughs, that fundamental unity of body and world that underlies all of our actions is repressed by mental and social structures that are those of Western civilization. Again as Marcuse has pointed out, many have benefited from the repression civilization imposes, for it enables human beings to control and manipulate nature and each other, enables them to acquire and assimilate, to consume, with a minimum of stress and tension.[2] But the result is not only the exploitation of many by a few, but the alienation of all from each other and from the world, hence the loss of personal freedom. Even when the consumer culture succeeds, when all, not just a few, have the means to assimilate and acquire goods and objects, the social structure that has produced that culture is still completely inadequate, for it is one in which consuming and being filled are the only dimension of experience. In terms of the description of growth given in the last chapter, this means the temporal dimension is eliminated: people literally have no future, for they are unable to leave themselves, to become, to grow. Personal existence is thus object existence and is itself arranged by shelves, floor plans, timetables, file cabinets, bureaucracies—by maps.

The kind of revolution needed to transform this system is a total one; in the apocalyptic tradition, it means much that we are familiar with, that has anchored our world, will be turned upside down and come to mean the opposite of what it has meant, just as the term "schizophrenia" has taken on two opposite meanings in this book. Surely there is a sanity that is madness, and that is the sanity of the consumer culture and middle-class society. One has only to turn on a television or drive along the motel and drive-in restaurant strips that surround all of our cities to see it. I have tried to show that in almost all respects the structures of this culture are the structures of classical Western thought: structures of discreteness and alienation, of control and manipulation, structures whereby the fantastic and the erotic content of existence are repressed, and

2. Ibid., chap. 2.

the body itself alienated, becoming a kind of feed bag, loosely attached to the self—a dead weight.

I have tried also to show that the opposite of this is true, that genuine madness, as manifest in Roethke, for example, is the sanest response to the world, for it is that in which body, self, and world are united. This unity penetrates all the coordinates of experience; it means that subject and object, fantasy and reality, and savagery and civilization are all one in a unity of plenitude and wholeness, in a becoming, fully open, erotic world. This is the ecology of human existence, the underlying interdependent structure upon which our very sanity—and survival—depends. But it is difficult to talk about a fully open, erotic world when the earth itself is being hollowed out, polluted, desexed. The aim, as in naturalistic fiction, is undoubtedly to transform the earth itself into a map, an aim perfectly expressed in Ronald Reagan's observation that the United States could, if it wanted, blacktop the whole country of Vietnam and make a parking lot out of it. This is "objectivity," the attitude by which the not-me is purely Other, hence regarded as inert raw material to be molded from without. Such an attitude applies not only to the natural world but also to people—to the Vietnamese, to blacks, to students at all levels, to the poor, to everyone "out there."

The reversal of meaning that accompanies the apocalypse is one that reaches into all aspects of our social and individual lives, and reaches back into our history, the history of Western thought. Its implication is that the "good life" is one of the most vicious that man has produced. In the United States, our mania for cleanliness, sanity, decorum, and moderation only serves to heighten our dirt, madness, barbarism, and excess. A "good" Stanford psychologist, studying violence in America, declares that the assassin lurks in all of us, and says he knows it because "we can arrange it in our laboratory so that anyone—anyone at all—can become assaultive and violent."[3] The violence of such

3. Philip Zimbardo is the psychologist, quoted in the "California Living" section of the *San Francisco Sunday Examiner and Chronicle* (15 June 1969), p. 7.

a statement and such an attitude goes all too easily unnoticed, since it is surrounded by an aura of scientific respectability; but it should be noted that such "arrangements" in laboratories are recurring incidents in Burroughs' novels. They are possible only in a structure of thought that is "objective," that distances itself for purposes of greater control and manipulation, that tears the human body out of the fabric of its actions in communion with the world and treats it as a machine, an arrangement of discrete parts, highly complex but fundamentally easy to unlock with the proper key—the key of "condition-response," for example.

The irony of such a structure is that the unity of body and world, which it denies, returns to haunt it anyway. There is, for example, a racism of the human body that is inseparable from the racism of American society today. For white Americans, the literal chasm that exists in Harlem, Watts, or Oakland is a chasm in each of our bodies; the relationship is more than reciprocal—it is identical. Just as the body contains "Other Halves," to use Burroughs' phrase—Other Halves such as the siphoned-off sexual area of the body, or in general the sub-liminal unconscious area of the psyche—so the society contains Other Halves, pure pools into which it has channeled all of its blackness. Spatially these are the same areas; the shadow the body casts inside and the shadow the society casts into the hole of its ghettos are one shadow, and constitute one fear. The reason for both of these shadows is also the same: civilization has needed a pure space into which it could siphon all the di-mensions of experience that might in any way hinder the smooth mechanisms of its operations. All of this is the theme of Conrad's *Heart of Darkness*, and the schizophrenia Kurtz finally succumbs to is the condition of American society today. Not only is a whole dimension of our experience inaccessible to us, as it was to Kurtz, but it is positively antagonistic, threatening us by its very existence.

There is hope at least in the surfacing of that shadow, in the acknowledgment of its existence. But any hope must be ex-tremely cautionary, because that shadow *is* a shadow and is ab-solute, and in most respects is no closer to being integrated into our lives than it ever was. With regard to the human body, this can be seen in the fascination with violence and pornography in middle-class society, the implication being that the sexual and subliminal can be encountered by many people only as a pure space, as Other, as evil. With regard to the social body, it can be easily seen by a visit to any major city: ghettos still exist, and segregation is still as absolute as it has always been. Of course most intelligent black men know that integration into American society as it now exists would simply be mergence, assimilation. The "melting pot" concept of American society is the polar opposite of the segregation by which it has created its black ghettos, and both are results of a map consciousness that separates discreteness from mergence. An ideal community would unite discreteness and mergence by preserving individual and cultural differences in one common body, the body of its people— and the result would be freedom in the truest sense. But there is little freedom for American society, even for those who are in economic and social control, the white middle class, because discreteness and mergence are not united but are polarized to such a degree that they are reduced to each other, to a common condition of confinement and unfreedom. That is to say, middle-class society is both atomistic, in that its members are sealed off from each other, and blocklike, in that all of them adopt the same life-style and the same values.

Despite the fact that almost all the significant movements of thought and literature in this century have been attempts to find alternatives to the structures of Western thought, these structures are anchored as firmly as ever in our society and its institutions and values today. The philosophers and the poets, the cliché goes, are supposed to have their antennae tuned to changes in the atmosphere, and can predict major cultural changes before they come about. But perhaps the cliché doesn't apply to a society that has so efficiently ignored its philosophers and poets; and perhaps their work—the work of the existentialists, the phenomenologists, and those who have turned to Eastern thought, or the literature of Joyce or Wallace Stevens, or the surrealists, or Roethke, or people like W. S. Merwin, Robert Bly,

Allen Ginsberg, and others—has all been mapped off into a pure separate space, where it is powerless even to indicate, let alone effect, a change.

It would be a temptation to say that none of this matters, that the garden is a condition of individual consciousness, and that the way to change the society is to change the minds of the people in it. But to say this is to accept the atomization of the world that Burroughs' novels describe. The fact is that the garden is a social as well as individual condition, and that to exist fully it must be in the outer world as well as the inner, and even more, it must break down the barriers between those worlds. This means that a sense of community has to exist, community between peoples and community between people and the natural world around them. That this community doesn't exist today is obvious. The "youth culture" has been pointed to as an example of such a community, but the youth culture, with few exceptions, has turned out to be another version of the consumer culture. And even if the youth culture did exist, it would be insufficient, since the community has to be between *all*—youth and age, men and women, black, white, and brown.

And yet there is a sense in which that community does exist. The problem is not exclusively one of social structures (capitalism, bureaucracies), but also of perceptual structures, of the ability to see and feel what exists in our primary experience. This ability must accompany social change—it must be *one* with social change—or else social change will be hollow. This is because social change will have to return us to that primary experience, to the world previous to map consciousness; it is here that our sense of community always exists, although often beneath layers of repression, for it is here that we find our common humanity.

> Our mothers and fathers plucked us
> from their laps
> it was easy
> and the past became a string.
> Now we think we have nothing in common

we think we are only passengers
who will die the first time.
Rain without claws
words without teeth
everything belongs to us
and nothing belongs to us.

You prisoners of air
open
we are all one.
Our hands are all one hand
our backs are one.
Open the eyelid of your skin
and come out.
Open the light, the frail
luggage of fire
we are all one.
Field mice walk through
their necks, water
points its inefficient knife
unraveling itself
open the cells
open the bones
and come out.
The tree swims
in every leaf
we are all one.
Crowbar and fly
in delicate balance
a stone remembers its Indian
open the first mouth
deep in your flesh
and come out.

We are all one.
A new taste
flows through the body.
We are all one.

Selected Bibliography

Allott, Miriam, ed. *Novelists on the Novel*. New York, 1959.

Arieti, Silvano. *Interpretation of Schizophrenia*. New York, 1955.

Auerbach, Erich. *Mimesis*, trans. Willard Trask. New York, 1957.

Barth, John. *Giles Goat-Boy*. New York, 1966.

———. "The Literature of Exhaustion," *Atlantic Monthly*, CXX (August 1967), 29–34.

———. *Lost in the Funhouse*. New York, 1968.

———. *The Sot-Weed Factor*. New York, 1960.

Baudelaire, Charles. *Les Fleurs du Mal*. Paris, 1942.

———. *Intimate Journals*, trans. Christopher Isherwood. Boston, 1957.

Beckett, Samuel. *Malone Dies*. New York, 1956.

———. *The Unnamable*. New York, 1958.

———. *Waiting for Godot*. New York, 1954.

Bellow, Saul. *The Adventures of Augie March*. New York, 1960.

Bergson, Henri. *Time and Free Will*, trans. F. L. Pogson. London, 1910.

Binswanger, Ludwig. *Being-in-the-World: Selected Papers*, trans. Jacob Needleman. New York, 1963.

———. "The Case of Ellen West," trans. Werner M. Mendel and Joseph Lyons, in *Existence*, ed. Rollo May, Ernest Angel, and Henri F. Ellenberger. New York, 1958.

———. "On the Manic Mode of Being-in-the-World," in *Phenomenology: Pure and Applied*, ed. Erwin Straus. Pittsburgh, 1964.

Blackmur, R. P. *Language as Gesture*. New York, 1952.

Boehme, Jacob. *On the Election of Grace*, trans. John Rolleston Earle. London, 1930.

Borges, Jorge Luis. *Labyrinths: Selected Stories and Other Writings*, ed. Donald A. Yates and James E. Irby. New York, 1964.

Born, Wolfgang. "The Art of Schizophrenics," *Ciba Symposia*, VII (January 1946), 217–24.

Boss, Medard. *The Analysis of Dreams,* trans. Arnold J. Pomerans. London, 1947.

Breton, André. *Poèmes.* Paris, 1948.

Brown, Norman O. *Life against Death.* New York, 1959.

———. *Love's Body.* New York, 1966.

Burke, Kenneth. *The Philosophy of Literary Form.* New York, 1957.

———. "Surrealism," in *New Directions 1940.* Norfolk, Conn., 1940.

———. "The Vegetal Radicalism of Theodore Roethke," *Sewanee Review,* LVIII (Winter 1950), 68–108.

Burroughs, William S. *Junkie.* New York, 1953.

———. *Naked Lunch.* New York, 1966.

———. *Nova Express.* New York, 1964.

———. *The Soft Machine.* New York, 1966.

———. *The Ticket That Exploded.* New York, 1967.

Capek, Milic. *The Philosophical Impact of Contemporary Physics.* Princeton, N.J., 1961.

Cassirer, Ernst. *The Philosophy of Symbolic Forms,* trans. Ralph Manheim. 3 vols. New Haven, 1955.

Caws, Mary Ann. *Surrealism and the Literary Imagination.* The Hague, 1966.

Coleman, James C. *Abnormal Psychology and Modern Life.* Chicago, 1956.

Coleridge, S. T. *Lectures and Notes on Shakespeare and Other English Poets,* ed. T. Ashe. London, 1893.

Conrad, Joseph. *Heart of Darkness and The Secret Sharer.* New York, 1950.

Crane, R. S., ed. *Critics and Criticism.* Chicago, 1952.

Defoe, Daniel. *Moll Flanders.* Boston, 1961.

Dickey, James. *Poems 1957–1967.* New York, 1968.

Dreiser, Theodore. *Sister Carrie.* New York, 1959.

Eliade, Mircea. *Cosmos and History: The Myth of the Eternal Return,* trans. Willard Trask. New York, 1959.

———. *Mephistopheles and the Androgyne,* trans. J. M. Cohen. New York, 1965.

———. *Patterns in Comparative Religion,* trans. Rosemary Sheed. Cleveland, 1963.

———. *The Sacred and the Profane,* trans. Willard R. Trask. New York, 1961.

Eliot, T. S. *The Complete Poems and Plays: 1909–1950.* New York, 1952.

Eluard, Paul. *La Jarre Peut-Elle Etre Plus Belle Que l'Eau?* Paris, 1951.

Feidelson, Charles. *Symbolism in American Literature.* Chicago, 1953.

Fielding, Henry. *Joseph Andrews.* Boston, 1961.

———. *Tom Jones.* New York, 1963.

Fingarette, Herbert. *The Self in Transformation: Psychoanalysis, Philosophy, and the Life of the Spirit.* New York, 1963.

Forster, E. M. *Aspects of the Novel.* New York, 1927.

———. *Passage to India.* New York, 1924.

Foucault, Michel. *Madness and Civilization,* trans. Richard Howard. New York, 1965.

Frank, Joseph. *The Widening Gyre.* New Brunswick, N.J., 1963.

Freud, Sigmund. *The Interpretation of Dreams,* trans. James Strachey. New York, 1965.

Frye, Northrop. *Anatomy of Criticism.* Princeton, N.J., 1957.

———. *Fearful Symmetry.* Boston, 1962.

Gysin, Brion. "Cut-Ups," *Evergreen Review,* VIII (April–May 1964).

Hegel, G. W. F. *The Phenomenology of Mind,* trans. J. B. Baillie. New York, 1931.

Heidegger, Martin. *Being and Time,* trans. John Macquarrie and Edward Robinson. New York, 1962.

James, Henry. *The Ambassadors.* Boston, 1960.

———. *Wings of the Dove.* New York, 1937.

Jammer, Max. *Concepts of Mass.* Cambridge, Mass., 1961.

Joyce, James. *Ulysses.* New York, 1961.

Jung, Carl. *The Structure and Dynamics of the Psyche* (vol. 8 of *Collected Works*), trans. R. F. C. Hull. New York, 1960.

———. *Symbols of Transformation* (vol. 5 of *Collected Works*), trans. R. F. C. Hull. Princeton, N.J., 1956.

Kafka, Franz. *The Castle,* trans. Willa and Edwin Muir. London, 1957.

———. *Selected Stories of Franz Kafka,* trans. Willa and Edwin Muir. New York, 1952.

———. *The Trial,* trans. Willa and Edwin Muir. New York, 1968.

Kasanin, J. S., ed. *Language and Thought in Schizophrenia: Collected Papers.* Berkeley, 1944.

Kenner, Hugh, ed. *T. S. Eliot: A Collection of Critical Essays.* Englewood Cliffs, N.J., 1963.

Kermode, Frank. *The Sense of an Ending.* New York, 1967.

Kinnell, Galway. *Body Rags.* Boston, 1968.

Knickerbocker, Conrad. "William Burroughs," an interview in *Writers at Work: The Paris Review Interviews,* third series. New York, 1967.

Koch, Steven. "Images of Loathing," *Nation* (4 July 1966), pp. 25–26.

Laing, R. D. *The Divided Self.* Baltimore, 1965.

———. *The Politics of Experience.* London, 1967.

Levin, Harry. *Contexts of Criticism.* Cambridge, Mass., 1957.

Lévi-Strauss, Claude. *The Savage Mind,* trans. George Weidenfeld. Chicago, 1966.

———. *Totemism,* trans. Rodney Needham. Boston, 1962.

Lewis, Sinclair. *Babbitt*. New York, 1922.

Lorca, Frederico Garcia. *The Selected Poems of Frederico Garcia Lorca*, ed. Francisco Garcia Lorca and Donald M. Allen. New York, 1955.

McLuhan, Marshall. "Notes on Burroughs," *Nation* (28 December 1964), pp. 517–19.

———. *Understanding Media*. New York, 1964.

Marcuse, Herbert. *Eros and Civilization*. New York, 1955.

———. *One-Dimensional Man*. Boston, 1964.

Marx, Karl. "Economic and Philosophical Manuscripts," trans. T. B. Bottomore, in Erich Fromm, *Marx's Concept of Man*. New York, 1961.

Melville, Herman. *The Confidence Man*. London, 1948.

Merleau-Ponty, Maurice. *The Phenomenology of Perception*, trans. Colin Smith. London, 1962.

Merwin, W. S. *The Lice*. New York, 1967.

Meyers, Bert. *The Dark Birds*. New York, 1968.

Miller, J. Hillis. *Poets of Reality*. Cambridge, Mass., 1965.

Minkowski, Eugene. "Findings in a Case of Schizophrenic Depression," trans. Barbara Bliss, in *Existence*, ed. Rollo May, Ernest Angel, and Henri F. Ellenberger. New York, 1958.

Muir, Jane. *Of Men and Numbers*. New York, 1961.

Nadeau, Maurice. *The History of Surrealism*, trans. Richard Howard. New York, 1965.

Neruda, Pablo. *Twenty Poems of Pablo Neruda*, trans. Robert Bly and James Wright. Madison, Minn., 1967.

Neumann, Erich. *The Origins and History of Consciousness*, trans. R. F. C. Hull. 2 vols. New York, 1962.

Norris, Frank. *McTeague*. New York, 1964.

———. *The Octopus*. New York, 1964.

Ortega y Gasset, José. *History as a System*, trans. Helene Weyl. New York, 1961.

———. *The Modern Theme*, trans. James Cleugh. New York, 1961.

Pascal, Blaise. *The Pensées*, trans. J. M. Cohen. Baltimore, 1961.

Poulet, Georges. *Studies in Human Time*, trans. Elliott Coleman. Baltimore, 1959.

Pynchon, Thomas. *The Crying of Lot 49*. Philadelphia, 1966.

———. *V*. Philadelphia, 1963.

Rapport, Samuel, and Helen Wright, eds. *Physics*. New York, 1965.

Richardson, Samuel. *Pamela*. 2 vols. New York, 1914.

Robbe-Grillet, Alain. *For a New Novel*, trans. Richard Howard. New York, 1966.

———. *In the Labyrinth*, trans. Christine Brook-Rose. London, 1968.

Roethke, Theodore. *Collected Poems*. New York, 1966.

Roheim, Geza. *Magic and Schizophrenia*. New York, 1955.

Rosen, Ephraim, and Ian Gregory. *Abnormal Psychology.* Philadelphia, 1965.

Sartre, Jean-Paul. *Being and Nothingness,* trans. Hazel E. Barnes. New York, 1956.

———. *Literary and Philosophical Essays,* trans. Annette Michelson. New York, 1962.

———. *Nausea,* trans. Lloyd Alexander. New York, 1964.

Scholes, Robert, ed. *Approaches to the Novel.* San Francisco, 1961.

Schreber, Daniel Paul. *Memoirs of My Nervous Illness,* trans. Ida Macalpine and Richard A. Hunter. London, 1955.

Seager, Allan. *The Glass House: The Life of Theodore Roethke.* New York, 1968.

Shackle, G. L. S. *Decision, Order, and Time in Human Affairs.* Cambridge, 1961.

Smart, J. J. C., ed. *Problems of Space and Time.* New York, 1964.

Stevens, Wallace. *Collected Poems.* New York, 1967.

———. *Opus Posthumous,* ed. Samuel French Morse. New York, 1966.

Storch, A. *The Primitive Archaic Forms of Inner Experience and Thought in Schizophrenia,* trans. C. Willard. New York, 1924.

Straus, Erwin. *Phenomenological Psychology.* New York, 1966.

———. *The Primary World of the Senses,* trans. Jacob Needleman. New York, 1963.

Sypher, Wylie. *Loss of the Self in Modern Literature.* New York, 1962.

Teilhard de Chardin, Pierre. *The Phenomenon of Man,* trans. Bernard Wall. London, 1959.

Trilling, Lionel. *The Liberal Imagination.* New York, 1953.

Turbayne, Colin. *The Myth of Metaphor.* New Haven, 1962.

Werner, Heinz. *Comparative Psychology of Mental Development.* Chicago, 1948.

Wheelwright, Philip, ed. *The Presocratics.* New York, 1966.

Whitehead, Alfred North. *The Concept of Nature.* Cambridge, 1920.

Yeats, W. B. *The Collected Poems of W. B. Yeats.* New York, 1956.

Zola, Emile. *The Earth,* trans. Ann Lindsay. New York, 1954.

———. *The Experimental Novel,* trans. Belle M. Sherman. New York, 1893.

Index

"Primitive Like an Orb, A," 142
Principle of Contradiction: and maps, 11–12; foundation of Greek philosophy, 12; and schizophrenia, 27
Principle of Indeterminacy, 46, 147–48
Property: and the Fall, 10–11; and mathematics, 11–12; in *Heart of Darkness*, 31; in novel, 37, 39, 58–59. *See also* Ownership
Proust, Marcel, 37, 41, 42, 142
"Provision," 157
Psychology: objective, 7, 20–21; Gestalt, 25, 71
Pynchon, Thomas: and parodies of novel, 41–42; *V.*, 53–54, 65–66; *The Crying of Lot 49*, 65–66; mentioned, 37, 63, 67, 75, 85

Quantity, 11–12

Racism, 195
Rationalism, 119
Ray, Man, 100
Reagan, Ronald, 194
Realism: reality and fantasy in, xi–xii, 42; subject and object in, xi–xii, 76, 84; maps in, xii, 49, 54, 55; time and space in, 27, 42–53; plot in, 39–41, 47, 48–51, 54, 164; analysis of, 39–55; structure of, 40, 44–52, 55, 74, 76; language in, 41, 44, 45, 101, 103; and visual sense, 41, 69–70; parodies of, 41–42, 63–66, 75; schizophrenia in, 43, 53–54, 55; imitation in, 44–48; 67–69, 75; one point of view among many, 46–47, 61, 63, 67, 68–69, 74; character in, 47–48, 49; chance in, 48; and freedom, 52; body in, 52–54, 83–84; objects in, 54–55; appearance in, 66–68; in Robbe-Grillet, 69–70; and labyrinth, 75; separation of mechanical and organic in, 81–84; in Burroughs, 103, 107, 108–9; mentioned, 141, 142, 143, 156

Reality: one structure among many, ix, 46–47, 61, 63, 67, 68–69, 74; insanity of, xi, 110; in Western civilization, 13, 19, 23–24, 45; and appearance, 13, 45, 66; in novel, 39–40, 42, 68–69; in Barth and Pynchon, 66; and labyrinth, 75; in Burroughs, 85, 86, 89–90, 98–99; underlying structure of, 110
—separated from fantasy, ix, xiii, 4, 110, 111, 112; in Western civilization, 23–24; in schizophrenia, 28
—united with fantasy, xii, 63, 110, 112, 113, 158; in novel, 68–69; in Robbe-Grillet, 73; in *La Nausée*, 79, 81–82, 84; in surrealism, 100; in symbolism, 125–26; in Kafka, 126–29; in Roethke, 188–90
Regression: in Roethke, 161–62
Res cogitans, 20
Res extensa, 20
Reverdy, Pierre: on surrealism, 100–101
Richardson, Samuel: *Pamela*, 44, 54–55
Rimbaud, Arthur, 99
Rise of Silas Lapham, The, 55
Rising: in time, 139–40, 153, 158, 181, 190
Robbe-Grillet, Alain: and fantasy, ix; and parodies of novel, 41–42; *Dans le Labyrinthe*, 42, 63, 69–74; *For a New Novel*, 73–74; mentioned, 37, 68, 84, 85, 110, 112, 126
Roethke, Theodore: schizophrenia of, 113–14, 160–61, 189–90; Garden in, 159–61, 187, 189–90; childhood in, 161–62, 163, 165–89 passim; time in, 161–62, 163, 166, 169–75, 177, 179–83; body in, 162–63; language in, 162–63, 165; growth in, 163, 177, 179–85, 190; being lost in, 169–73, 175, 178, 182; space in, 178, 187–89; objects in, 187–89; symbolism in, 189–90; mentioned, ix, xiii, 112, 146, 158, 191, 192, 194, 196

DISCARDED